Myths and Motifs of The Mortal Instruments

Valerie Estelle Frankel

Myths and Motifs in The Mortal Instruments

Copyright © 2013 Valerie Estelle Frankel

Zossima Press
a division of Winged Lion Press
Hamden, CT

All rights reserved. Except in the case of quotations embodied in critical articles or reviews, no part of this book may be reproduced or transmitted in any form or by any means, electronic or mechanical, including photocopying, recording, or by any information storage or retrieval system, without written permission of the publisher.
For information, contact Winged Lion Press www.WingedLionPress.com

ISBN-13 978-1-936294-23-7

TABLE OF CONTENTS

Introduction		1
Chapter 1:	**The Chosen One**	4
	Clary and the Heroine's Journey	
	Simon's Hero's Journey	
	Jaces's Hero's Journey	
	Tessa's Heroine Journey	
Chapter 2:	**The Bible Reimagined**	47
	The Book of Raziel	
	Mene Mene Tekel Upharsin	
	Nephilim	
	Lucifer and Paradise Lost	
	Ithuriel	
	Parabatai	
	The Mark of Cain	
	Magic	
	Runes	
	The Hero Sword	
	Angels	
	Greater Demons	
Chapter 3:	**Fantasy Tropes and Genres**	73
	All Myths are True	
	Urban Fantasy and the City	
	Angels in Popular Culture	
	Vampires	
	Slayers	
	Werewolves	
	Witches and Warlocks	
	Fairies	
	Steampunk	

Chapter 4	**Literary Allusions**	98
	The Mortal Instruments and the Classics	
	Will, Tessa, and the Library	

Chapter 5	**A Deeper Look at the Shadowhunters and their Book**	121
	Timeline	
	Names	
	Archetypes and Tarot	
	Easter Eggs	
	Themes and Motifs	

The Future of Shadowhunters	155
Bibliography	159
Index	165

Other Books of Interest

INTRODUCTION

With the arrival of the 2013 summer movie, Cassandra Clare's fans have reached an overwhelming level of excitement. And the fans are many: Clare's novels have been translated into 35 languages, and *The Mortal Instruments* series has 16 million copies in print worldwide, with 7 million of *The Infernal Devices*.

The story began years ago, in New York, as the author tells it:

> The idea for the Mortal Instruments came to me one afternoon in the East Village. I was with a good friend of mine, who was taking me to see the tattoo shop where she used to work. She wanted to show me that her footprints were on the ceiling in black paint – in fact the footprints of everyone who'd worked there were on the ceiling, crisscrossing each other and making patterns. To me it looked like some fabulous supernatural battle had been fought there by beings who'd left their footprints behind. I started thinking about a magical battle in a New York tattoo shop and the idea of a secret society of demon-hunters whose magic was based on an elaborate system of tattooed runes just sprang into my mind. (FAQ)

As Clare recounts the story, her friend and fellow author Holly Black took some chapters of the book to her agent, and the publishing process began. "This was pre-Twilight, so the genre wasn't considered a bestselling genre," Clare notes (*Cassandra Clare's Clockwork Princess Bus Tour*). Teen paranormal fantasy existed, but it wasn't the enormous, shelf-splitting genre it is today. She added: "Harry Potter came out and said these books are about kids, but not necessarily for children. And that made it okay, for people of all ages, from all walks of life, to read fantasy. I feel these books really opened up the gates for people like me" (Nathan).

Of course, young-adult fiction is "genre-busting." Adult fiction, Clare says, tends to be labeled "either romance or sci-fi or historical fiction or literature. They're in different sections of bookstores. But YA novels, whether it's *Twilight* or *The Hunger Games*, combine all or most of those elements." Clare adds that her own series are a "combination of urban fantasy, adventure and romance" (Minzesheimer). With vampires, fairies, angels, modern teen romance, and steampunk all in one series, she certainly bends genres to her will.

Like many works of fantasy, *The Mortal Instruments* offers a strong young woman embarking on the heroine's journey. Clare's steampunk series, set over a century earlier, also follows a young woman questing to discover her own secret powers. Along with Bella, Katniss, Lucy Pevensie, Lyra Belacqua and others, Clary and Tessa have unique powers that can save the world. Clare notes:

> For me, the triad of Harry Potter, the Hunger Games and Twilight feature strong women and as a declared feminist, it's a wonderful thing. These women have really opened up this particular world of storytelling, which I'm very grateful for.
>
> …
>
> She does keep in touch with Stephanie Meyer and Suzanne Collins, saying: "Stephanie has been lovely, super-promotive and she's recommended my books to a lot of people. She read the manuscripts of two of my books early on and was also one of the first big promoters of The Hunger Games, she talked about it everywhere. And Suzanne worked as a screenwriter for a long time and she gives great advice." (Nathan)

Like *Harry Potter* and *Twilight,* her series incorporates religious themes, as her heroes battle demons from the Jewish Apocrypha. All the religions of the world unite to aid the Shadowhunters on their holy quest. While Muslim angels and Hindu prayers appear, most of the Shadowhunters' beliefs come from the Judeo-Christian Bible and its teachings. Characters are named Jonathan, Simon, and Zachariah, as they summon angels. Nephilim, themselves a Biblical concept, use sacred runes from the Book of the Angel Raziel. They don't cast spells themselves, as Jace notes – they petition angels to bless their blades and bring them protection and holy grace.

The series also contains many references to great literature. Jace quotes Catullus and Coleridge, while his ancestor Will sees himself as the unworthy Sydney Carton from *A Tale of Two Cities*. His true love Tessa, who is obsessed with books herself, encourages him to write his own story. Clare wrote the series as an allegory of both Dante's *Divine Comedy* and Milton's *Paradise Lost*: The characters journey through a purgatory of darkness and despair to the light of joy and the heavenly city. At the same time, they must battle Idris's fallen angels—those who have grudges against the Shadowhunters and seek their destruction. Themes range from tolerance to the value of faith and forgiveness, like many other top fantasy works.

With many more series to come, and more movies optioned from top studios, one thing is clear: Cassandra Clare's bright future is only beginning.

CHAPTER 1
THE CHOSEN ONE

Clary and the Heroine's Journey

One of the reasons we're often drawn to tell stories about adolescents who discover they're gifted in some special, often supernatural way, I think, is that they function well as allegory. It's the time in your life when you feel you don't belong and you're not like your parents, and you're not like anyone else, so who are you? And it's also the time when you discover that talent, that gift that makes you you. – Cassandra Clare ("Cassandra Clare: Bringing the Shadows to Light")

The hero's journey, or story of the Chosen One, is the basic format for most myths, epics, and fantasy novels. The Chosen One is a heroic child like Harry Potter or Luke Skywalker destined to fight the forces of evil. In the darkest place of all he faces his tyrant father or wicked stepmother, the darkest impulses he keeps buried within himself. He faces death and returns to life stronger than before, for death is a metaphor for crossing from child to adult.

Heroine's journeys are equally common in fantasy, originating mainly in fairytales rather than in the longer epics. Andersen's "The Six Swans" or "The Little Mermaid," the myths of Cupid and Psyche or Demeter and Persephone, all are perfect heroine's journeys. Children's and young adult novels give us *The Wizard of Oz*, *The Chronicles of Narnia*, *The Hunger Games*, *Twilight*, *Divergent*, *The Song of the Lioness Quartet*, *The Golden Compass*, *The Gemma Doyle Trilogy*, *Tithe*, and so forth. Clare acknowledges that she was deliberately writing a classic hero's journey for Clary, adding, that her two goals were "that it not be terrible (finger crossed!) and that it center around a female heroine, instead of a male hero" ("Introduction," xiii).

The heroine's most typical quest is rescue of family members, especially the little sibling that represents her child.

> Her goal is to become the all-powerful mother. Thus, many heroines set out on missions to rescue their shattered families: Meg Murray

Myths and Motifs in *The Mortal Instruments*

of *A Wrinkle in Time* quests to save her father then her little brother. Coraline tries to save her parents, Meggie of *Inkheart* and Clary of *The Mortal Instruments,* their mothers. Tim Burton's Alice tries to rescue the Mad Hatter. Scores of young women in folklore rescue their lovers from fairies, demons, and ogres. Demeter forces herself into the realm of the dead to reclaim her daughter, while Isis scours the world for her husband's broken body. Katniss, of course, spends the series protecting Prim and her growing adoptive family, from Peeta to the children of Panem. (Frankel, *Many Faces of Katniss* 113-114)

The heroine quests to find her best friend or little brother, in *The Golden Compass*, *A Wrinkle in Time*, and other series. Clary spends *City of Bones* questing for Simon the rat then kidnapped Jace, all while seeking her mother. Jace calls Clary "the girl who walked into a hotel full of vampires because her best friend was there and needed saving" (*Lost Souls* 522). He adds, "You came for me…when almost everyone else had given up" (*Lost Souls* 523). Unarmed and alone, Clary chases after Hodge because she's determined to stop Valentine from slaughtering mundane children. As she rescues Simon and Jace over and over, while saving her mother and stopping her father's slaughter of the innocent, Clary's family sphere becomes the motivation for a much larger epic. At last, she becomes the savior of all the Shadowhunters, teaching them to bond with the Downworlders and save them as well. Her inspiring love and creativity preserve the world of magic in the ultimate triumph.

The Call to Adventure: Losing the Mother

Clary grows up in Brooklyn, living a normal childhood. When her geeky friend Simon takes her clubbing, she sees three powerful teens destroy a demon…and no one else sees anything. Her mother is so worried she tries to drag Clary off to the country. One of those teens, Jace Wayland, seeks Clary out later to tell her she has the sight and is clearly more than she seems. However, at that moment, demons invade, destroying her home and kidnapping her mother. The quest has begun.

Clary's quest begins with her mother's kidnapping, as Clary struggles through three books to save her. Of course, the mother is usually absent during the heroine's story. Disney's Beauty, Ariel, Jasmine, Mu Lan, and Pocahontas are raised by their fathers. Snow White and Cinderella have stepmothers. Fairytales, like other heroine's journey tales, follow this pattern for a reason. The mother, who was the childhood protector, cannot continue shielding her daughter from everything or there will be no adventure. It's time for independence. Sheldon Cashdan explains in the fairytale study *The Witch Must Die*:

> The mother's exit, paradoxically, is empowering in that it forces the children in the story to confront a cruel and dangerous world on their own. Lacking a mother or protector, the hero or heroine must draw on inner resources that might not have been tested were the mother still around. (42)

This is particularly true in *City of Bones:* Jocelyn has more than sheltered Clary from the hazards of the demonic world and threat of Valentine: She has hired Magnus Bane to erase all of Clary's paranormal sightings and memories of them in order to keep her completely innocent. She seeks to blind Clary of the sight and strip her of her magical perception as well as her heritage. In this way, the mother becomes too protective, to the point of stifling the heroine and preventing her from adventuring. She has become the adversary, like Rapunzel's stepmother, who locks her in a tower. The dark side of the loving mother is "anxious nursing and over-instructing, far beyond the needs of her charges. She may fail to affirm their own need for a sense of strength and independence, and thus delay the maturing process" (Molton and Sikes 42). With Jocelyn's kidnapping, Clary is released, and discovers the world of magic and evil for the first time.

> The Good Mother is perfect kindness, love, and protection. As such, she has few defenses. To have the forces of wickedness kill the mother would be like having one's inner demons devour one's gentle, kindly side – a horrifying development for the psyche. The best way to protect or insulate the mother from such a fate is to leave her out of the story (as fairytales often do) or even have her quietly perish. "Though her absence makes the child highly vulnerable, her peaceful departure is preferable to a scenario in which she dies a violent death" (Cashdan 42). Such a thing is its own death-rebirth cycle, as the death of the mother leads the child to sink into despair and then rise strengthened, channeling the mother's spirit into her own developing self. (Frankel, *Buffy* 121).

Another reason for the mother's vanishing is the Jungian Mother Complex, which is one of the earliest and most central forces in a girl's psyche. A baby views the mother and itself as inseparable – one person in fact. Therefore, it's impossible that the mother should yell or punish or upset the baby, any more than its own arm might. Therefore, the baby imagines two mothers: one completely loving, selfless, and perfect, the other the "Terrible Mother" – the punisher and evil force. She is a killer of children, like the White Witch of Narnia or Wicked Witch of the West. These two figures – protective, angelic mother and vicious cruel mother – represent two conflicting voices within the self.

Myths and Motifs in *The Mortal Instruments*

Valentine, though a man, is the child killer and evil parent of the first trilogy. He's a slayer of children: decades ago, he experimented on Downworlder young. He tortures and experiments on his own children as well, as Jace and Clary soon discover. Now he will kill all the marked Nephilim who haven't pledged loyalty to him.

The protective mother is the force inside Clary that wants to keep her a child, safe and innocent yet unable to affect the world or find her destiny. The dark mother within wants to force experience and pain on her to compel her to grow. Lilith, the evil mother figure, takes this role in the second trilogy. The Inquisitor is another monstrous mother – burned by grief, she becomes a figure of ruthless, merciless, cruel order corrupted by revenge. Watching her, Clary decides who she doesn't want to become. The capricious fairy queen and Dorothea, inhabited by a demon, represent other cruel mothers who echo the darkness inside Clary herself. Without Joyce for protection, Clary must confront all these forces and learn the harsh skills she needs to survive. Luckily, she has friends.

The World of Magic

The first gift Clary receives from the magical world is the Sensor, which she takes from Jace, her first guide. The Sensor is an appropriate tool as heroines often receive tools of perception as their talismans on magical adventures: golden compasses, magic mirrors or spectacles. Of course, Clary doesn't use the sensor to see the magical world but to combat her enemies, and she shoves the sensor into a demon's mouth, slaying it with the protective runes. This signals that Clary will certainly not be a passive damsel on her adventure.

In the first book, she uses her new power of perception to sweep away glamours and see the Shadowhunter world for what it really is. Perception is a significant part of her life, joined with her prophetic visions, magical sight, and lost memories of the Shadowhunter world. Further, visions and images define her: Clary keeps a sketchbook because, as she explains, she thinks in pictures, not words (*Bones* 204). When she pushes aside a glamour, she imagines cleaning it away like old paint under a rag of turpentine (*Bones* 133). "Clary is every bookish, fantasy-loving girl who grows up wielding a pencil and a sketchbook instead of mutant powers or a sword," Sarah Cross explains in her essay on Clary (20). She may be ordinary, but she can use her abilities from our world to change everything.

Jace teaches Clary the basics of the Shadowhunter world, and his teacher Hodge offers her other facts. However, neither acts precisely as her mentor.

The child on the Chosen One's path leaves his or her unsatisfying birth family to find a better one, a "real" one. "My parents don't appreciate me, and they're so boring. I must be adopted and belong somewhere more magical and special," the child thinks. In fact, Clary's impulses are correct, as generally happens in Chosen One stories – she has the perception of a Shadowhunter, and with it magical gifts. She's even uniquely powerful among Shadowhunters, as she eventually discovers. She is not the daughter of Jocelyn Fray the prosaic artist and her husband Jonathan, the dead soldier. In fact, her father is the infamous and villainous Valentine, and her mother was once his revered and powerful wife. Even Clary's "stepfather," Luke, is a werewolf.

With her mother kidnapped and Luke rejecting her, Clary must find another guide to who she really is. This she finds in the ancient warlock Magnus Bane, her first mentor. Magnus comments: "Every teenager in the world feels like that, feels broken or out of place, different somehow, royalty mistakenly born into a family of peasants. The difference in your case is that it's true. You *are* different" (*Bones* 231). He has been hiding Clary's memories at her mother's insistence. Like Gandalf and other great wizards, he provides help whenever the heroes cannot solve their own problems. Clare notes: "In writing about Clary, I am writing about the feeling that a lot of teenagers have that they are different somehow, alienated, unlike others. Only Clary actually very literally is another kind of species of human" (*Enchanted Inkpot*).

The mentor's task is to give the hero or heroine a talisman to protect and strengthen her. Most male heroes receive swords, from Sting to Excalibur to Harry Potter's dueling wand. For heroines, along with tools of perception, books are very common, appearing in *Inkheart, Ella Enchanted, The Spiderwick Chronicles, The Kane Chronicles,* and *A Series of Unfortunate Events.* Katniss of *The Hunger Games* has her father's logbook as well as his bows and jacket. Clary is no exception, as Magnus offers her part of her birthright by handing her the Gramarye of runes, which will teach her to understand the hidden world. She hears a click in her head, like a key turning in a lock. After, everything seems clearer, and she's gained stronger powers of understanding and remembrance. She soon begins writing runes, not only from the book but from heaven itself – runes only the angels know.

Women's powers often come, not from fighting, but from crafting. Cheyenne and Micmac women cast spells of magical protection through their weaving and beading skills. In Hopi myth, Spider Woman molded people from the clay of the earth and attached a strand of her web to each of them, weaving them together. The Inuit Aakuluujjusi created the caribou from a pair of her discarded trousers and the walrus from her lumpy jacket. Ix Chel, water and moon goddess of the Maya, is a weaver, whose whirling drop spindle twirls the Universe. The Fates and the Norns likewise spun lives, with the gods themselves unable to change their wills. Goddesses are creators, but they use the magic of crafting and creating as much as birth magic.

This too is Clary's power, as she grows from an artist with a sketchbook to a creator of powerful runes, summoned from heaven itself. She "finds a way to turn her natural talents into the tools of her survival...she draws a better world into existence and she never lets the word *impossible* stop her. In Clary's hands, the stele truly is mightier than the sword" (Cross 33).

In *Ashes*, she puts her enormous power into an Opening rune and blasts open the door of Jace's cell. She later creates a Fearless rune and gives it to Jace to protect him. When she creates it, she thinks of her mother and when a "soft voice" in her head challenges her, she responds, "I am Jocelyn Fray's daughter" (*Ashes* 282). As she imagines her mother's paintings, the voice fades away. On Valentine's ship, as she tears it open with her mother's stele, she even hears her mother's voice inside her head. Once she's opened herself to creative, feminine magic, Madeline Bellefleur appears and tells her how to get her mother back. Clary's feminine side is awakening.

The Lover

Jace takes Clary to the Institute, home of the Shadowhunters. These are the warriors who fight demons, protecting mortals who don't even know they exist. It's filled with motifs of angels and swords, suns and roses. Angels and swords suggest defense and offense in their constant war, along with the sacred trust to defend the world from demons. The sun is a popular hero symbol, while the rose is a symbol of perfection, round like a mandala or the world.

There, Clary discovers that she is tied to this ancient birthright. She and Jace squabble, but she's drawn to him as well, far more than to her childhood friend Simon. Jace is mysterious and powerful, magical as she is mundane, aristocratic and old-fashioned. He's everything she's not, and thus, incredibly captivating.

The romantic figure in the heroine's journey represents the unconscious world of dreams and power she's seeking in herself. By learning from him, she grows beyond her ordinary self to embrace the magic he offers. Jace is not just a Shadowhunter with the dazzling good looks and charm Clary feels she lacks. From her perspective, he's described with his hair in a "halo of damp gold" (*Bones* 306) and as a "wounded prince" (*Bones* 297). He's also incredibly perceptive, seeing all the nuances of Clary and Simon's relationship when Clary often misses details.

The heroine's love is usually a shapechanger, a frog prince or beast. This reflects the constant indecipherable moods the other person has in a romance – he seems so foreign and incomprehensible that this lover must have turned into another person entirely. Jace becomes another person when possessed in the fifth book, but there are earlier echoes: When Jace discovers Valentine's his father, Clary is horrified by the new obedient Jace, who surrenders all of his beliefs: "This new Jace, fragile and shining in the light of his own personal miracle, was a stranger to her" (*Bones* 436). His belief in Valentine is described as a kind of glamour. Similarly, Jace shifts names throughout the series, from the moment he's revealed as Jonathan Morgenstern through his struggle to find the last name that fits him.

The greenhouse he and Clary share is a magical place – it even smells like Idris. The glass roof shines like the lake in reverse, and strange, magical flowers bloom there, in an enclosed magical world. In the greenhouse, Jace gives Clary a witchlight stone for her birthday. He tells her all Shadowhunters have them and adds, "It will bring you light…even among the darkest shadows of this world and others" (*Bones* 313). Later it pulses in her hand "like the heartbeat of a tiny bird" and shines in her hand "as if she'd cracked a seed of darkness" (*Bones* 423). Birds and seeds are feminine symbols, of freedom and potential respectively. As Clary uses the stone, she claims both powers and takes her place as a Shadowhunter. The gift of light in dark places is a feminine tool of perception, like Galadriel's phial or Ariadne's thread, a flashlight that will let Clary find her way.

When Jace gives it to her, Clary makes an engagement joke about how girls don't literally want a "big rock" but a diamond. This mention emphasizes how Clary is already thinking she wants an engagement ring from Jace, and thus the "big rock" he gives her takes on that meaning, binding them together. Indeed, Jace follows his gift with their first kiss. In the greenhouse, this kiss is filled with the magical plants of Idris like an Eden or a place of creation magic. He also gives her apples in the greenhouse, a sign of temptation and sin, though apples were also beloved of Aphrodite. His birthday gift of the blooming flower "dusted with pale gold pollen" blooms only for a moment, symbolizing the short-lived nature of happiness in the world. In fact, the symbolism echoes this: they have a perfect moment, a perfect kiss, and then Clary's messy love triangle ruins things as she stumbles into Simon.

When they leave for Magnus's party, Jace offers Clary "a long thin dagger in a leather sheath. The hilt of the dagger was set with a single red stone carved in the shape of a rose." He tells her the knowledge of how to wield it is in her blood (*Bones* 214). This is a feminine dagger – containing a red stone like Isabelle's pendant and a rose shape – but set in a masculine weapon. It's a talisman of the Shadowhunter world and an acknowledgement that Clary can be a fighter like Jace, Alec and Isabelle. Later, it's revealed that the *kindjal* dagger was Valentine's, with his falling star emblem. Luke has its match. As Jace, then Clary take Valentine's red dagger, they become part of the war he began with the Downworlders decades before. They are the heirs to his dark legacy as well as his weapons.

In the third book, Jace gives Clary his Morgenstern ring when he goes to face death. Though their single night together in Idris is chaste, combining it with the ring symbolizes a marriage. It's revealed in *Clockwork Prince* that Shadowhunters give their ring as a betrothal gift, like an engagement ring. While Clary doesn't know this, Jace certainly does (as do Luke and Jocelyn). She wears the ring through the second trilogy, indicating that she's given Jace her heart and more. In folklore, a ring is given as a promise of fidelity, betrothal, or marriage. Jace tells her later "It means I trust you with my past and all the secrets that past carries" (*Fallen Angels* 410). It's the Morgenstern ring, symbol that Jace's past will always be his childhood with Valentine but his future will belong to Clary.

The Animus

Simon's mom notes that "you only need three people you can rely on in order to achieve self-actualization" (*Bones* 303). For Clary, these are her adoptive father Luke, best friend Simon, and boyfriend Jace. Clary notes that through her childhood she has only ever loved her mom, Luke, and Simon. In the first book, her mom is taken and Luke (temporarily) rejects her, and in the second, Simon dies and turns into a vampire. She must learn to do without all of them. She opens her heart to Jace, but discovers he's Valentine's son and her brother. Thus one of Clary's greatest quests is to discover her identity without leaning on any of the men in her life.

Followers of Carl Jung's philosophy, itself one of the roots of the hero's journey, saw the need for women to actualize the so-called "masculine" side, the power, authority, and rational thought waiting to be developed within them. The next step is to "legitimize women's power and authority in its own right" (Wehr 46). In Jungian psychology, the animus is another word for the heroine's hidden masculine side. All characters represent part of the self, and Luke, Simon, Jace, and even Valentine and Sebastian all act as different types of animus, challenging Clary and forcing her to grow while offering different kinds of comfort and protection. When they are seen as aspects of the questing heroine, rather than individual characters, it becomes clear that their growth is mirroring hers in a traditional pattern. This Animus "evokes masculine traits within her: logic, rationality, intellect. Her conscious side, aware of the world around her, grows, and she can rule and comprehend the exterior world" (Frankel, *Girl to Goddess* 22).

As Clary matures, the animus figures in her life grow wiser and more useful, or are replaced by other, stronger, allies and enemies to challenge her. The highest level of Animus is as catalyst to wisdom. It "connects the woman with her spiritual side, making her even more receptive to her own creativity. Thus, the heroine, as well as the hero, obtains the mystical feminine energy that offers endless emotion, sympathy, nature, magic, insight, and perception," as the first book on the heroine's journey in myth and legend explains (Frankel,

Girl to Goddess 23). These wise guides appear to Clary in the third book, as Luke, Simon, and Jace show her how to defeat evil with the power of her runes.

THE ANIMUS (Frankel, *Buffy*, 46)

The Animus Growth Within the Heroine	Trait	Positive Aspect	Negative Aspect
Passion and Physical Growth	Emotion	Mutual Devotion	Mutual rage and destruction
Initiative and Planning	Body	Useful plans and action	Harmful, ill-considered acts
Law, Rule, and Order	Mind	Self restraint and moral advice	Inflexible obstruction
Wisdom and Spiritual Fulfillment	Spirit	Guide to self-knowledge and ascension	Deceiver and distorter of the future

Simon, of course, is all passion without stopping to think. He lusts after Isabelle, snaps at Jace, and gets transformed into a rat because he wants to participate during Magnus's party. The adventure in the vampires' house nearly destroys them all. Still, when Simon is transformed into a rat, he acts as Clary's perceptive animal companion, scouting exits and warning her that dawn is coming.

Several times, Clary is menaced by werewolves, which it turns out have all been sent by Luke. Though he protects her with violence and action, much as Jace does, his rejecting her early in the book has damaged their paternal relationship – he is not seen giving her much fatherly advice. In the first book, both are stuck in the early stages – Luke's wisdom is seen more in the third book.

At the same time, Clary meets the Silent Brothers, described as being warriors of the mind rather than the body. They're the ones who aid Clary with their advice and lead her to find her lost memories. Magnus Bane does the same, offering her the Grey Book and runes of her Shadowhunter heritage.

In the second book, Simon is transformed into a vampire because he follows his impulses and destructive jealousy. Jace likewise has become a destructive force for Clary, offering only a forbidden, confusing love. Both boys are eager to rush into battle, but less helpful when they should show restraint. Jace's passion is his undoing – a fear demon nearly destroys him and the Fairy Queen makes him kiss Clary to upset him. However, he asks Clary for a Fearless rune, as he's determined to master his weaknesses and become a figure of strength in the coming war. As he strengthens, Clary does likewise.

MYTHS AND MOTIFS IN *THE MORTAL INSTRUMENTS*

By the next book, Jace has become a model of order and law, only holding Clary's hand as they lie together for the single night he requests. He decides to track down Sebastian and offer his life for a chance to kill him and Valentine. However, Jace is too emotional to defeat his father, when he shows up, full of sorrow at his brother's death. Similarly, Luke's life is all about restraint – he loves Jocelyn but can't bear to tell her. All his life is about keeping secrets. In book three, however, Luke becomes Clary's guide into the world of Idris. Luke takes his place on the Council as the lone voice of wisdom and Clary's representative to the Clave, standing on the podium and dictating to them all. However, his inflexibility leads him to walk away from Jocelyn and nearly give her up. Luke as he insists on forming an alliance between Shadowhunters and Downworlders, Jace as he tracks Sebastian, and Simon who understands how to defeat Raphael, all learn wisdom in the course of the first trilogy and finally defeat their enemies.

Valentine and Sebastian are the crafty masterminds of the story and stronger adversaries than untrained Clary can defeat. Valentine, like the queen of the Seelie Court is "cool, menacing, calculating" (*Ashes* 256). He's the patriarchy, determined to rule the world as the force of pitiless rigidity. While both may begin as incarnations of violence (Valentine leads the Circle in an uprising sixteen years in the past; Sebastian murders Max), they grow beyond this stage into master liars and manipulators. Valentine's lie that Jace is his biological son haunts Clary and Jace's relationship for most of two books. Sebastian deceives Jace so well that Jace believes they're allies and best friends in the fifth book, just as he misleads them all when he first appears. Clary and Jace will need to learn true wisdom and perception, not to mention their own power of deception, in order to win against them.

At the climax of *City of Glass*, Clary risks her life portaling to the lake to warn the other Shadowhunters there's a threat. She half-drowns, just like at the book's beginning, only to discover Valentine has saved her. If Luke represents benevolent rationality, Valentine is the evil: inflexible obstruction and even madness. Clary reflects that he has "lost the ability to distinguish between force and cooperation, between fear and willingness, between love and torture" (*Glass* 482). He's an evil Jonathan Shadowhunter, the second to summon Raziel to make a new Shadowhunter race. And he's killed when Raziel administers the "Justice of Heaven" (*Glass* 495). The evil force of patriarchy and cruel order is killed by a greater force of order than himself, thanks to the wisdom and perception Clary uses for her final trick against him. In fact, only Clary can defeat him, not through force of arms but through her own cleverness. With intuition, faith, and love, all inspired by her friends, Clary finds the power to fight back silently, subtly. The patriarch, determined to seize total power considers her weak and helpless – very well, she will use that helplessness to defeat him.

The Feminine Sphere

Clary is surrounded by feminine role models, though she spends more time with masculine ones.

Toni Wolff, longtime mistress of Carl Jung, described four main feminine archetypes: Mother, Hetaera, Amazon, and Medial Woman. The Amazon is a virginal warrior-girl like Artemis or Katniss. This is Isabelle's role in the story. (Though Isabelle, like Artemis, has occasional relationships, she remains single and fiercely independent). Jocelyn of course is the nurturing, kindly and absent mother who can no longer shelter Clary.

The Hetaera (a sacred bride of ancient times) discovers her inner sensuality by relating to her consort. She is his lover or soulmate, inspiration or goddess figure, or on the dark side, femme fatale. She thinks in terms of her companion, just as the mother relates first to her child. Clary has few examples of this, but as she watches Jocelyn examine her past with Valentine and her future with Luke, she decides what she wants with Jace.

The Medial Woman is the most enigmatic of these figures. She is the seer, sage, prophetess, witch, or sorceress. "She is both a puzzle to herself and a mystery to those she encounters. In contrast to the other types, her primary relationship is to the other, the unknown, to God or gods" (Molton and Sikes 225). Thus, her shadow or negative side is in service to the demons. Madame Dorothea, who doesn't realize a demon has taken her over, is the perfect embodiment of this archetype. Clary seeks out Madame Dorothea for guidance, but Dorothea is a false guide. She is a conduit between the real world and that of dreams and the deep unconscious – it's no accident that Clary takes the feminine cup from her house.

"A woman's self-nurture includes an invitation for her to explore and integrate all four of the types into her awareness and understanding, one by one, over time" (Molton and Sikes 295). If she integrates all four types into her personality, she can use them as tools at need. Thus the Divine Child Clary is not clearly any of these types, but she tries each on at various moments as she decides who she wants to become. Mystic Clary receives visions from angels and scribes runes, Mother Clary offers to take Max shopping and cradles Simon as he lies dying. She is Hetaera Clary around Jace and Amazon Clary around the demons. The Shadow, in Jung's psychology, is "aspects of oneself which are considered by the ego to be undesirable or not useful and are therefore relegated to the dark" (Estés 85). However, the heroine will need to explore these aspects to understand the emotions she refuses to confront in herself.

Myths and Motifs in *The Mortal Instruments*

Wolff's Archetypes

	As creator	As destroyer	Power	Animus
Amazon	Competitor, hard worker, builder	Fighter and death-dealer	Man's world of war and intellect	Father
Hetaera	Inspiratrice, lover, enabler	Femme fatale	Woman's world of relationships and self-knowledge	Lover
Mother	Nurturer, protector, teacher	Devouring mother	Life, birth, and creation	Son
Medium	Seer, magician, wisewoman	Deceiver and distorter of the future	Death, rebirth, and the future	Wiseman

In the first book, Clary's mother is kidnapped, Isabelle's mother is absent. The Institute suffers from the lack of a mother-figure – mud is tracked everywhere, meals are disgusting, Hodge is unable to perform the healings needed. Book two sees a stronger feminine presence with Maryse and the Inquisitor taking charge. However, both are the cruel mothers who torture children or push them away. The Inquisitor has learned to dominate the patriarchy as she confines the powerful Jace and orders him to shut his sharp mouth. "A woman with a highly developed animus becomes overly aggressive, intellectual, and power-hungry" (Zweig 188). This is the Inquisitor, determined to best men at war. She issues ultimatums to Valentine, demanding he obey orders if he wants his son returned. However, she is a brittle figure, confined by the same narrow thinking that defines the Clave and sometimes Valentine himself. When Valentine doesn't play by her rules, she crumples in despair. From the Inquisitor, Clary, Jace, and Alec all learn that leaders can be wrong or follow personal vendettas. This is a step along the path to defying the Council and demanding change as Clary does at the book's end.

Clary lacks a wise female mentor or a romantic role model who's happily in love – Isabelle the Amazon and Jocelyn the Good Mother are only half the archetypes. However, by looking deep within, and listening to the wisdom of Jace, Magnus, Simon, and Luke, Clary manages to become a lover and mystic by the end of the trilogy, saving Jace and the world together with heart and spirit combined. By the third book, and especially the second trilogy, she becomes a nurturer for Simon, a lover for Jace, an amazon warrior who can battle Sebastian, and a seer who dreams with the angels.

The Double

The Double is a same-sex friend or companion. Like Frodo and Sam or Don Quixote and Sancho, this is a partner with opposite knowledge and abilities. This double can unlock the creative process and inspire the hero to great heights.

The negative side of the partner is the competitor. Jessamine and Tessa or Clary and Isabelle spend time as both friends and enemies. When they are on the same team, their contrasting skills and outlooks prove an invaluable partnership. When they argue, the Double's cruelty can spur the heroine to make daring choices and grow from the experience. "The competitor presents a challenge to overcome and thus provides an image of oneself to grow into" (M. Walker 51).

Isabelle is the story's Amazon, for whom "relationship with a man is through a role of being competitor or that of a comrade and rival who makes no personal demands" (Molton and Sikes 208). Isabelle has only platonic relationships with the boys of the story until the final pages of the third book, when she grows closer to Simon. She is a model for Clary of strength and independence but also their dark side: the Shadow Amazon may spend all her time trying to prove her toughness and superiority but is in fact insecure and displays anger and over-competitiveness. "Socially she can become a social hyena, and at home a jealous fury. She takes little time for a social life. Her relationships are mostly impersonal" (Molton and Sikes 189).

Isabelle goes to Magnus's party dressed all in silver "like a moon goddess" (*Bones* 208). To Clary, she's all Clary isn't – she's taller and dresses older and much cooler and more elegantly. Isabelle uses her beauty "like a whip," while Clary doesn't know she's beautiful (*Bones* 324). Isabelle always makes Clary feel scruffy – wearing Isabelle's clothes, at the Institute, Clary feels her shortness and lack of cleavage more than ever. In *Lost Souls*, Clary wishes she were like Isabelle, "so aware of your own feminine power you could wield it as a weapon" (244). "The double often appears with an aura of beauty, youth, and perfection or near-perfection" (M. Walker 49). She's all the heroine aspires to be, and thus a spur for growth and change.

Isabelle's room is black with gold and hot pink. Inside, the tables are covered in makeup bottles, vanilla perfume, glitter, and sequins. Filled with beautiful clothes and weapons, it reflects Isabelle – and all Clary isn't. Her room is orange, a cheerful, androgynous color. Clary usually wears braids, jeans, and plain shirts, while Isabelle wears sexy, dangerous black, white, red, and silver – goddess colors. Above it all shines her red pendent, like a fierce heart.

The ruby at Isabelle's throat pulses "like the beat of a distant heart" and warns her of danger (*Fallen Angels* 342). If the heroine has talismans of perception that make her stronger, Isabelle has already completed that journey. When bestowing the necklace on Isabelle's ancestress, Will says, "It will help keep you safe which is how I want you, and help you be a warrior, which is what you want" (*Clockwork Princess* 252). When her mother or grandmother passed it on, she offered it to Isabelle with similar sentiments. Its inscription reads, "True love cannot die," offering another stage for both Isabelle and Clary to reach in time.

However, as Clary puts on Isabelle's borrowed dress, she takes steps toward becoming a Shadowhunter, dark, powerful, and dangerous. Isabelle dresses Clary in a black spaghetti strap dress with fishnets and boots so that Clary looks "fairly badass" (*Bones* 210). She even offers Clary a thigh sheath. Isabelle puts Clary's hair up in an elegant swirl, and Clary finds herself remembering her romantic dream of dancing with Jace and Simon at an Idris ball. Under Isabelle's ministrations, Clary is suddenly grown up and alluring.

Feminine Magic

In the first book, she follows receiving Magnus's book with questing for and finding her mother's Mortal Cup. "Raziel's Cup, in which he mixed the blood of the angels and the blood of men and gave of this mixture to a man to drink and created the first Shadowhunter" is a grail of sorts (*Bones* 346). As Cassandra Clare comments:

> The Cup draws from all sorts of Cup legends – the Grail legend, for one, though it's not meant to be the Grail. It also draws from the imagery of the Tarot card class of Cups. The Cup is also a symbol of faith, and Shadowhunters are all about faith. ("Interview: Cassandra Clare")

Grail symbolism goes back for millennia: The top of the chalice is open to spiritual matters, the bottom is grounded in earth (Cirlot 43).

This cup has been hidden in Clary's mother's craft, her painted tarot cards. "Jocelyn clearly wanted only one person to be able to find the Cup, and that is Clary, and Clary alone" (*Bones* 329). The grail symbolizes the quest and is a source of illumination. Losing the grail is like losing one's inner ties (Cirlot 121). The cup is also a feminine symbol – it's no accident that Clary is the one to draw it from the Tarot deck where her mother hid it. The feminine is generally hidden in stories: Arthur has Excalibur but must quest across the world for the grail's elusive power.

> The cup, as a universal symbol of the mother-element, water, reflects the womb-vessel, and later, the chalice of resurrection, "the female-

symbolic bowl of life-giving blood." As for its feminine characteristics, the Grail dispenses both material food and spiritual solace. It preserves youth and maintains life. It heals knights wounded in battle. It radiates light and a sweet fragrance; it rejoices the troubled heart. In all these ways it is a source of solace and spirituality, elevating man above the animal and toward the divine. It is the guiding symbol, the anima, for which man quests. (Frankel, *Girl to Goddess* 58).

In this series, the cup gives birth to Shadowhunters, though Sebastian and Lilith seek to corrupt it and create a race of demonic Shadowhunters through evil birth magic in the second trilogy.

However, Clary must discover that her mother had the Cup's power all along, as has Clary – it's been waiting in her house all this time, like the ruby slippers on Dorothy's feet, waiting for the heroine to call it forth. "Men may quest for the grail, but each woman already bears the feminine deep within, and only needs evoke it" (Frankel, *Girl to Goddess* 58). Drawing it from the tarot deck indicates Clary is claiming her feminine strength.

The Ace of Cups or "love card" has a rayed sun. Madame Dorothea warns her that love can be terrible and powerful. The suns and rubies decorating the golden cup represent the heroic principle – the heir inheriting the throne. As Clary claims the card, she is taking on her role as Shadowhunter and Chosen One. The sun represents courage, passion, and creative energy, all traits Clary is known for. In tarot, on the positive side, it means glory, spirituality, and illumination, all gifts Clary needs to beat Valentine. On the negative side it is vanity and unrealistic idealism (Cirlot 317-320). These latter traits show up as the teens are overconfident when fighting the demon in Dorothea and Alec is severely wounded.

Facing Death

In the first book, Clary follows Jace to Valentine's base on Roosevelt Island. This ancient Shadowhunter fortress bears the Circle's symbol on the floors – it is Valentine's stronghold. In many tales, the heroine ventures from her place of power, like the Little Mermaid's magical ocean, into the patriarchal castle where she is powerless. As Clary explores, the very building oppresses her. The weapons won't pull free of the walls, and the rooms are thick with dark shadows and the screams of the forsaken. Worst of all, her mother is chained to a bed helpless and unconscious.

This withdrawal and magical sleep is a time for the woman to adjust to new roles and new situations. "Women and artists know instinctively that there are times in life where we must be unreachable, times when we must insist that those around us, especially those nearest and dearest, remain at a distance if anything significant is to develop inside us," explains Joan Gould, author of the fairytale analysis *Spinning Straw into Gold*. (98).

Clary falls asleep or faints several significant times in the series, the first being when she is poisoned and awakes three days later in the Institute. Literally overnight, she has become a Shadowhunter. Metaphorically, she needs time to absorb this change, this entry into a new world, thus the sleep state. Sleeping Beauty and Snow White have similar withdrawals during their own stories. Jocelyn enters the coma herself as a defense mechanism. She awakens to find her own world has changed – Clary is a Shadowhunter and Jocelyn must return to Idris and face the path she thought she'd left forever.

Spiritual gifts are just as important as the physical. Clary's greatest runes are created in moments of love and classically feminine emotion. At the second book's climax, the world falls away and she pours all her power, love, and hope, and rage into an Opening rune. Her pure love and desperation tear apart the patriarchal stronghold of Valentine's ship with all his demons in it. They fall into the purifying feminine ocean, with magical Nixies waiting to save them all (as Jace has called the feminine powers of the cavalry to the rescue). As she falls into the dark ocean in a near-death, she sees a nixie come for her and imagines it is her mother, source of protective feminine power. "Water evokes the deep feminine, interconnectivity and flexibility. It offers a chance to let go, to let intuition and nature buoy the woman forward" (Frankel, *Girl to Goddess* 63). Before the Council in the third book, Clary feels intimidated. However, she gazes out at Simon and thinks of Jace. Knowing their love and faith in her, she draws a new rune. She creates an illusion of everyone's loved one – she feels love so she can create it in turn.

Clary's journey to Jace's childhood home is a different kind of descent. It is another of Valentine's strongholds, but this one is hidden underground, the place of initiation. Further, the angel waiting below is the source of Clary's feminine magic – dreams, prophetic visions, and runes. This place stands on the threshold, blending science and magic, Valentine's cruel experiments with the inexplicable miracle of a true angel. Clary and Jace together free the angel and decipher its message, returning to the world above with a new understanding.

At the climax of the third book, Clary risks her life to save Jace and stop Valentine. However, Valentine is too powerful for her: Clary is incapacitated and robbed of her voice when Jace arrives, confronts Valentine, and dies. The silenced heroine is common in myths and fairytales, from the story of Echo to The Six Swans and more:

> Fairytales show silent, virtuous maids like Cinderella and the little mermaid, who never complain of their vicious treatment, and even more silent, virtuous but dead mothers. Contrasted with this are the

vocal witches and stepmothers giving orders. (Frankel, *From Girl to Goddess* 22)

This theme is found throughout the world, from sleeping princesses to gagged and enchanted questing girls. Disturbingly, this best reflects the real status of women through history: illiterate and confined to cleaning and childbearing. Valentine binds and silences his daughter, then dismisses her as a helpless sacrifice who can do nothing to stop him. The rune Clary carves is tiny, unlike the great binding rune or Mark of Cain. At the height of Valentine's master plan, he is defeated by his neglected, bound, ignored daughter, who scribbles a single word. This too is the heroine's journey, often the path of silently knitting coats of nettles or keeping faith for seven years to rescue loved ones and bring an end to evil.

Clary comes to understand Valentine, and even sympathizes a bit with the man who honestly mourns Jace as she does. By watching him, Clary understands how to defeat him with his own runes when he won't look for a quiet act of desperation. Valentine's misogyny has made him dismiss her as a threat, just as he once dismissed a pregnant, despairing Jocelyn. This narrow thinking proves his downfall. Further, she makes a wiser choice than he does when Raziel offers her a boon: Valentine chose death, she chooses life.

Like Clary's other great moments, this one springs from emotion. Jace's death gives her the clue she needs, for, as she reflects, "there was so much power in a name (*Glass* 489). As with the rune she draws for the Council, she thinks of Jace and realizes he'd be disappointed if she stopped fighting. When the Angel Raziel offers her anything in the world, Clary once more relies on love and asks for the only person she truly wants: Jace. Her love brings him back to life in one of the heroine's classic quests. She's succeeding with the "deep magic" of Narnia or the brave desperation of Katniss and her berries – the older, quieter wisdom the powerful tyrant has discounted.

She ends the trilogy strong enough in herself to face down the all-powerful matriarch, the fairy queen, and refuse her offer of a favor. Further, Simon points out Clary's strong enough to defend herself with a variety of weapons. By defeating Valentine the Patriarch, Clary can usher in a better world with peace between Downworlders and Shadowhunters. With the lessons she's learned, she demands that her mother marry Luke and treasure the love in her life, just as Clary has brought Jace back from the dead.

Myths and Motifs in *The Mortal Instruments*

Comparison of Models – The Steps of the Journey

The Heroine's Journey	City of Bones	The Mortal Instruments
The World of Common Day	Clary grows up in Brooklyn	Clary grows up in Brooklyn
The Call to Adventure	Clary enters a club and discovers demons are real. Her mother is kidnapped directly after.	Clary enters a club and discovers demons are real. Her mother is kidnapped directly after.
Refusal of the Call	Clary's mother tries to take her away.	Clary's mother tries to take her away.
The Ruthless Mentor and the Bladeless Talisman	Rune powers woken by Magnus Bane	Magnus Bane, Fairy Queen, Grey Book, Mortal Cup, Mirror.
The crossing of the first threshold / Opening One's Senses	Clary enters the Institute and learns about Shadowhunters	Clary enters Idris
Sidekicks, Trials, Adversaries	Simon at the hotel Dumont, battling Abbadon	Battling demons and Valentine's followers
Wedding the Animas / Facing Bluebeard / Finding the Sensitive Man / Confronting the Powerless Father	Meeting Jace in the greenhouse	After spending the night with Jace before they face death, she convinces the patriarchal Clave that she can end the war
Descent into Darkness / Atonement with the Mother / Facing Destroyer / Integration and Apotheosis	Clary enters Valentine's stronghold on Roosevelt Island	Clary Portals to the Mirror. Silenced, with Jace dead, she redraws the rune. She ends the threat to Jocelyn, Luke, and the Lightwoods and saves Jace
Reward: Winning the Family	Clary saves her mother, still unconscious	Clary restores Jace to life

The Heroine's Journey	City of Bones	The Mortal Instruments
Torn Desires The Magic Flight Reinstating the Family Return	Clary returns to the Shadowhunters	Clary celebrates with the Shadowhunters
Power Over Life and Death Ascension of the New Mother		Clary becomes a Shadowhunter with Jace

Lilith Rises

Changed by her adventure, the heroine realizes that her father is not the omnipotent god in whom she had once completely believed. She has her own power now and her own success. In this moment, the heroine realizes that she need not depend on her father, or men at all, to rescue and protect her. She is the heroine, equally as valid as the hero.

Often, this encounter takes place in the middle of the epic quest, before descending into the final conflict with the witch. Though a resting place, it is also a revelation. By returning home, the heroine can see how far she has evolved. Beauty visits her family and chooses between magic and the mundane. Dorothy returns to the Wizard but discovers him a humbug. Cinderella returns from the magical world of the ball. Now she must cater to her stepsisters and pretend that she is the same person. Her night of glamour is over. Yet, she finds that the status quo no longer fits her, if indeed, it ever did. She is a different person more suited to the prince's world than her own. (Frankel, *Girl to Goddess* 104).

The two trilogies fit together as the two halves of Clary's heroine's journey – on the first, she faces the patriarch, Valentine. Her second, deadlier adversary will be the Dark Mother, Lilith. The first trilogy is about beating Valentine and the patriarchal Council, both too rigid with their desire for order. The second trilogy is more concerned with the spirituality of Clary's power as she quests to become lover and mystic, the one who can stand by Jace through the darkest of evils and harness the angels' power.

However, her first adventure has taught her a great deal. She begins the second trilogy having fully integrated into Jace's world of the supernatural. She trains in fighting and is fully committed to her new boyfriend. Isabelle and Jocelyn have integrated the lover archetype into themselves, reflecting Clary's happiness with Jace. Magnus and Alec are equally blissful. All is well in the Shadowhunters' world.

Myths and Motifs in *The Mortal Instruments*

The second series reflects a shift from male power to female: Robert Lightwood abandons his family. Magnus and Alec quarrel constantly, and Magnus finally leaves the cause. The Council drifts, uncertain how to rule in this new world. Luke is wounded critically, as Jocelyn was in the previous trilogy. Simon loses his godlike power. Jace is possessed and kidnapped.

By contrast, Isabelle is gaining confidence. When Clary loses Jace, Isabelle, her strong female side, grows even stronger and becomes "her staunchest defender" (*Lost Souls* 12). Isabelle marches her protectively past the glaring Shadowhunters and accompanies her to bargain with the treacherous fairy queen. This time, Clary must confront her without Jace's clever tongue. When Jace is taken from her, Clary turns all her energy toward getting him back. However, with Isabelle and the fairy queen as allies, she's coming from a stronger position, with her feminine energies marshaled. Clary also begins wearing the fairy queen's silver bell rather than Jace's ring around her neck. She's seeking feminine power without her boyfriend. Camille replaces the weaker Raphael as another selfish yet strong female, glowing with power. Maia takes a larger role. Clary herself has been trained in battling demons, and she becomes strong enough for a physical battle with Sebastian.

However, Clary struggles with her rune powers because she hasn't yet explored her dark side, only the lighter side of her nature that mastered physical power over Valentine's ship, Valentine's summoning circle, and the hierarchical Clave. Clary has not delved into the mystical feminine side of her abilities. In *City of Fallen Angels*, she finally tries. However, her first foray into the dark side terrifies her: She revives a Shadowhunter from the dead and is horrified at his agony. Luke warns her that she needs to train and not only use her power for big moments: He comments, "Think of Magnus: His power is a part of him. You seem to think of yours as separate from you. Something that happens to you. It's not. It's a tool you need to learn to use" (*Fallen Angels* 137).

This is good advice modern psychologists would agree with: Clarissa Pinkola Estés, author of *Women Who Run with the Wolves* explains, "We find that by opening the door to the shadow realm a little, and letting out various elements a few at a time, relating to them, finding use for them, negotiating, we can reduce being surprised by shadow sneak attacks and unexpected explosions" (236). The Shadow is all one's buried or rejected impulses – rage, selfishness, misbehavior. However, a Shadow is also a force of strength and motivator for growth – it has positive qualities to teach the too polite, too-repressed Chosen One. But Clary has only begun exploring this side of herself. To understand her dark side, Clary will need to face the Dark Mother.

Lilith is the powerful mother to the reborn Jonathan, and to the race of dark Shadowhunters that follow. As she shows in *City of Fallen Angels*, she will do anything, even kill, to protect her unnatural child. This is a lesson that Clary, future mother to Shadowhunter children, must learn. Her mother cannot teach her the lesson. Estés says that to defend her unnatural child, the mother needs fierce qualities such as fearlessness, vehemence, and fearsomeness (176). Jocelyn, however loving, backed away from raising a Shadowhunter child and instead robbed Clary of her powers, forcing her to grow up "normal" in the mundane world. To learn how to fight and kill to protect her dangerous, powerful future child, to keep her child safe to the exclusion of everything, Clary must learn from Lilith.

She is the strong shadow of femininity, all Clary isn't. She tells Jace: "I am not a *man*. I have no male pride for you to trick me with, and I am not interested in single combat. That is merely a weakness of your sex, not mine. I am a woman. I will use any weapon and all weapons to get what I want" (*Fallen Angels* 371). Ironically, this is the lesson Jace has tried to teach Clary in combat: to be ruthless, pitiless, clever and determined. "It's the Mother Goddess in her dark aspect, devoted to fertility and death but caring nothing about personal happiness, who forces the girl to grow up" (Gould 20).

Lilith is "the demon goddess of dead children" whose temple is filled with dead babies (*Fallen Angels* 355). Lilith collects young women off the street then drives them to get pregnant and poison their unborn children with demon blood. Lilith is cursed with barrenness: her thousand babies died. Further, she's Sebastian's "mother," who created him with her demonic blood. As such, she's Clary's wicked stepmother. She is the one to take over Jace's mind, seducing him away from the immature virgin.

She plots to resurrect Sebastian, keeping him in a glass coffin like Snow White's. She adds, "As Jonathan Shadowhunter led the first Nephilim, so shall this Jonathan lead the new race that I intend to create" (*Fallen Angels* 331). In *The Uses of Enchantment*, Bruno Bettelheim observes the destructive safety of stagnation in Snow White's coffin:

> Whether it is Snow White in her glass coffin or Sleeping Beauty on her bed, the adolescent dream of everlasting youth and perfection is just that: a dream. The alteration of the original curse, which threatened death, to one of prolonged sleep suggests the two are not all that different. If we do not want to change and develop, then we might as well remain in a deathlike sleep. During their sleep the heroines' beauty is a frigid one; theirs is the isolation of narcissism. In such self-involvement which excludes the rest of the world there is no suffering, but also no knowledge to be gained, no feelings to be experienced. (234)

Sebastian's sleep is likewise one of icy preservation, but not growth or change.

Myths and Motifs in *The Mortal Instruments*

Clary may think she has nothing in common with this dark mother, but Lilith reveals the truth: Clary's reviving Jace has let Lilith revive Sebastian: "Thinking you could be the only people in the world who could have their dead loved one back, and that there would be *no consequences*. That *is* what you thought, isn't it, both of you? Fools" (*Fallen Angels* 385). Clary and Jace have been living in a world in which their love only affects them, but it matters to their families, as the next book will reveal. Clary has played with the power of death, not merely life, and she didn't understand the gravity of the consequences. Now she is learning them, directly from the dark goddess of the series. Being able to speak with the dead and conjure angels is useless until she can harness her power and understand how to control it.

Clary is dragged into Lilith's temple in *City of Fallen Angels*. The words on her altar reference Proverbs from the Bible, describing the woman who forsakes God, as Lilith has:

> For her house inclineth unto death, and her paths unto the dead. None that go unto her return again, neither take they hold of the paths of life. (Proverbs 2:18-19)

Inside, all is the dark reversal of the Shadowhunters' blessed Institute: Clary reads an evil book of runes and is revolted. She also takes an athame, a sacrificial knife used to summon demons as it's described, and marks it into a Shadowhunter blade, turning Lilith's dark magic into a source of light.

Lilith's temple is a place of terror, with dead and dying perversions of childbirth all around. This stronghold is the dark side of love: obsession, torture, singlemindedness. However, facing this is a part of growing up: Clary, Isabelle, and Maia all must accept that there's no ideal, perfect love – that their boyfriends can sin and even do unforgiveable acts. All three enter Lilith's temple to save their loved ones and discover that they can indeed forgive their men. The innermost cave is a place of total truth with all illusions burned away. By accepting this lesson, all these couples can grow and find a real love, accepting the other person's all-too-human flaws.

Around her, Clary's males have been weakened: Jace is possessed, Simon held hostage by the threat to her. Sebastian is frozen in his coffin. Lilith says, "We are all needed here. Simon to die. Jace to live. Jonathan to return. And you, Valentine's daughter, to be the catalyst for it all (*Fallen Angels* 341). Clary uses trickery and love once more to write on Jace with his father's dagger and erase Lilith's rune on his heart. Her rune power and force of love save her, along with cleverness – Simon, Clary's creation and appointed warrior, also uses all three to destroy Lilith. With the Mark burning on Simon's forehead, Clary asks herself "*What have I done?*" (*Fallen Angels* 391). She bears the responsibility for his acts as she fashioned him into an invincible warrior.

Jace as Destroyer

In the new trilogy, Jace and Clary are finally allowed to be together. In fact, he becomes her occasional weapons tutor and Shadowhunter partner as well as boyfriend. Clary decides that they are soulmates, eternally, perfectly in love. She gives up her mundane world for his, and might even have given up her mother if the laws weren't in chaos. They spend training sessions making out, and Clary neglects her friends to stare moonily at her boyfriend. He's taking over her entire world, so much that the old her is in danger of vanishing. The journey involves finding balance between the daylight world and the magical world that represents the subconscious. However, Clary is giving up on all aspects of her former life to spend her days with Shadowhunters. She's acting like *Twilight*'s Bella Swan, who offers to give up parents, Jacob's friendship, college, children, her soul, and her sanity just to be with Edward.

Jocelyn points out that the universe has thrown so many obstacles at their love, from the brother-sister relationship to Jace's possession that "the two of you are *not meant to be together*" (*Lost Souls* 122). The strong feminine voice in Clary's life, missing from the first trilogy, has returned, and is trying to protect Clary from being completely subsumed in the new relationship. "You love him so much. It scares me," she worries, voicing the defensive fears inside Clary herself (*Fallen Angels* 288). Clary hasn't yet found her identity – she's hiding from her rune powers and hasn't decided who she wants to be, aside from Jace's perfect girlfriend and Shadowhunter partner. As such, the new her could easily become lost.

"There isn't anything I wouldn't do for Jace," Clary insists (*Lost Souls* 142). Simon must point out how destructive this philosophy is: He would do almost anything for Clary. But he wouldn't kill innocents or destroy the world. Evil Jace might ask her to do all that and more. In fact, that is what Jace asks, and Clary must make her choice. Describing Jace's possession, the author adds:

> Jace is in this place where he needs to be saved. But he's not really Jace anymore. So the question is, how much would you do for love? And what if you have to do an immoral thing for a moral reason because you love someone so much? At what point do you have to stop trying to save this person because it's bad for the world in general, even if you love them very much. That's the central tension that kind of rips up the characters in *Lost Souls*. The group that wants to save him more than anything else, and the group that is willing to sacrifice him for the greater good. (Bressia, "Cassandra Clare talks 'Clockwork Prince'")

"When a woman is attempting to avoid the facts of her own devastations, her night dreams will shout warnings to her" such as "flee," or even "go for the kill," explains Estés (54).

Myths and Motifs in *The Mortal Instruments*

Clary struggles to commit to Jace completely. Their brother-sister barrier is gone. However, when she considers making love with Jace, he takes the Herondale knife and stabs her with it. These are Jace's nightmares, but they are directed by the dark feminine presence of the story. If all characters are aspects of Clary, Lilith is the cruel Shadow but also Clary's fierceness, determined to stop Jace from taking her over. The dreams she sends reveal Jace as a killer who could tear Clary to pieces. In the next book, his predatory side is even more pronounced, as he tries to make her drink a demon's blood "for her own good." Evil Jace is the Predator without disguise or apology.

Later, he asks to put a binding rune on her, but it ends up being a rune of coercion: 'Something darker that spoke of control and submission, of loss and darkness" (*Fallen Angels* 305). All this is the dark side of love, and it frightens her. Clary swoons like Sleeping Beauty confronted with the spindle's prick (a metaphor for sex, as the rune of total commitment is). The powerful feminine inside Clary is raging against her giving up her identity completely. Once again, Jace is revealed as the Predator, his rune selfish and coercive. With Lilith's mark on him, Jace becomes a stranger. "Like a recording of him, she thought, all the tones and patterns of his voice there, but the life that animated it gone" (*Fallen Angels* 336). "Now the naive self has knowledge about a killing force loose within the psyche," Estés explains (55).

Clearly, Simon was right to warn her that she needs to reprioritize. "Today, it is generally understood that the romantic and spiritual man-god – the male ideal worthy of a woman's self-sacrifice and worship, for whom she is expected to set aside herself and her life – simply does not exist" (Pearson and Pope 35). This is the lesson Clary must learn – that overpowering love is wonderful, but she cannot sacrifice the world for Jace. Only if she sees him as an equal partner, not her golden angel, can they have a real relationship.

Blurred Morality

In *City of Lost Souls*, Clary comes to realize the world isn't as black and white as she'd envisioned. With Jace in danger, she would break any rule, betray any loyalty to get him back.

First, she bargains with the fairy queen and steals magic rings from the Institute. After, she keeps the rings for herself. In Venice she happily steals a gondola with Jace and tries fairy drugs. This is Clary dipping into her Shadow, just to try it out. It's more delightful than she'd expected to ignore her mother's chiding and her own knowledge of consequences.

Jace, flirting with her, urges her to abandon all control. She sees that Jace has given up his principles and only lives for the moment now – and is happier without ethics. This makes her question her own rules. Together they kill a demon and steal its possessions, and for the first time she feels the rush and joy of fighting. The silvery adamas they had bargained for is darkened as she is, its pure angelic silver marred by her blood. She puts on the dress Sebastian brings her – black lace and beads. In it, her eyes are smudged with "dark shadow" and she has "a certain toughness" (*Lost Souls* 300). She remembers wearing Isabelle's dress in book one and taking her first steps into the demon world as she enters an even darker realm this time.

Jace guides her into the Bone Chandelier and references the quote "Easy is the decent into hell." There, a black-winged angel drips strings of garnets like blood. The gruesome bone chandelier dominates, sprinkling the room with silvery fairy drugs. Under its light, Clary gives in to temptation. She makes out with Jace and drinks the drugs, discarding her good girl role.

When Clary turns into her own evil twin, dressing provocatively and slipping into a demon party (as she did in *City of Bones*), she's allowing her Shadow to take over – all the impulses she's always buried, all the sexy, provocative, bad girl impulses she never allows to surface. With the catalyst of various Shadows – Sebastian and Isabelle, who both offer her sexy dresses, Clary feels her unacknowledged, unexplored bad girl side pushing through. And she revels in it. Campbell describes facing this Shadow as "destruction of the world that we have built and in which we live, and of ourselves within it; but then a wonderful reconstruction, of the bolder, cleaner, more spacious, and fully human life" (8). Allowing the Shadow out, learning its lessons and acknowledging its place in the day to day world is the process of being human.

In *Lost Souls*, Jace must contend with his Shadow of evil Jace: Clary must contend with Sebastian. He tells her that he needs Jace "But in his heart he's not like me. You are" (*Lost Souls* 358). Sebastian even holds up hands like Jocelyn's and talks about painting. In fact, he represents her buried side: all the seething emotions, power, and desire to lash out people keep hidden under their skins. Sebastian tells her unpleasant truths, pointing out that Jocelyn isn't as wonderful as Clary always thought: She betrayed her husband, lied for months, and arranged the slaughter of all their friends. "She stole your memories. Have you forgiven her?" he adds, like the angry voice deep inside Clary (*Lost Souls* 358). He points out Clary too has the potential for evil – she killed their father and doesn't mourn what she's done.

As she tries on his lifestyle like the black dress, she finds herself seeing Sebastian's side, acting on the dark voice that whispers within her. Under the drugs' influence, she finds herself liking Sebastian. She's become her own evil twin there in the club, as she thinks of him as her brother and can't recall why she should fear him. Side by side, they gaze into a pool, and Sebastian tells her how much they share. "You have a dark heart in you, Valentine's daughter… You just won't admit it" (*Lost Souls* 316).

In one of her posted deleted scenes, Clare shows Sebastian's thought process.

> Clarissa was Father's real daughter too, and who knew what strange brew the combination of Father's blood and Heaven's power had formed to run through Clarissa's veins? She might not be very different from himself.
> …
>
> Jonathan dreamed of a girl standing in the sea with hair like scarlet smoke coiling over her shoulders, winding and unwinding in the untameable wind. Everything was stormy darkness, and in the raging sea were pieces of wreckage that had once been a boat and bodies floating facedown. She looked down on them with cool green eyes and was not afraid.
>
> Clarissa had done that – wreaked destruction like he would have. In the dream, he was proud of her. His little sister. ("City of Glass: A Dark Transformation.")

He shares her prophetic dreams and also her longing for someone like him, someone who will understand his unique powers. On some level, he respects her and cares for her as Valentine does not.

Talking with Sebastian, Clary comes to realize he isn't all evil either – he genuinely likes her and Jace, and wants them to be a family. He tells her, "You can't go back. You've already thrown your lot in with Jace. You might as well do it wholeheartedly" (*Lost Souls* 257). Fighting beside him, she discovers the high of battle, and it makes her feel invincible. "Amazing that it had taken fighting alongside *Sebastian* of all people to flip the switch inside her that seemed to turn her Shadowhunter instincts on" (*Lost Souls* 298). By abandoning her good self, she's embraced the fighter side of her heritage. The gold ring of responsibility, link to her mission and family back home, is her only tether.

After she parties all night, tries fairy drugs, and nearly gives in to Jace, her ring vanishes. Like Bluebeard's wife, she's done the forbidden and so been stained with its consequences: she can no longer reach her friends. Of course, cut off from them, she must choose for herself and find a way to save the world without outside help.

By trying to beat Sebastian, Clary must become him, resorting to dirty tricks she would never use under ordinary circumstances. However, pretending to be their ally is bringing her closer to their side. "You're everything like me," he hisses. "You infiltrated us. You faked friendship, faked caring" (*Lost Souls* 446). In the end, Clary realizes she's come to understand Sebastian, an invaluable skill for their next encounter.

Though she is more comfortable with her dark side, Clary is still a warrior of the light, In the battle, Simon gives her the sword "and in that moment, she was no longer Clary, his friend since childhood, but a Shadowhunter, an avenging angel who belonged with that sword in her hand" (*Lost Souls* 485-486). The sword, named Glorious, was once given by the Archangel Michael to lead God's chosen in battle. Clary accepts the sword to do just that.

Clary stabs Jace and Sebastian, and far off, the evil side of herself that has been allowed to whisper to her, screams in agony. It's over. Clary has another near death as she crumples, feeling like she's burning alive alongside Jace.

Looking at Jace, Clary realizes evil Jace doesn't love her, only an idealized picture of her. For fairytale heroines, the test is often to withstand pity – if the heroine turns from the path at every cry for help, she will never reach her goal. Clary's task is to destroy the Predator taking over her life and ignore the maternal impulse that urges her to spare her lover pain. For Evil Jace to be broken apart and Good Jace to return, Clary must be ruthless. She summons the cruel, expedient side she's learned from Sebastian, the side that would sacrifice a loved one to win a larger goal. With it, Clary stabs Jace with Glorious, burning away the false images and blurry glass through which each has been seeing the other.

Jace is broken down with the sword and burned by heavenly fire until the evil shatters. After he returns to life, he and Clary begin a more balanced relationship. They discuss their priorities and agree to trust each other in the future. There will be further trials as Clary explores her darker nature and faces death, together with the world's end, one last time, but she and Jace will approach the quest from a more honest and united place.

Simon's Hero Journey

Some characters don't have hidden powers or destinies: they're ordinary people dragged into events until they develop the magic. This is Bilbo Baggins, the Narnia children, Dorothy Gale, Peter Parker. And this is Simon Lewis, the most ordinary boy of the series…at least at the start. However, he shouldn't be discounted because he's ordinary. With his camp skills, he saves all the heroic Shadowhunters through cleverness, shooting out a window in *City of Bones* to burn the greater demon with sunlight. His status as the ordinary guy of the story is emphasized on every page with his geeky references that the mysterious Shadowhunters don't get. In fact, they're all in a fantasy adventure and Simon reads fantasy adventures. As such, he has a power of practicality and wisdom in the magical world. "Never believe the bad guy is dead until you see a body" he says in *City of Ashes*. "That just leads to unhappiness and surprise ambushes" (428).

Facing death and returning from the experience with new knowledge is the crux of the hero's journey. Through this journey, the hero must accept his dark side – Simon is questing to understand his new vampire powers and accept them as a strength rather than damnation. Simon has three transitions into the magical world: he becomes a vampire (otherworld), he becomes a daylighter (unique power), he gets the mark of Cain (his talisman from Clary, his Galadriel). And that's just the first trilogy.

He meets Isabelle as he first discovers magic exists: she's his guide into that world, as Jace is Clary's. In fact, he drinks a fairy potion to impress both girls; he feels jealous that they are part of the magic world and he is an excluded "mundane." "I've always been the one who needed you more than you needed me," he tells Clary sadly (*Bones* 303). This commences a mini adventure as Simon becomes a rat, gets kidnapped by vampires, and bites one to save the day. Though Clary saves him, he's already tasted a vampire's blood. In *City of Ashes*, a jealous Simon returns to the vampires' hotel and is transformed. He dies, quite literally in front of Clary and her friends, and revives as a fledgling vampire. Now he has truly entered the magical world, by becoming a Downworlder.

On Valentine's ship, Simon faces death a second time, and only survives by feeding off Jace. However, he returns much stronger, even before he's revealed as a Daylighter. Clary realizes Simon sounds different: "He sounded like someone who felt like he could face Valentine Morgenstern on equal footing" (*Ashes* 418). After they escape the ship, the sun shines on Simon and highlights him in gold. Simon accepts death as they sail into the sunrise with Clary cradling him.

Facing death is the central moment of the hero's journey, coming to terms with the fear of mortality and growing stronger. Both of Simon's moments have made him near-invincible and given him supernatural strength. "The conscious personality here has come in touch with a charge of unconscious energy which it is unable to handle and must now suffer...while learning how to come to terms with this power of the dark and emerge, at last, to a new way of life," Joseph Campbell explains (146).

In the third book, Simon offers his life to the vampire Raphael in return for the vampires joining the war against Valentine. To do this, he realizes he needs a talisman, so he asks Clary to protect him with the Mark of Cain. She gives it to him, like Galadriel's phial of light given to Frodo, or the Lady of the Lake's protective scabbard. With Clary's mark on him, Simon walks into possible death, faces Raphael, and wins his alliance. He returns from his ordeal strengthened once more: In battle, he needs to be "vampire Simon, a creature he barely even knew" rather than the gentle geeky human (*Glass* 470). His dark savage side frightens him, but it offers extraordinary strength and speed if he's willing to tap it. For the first time, Simon accepts he's a vampire and demands the right to win his people a seat on the Council and bind Shadowhunters and Downworlders together.

In the second series, he finds himself seeking normality. He's torn between two women: magical Isabelle and prosaic Maia who wants to play Halo and discuss comics. Simon tells her, "You treated me like I was normal. You've never called me 'Daylighter' or 'vampire' or anything but Simon" (*Fallen Angels* 300). "Maia was calm and grounded; Isabelle lived at a high pitch of excitement. Maia was a steady light in the darkness; Isabelle a burning star, spinning through the void" (*Fallen Angels* 95). Both call to different sides of his personality.

However, his attempt to be normal fails. When his mother rejects him, Simon realizes he can't continue faking being human. He loses his mother, and Maia breaks up with him. Clary is no longer his comic book buddy but a Shadowhunter. He's quickly leaving the normal world behind as he becomes part of the magical one. Simon has his new werewolf brother (responsibility) pitted against temptation (Camille and Raphael's war). He struggles between these two impulses and lets these three mentors (of a sort) counsel him on his choices. At last he betrays Camille and chooses the Shadowhunters.

If one denies his or her Shadow and pretends one is only good, with no angry impulses, the Shadow can take over. Simon spends all his effort pretending to be human, reluctantly drinking blood or ignoring his need to do so. Worse, Simon doesn't realize that animal blood isn't enough for him, and that skipping meals will make him attack humans. "When someone is always well-behaved, kind, and restrained, they are not taking the time to be moody and angry, to connect with their Shadow. Thus it can unexpectedly take over the entire personality" (Frankel, *Buffy* 169). Without warning, Simon bites the innocent Maureen, and he mourns his act through most of the book. At the end, she turns up a vampire – a walking proof of his guilt that will live forever.

At the climax of the fourth book, he uses his Mark of Cain deliberately as a weapon to save Clary. By doing so, he accepts it's a gift. After, he tells Luke about feeding off Maureen. "The more you try to crush your true nature, the more it will control you," Luke warns (*Fallen Angels* 419). Simon cannot ignore his dark side or it, like his urge to feed, will rise and take him over. He must use his powers if he doesn't want them using him. With this new knowledge, Simon decides to go home and face his mother.

However, Simon still hasn't truly accepted being a vampire. It takes Isabelle to help him with that. She tells him, "Being a vampire is part of you" (*Lost Souls* 264) and makes him know that she loves every part of him – including the vampire part. For the first time he experiences what it really means to drink the blood of someone in a mutual loving relationship and he finds a measure of pride and peace. When he leaves behind Maia, who makes him feel normal, and commits to Isabelle, the bad girl who dates Downworlders, he turns his back on his human life.

Myths and Motifs in *The Mortal Instruments*

He faces the Angel Raziel and accepts possible death once again to seek help for Clary, Isabelle, and Jace. But Raziel demands a different price. The Mark of Cain helps Simon feel "like a conductor for a lightning bolt, sheer energy passing through him with deadly force" (*Lost Souls* 426-427). It's what makes him special. Still, he gives it up for the Shadowhunters in a sacrifice like the ones he makes in each book.

Raziel observes, "You are a warrior of Heaven, Daylighter, whether you like it or not" (*Lost Souls* 427). By giving him the sword, Raziel appoints him as a soldier for the side of light, adding that the sword "possesses the power of Heaven's fire" (*Lost Souls* 428) – Simon has proof at last that he is on the side of the angels. Clary points out at book's end that thinking he's evil because he's a vampire is a question of how he sees himself – he can't say God's name because he fears he's corrupted, but he's actually not. As always, she is his light in the darkness who helps him see the truth. With heaven's blessing, he begins to quest toward balance once more.

Clare revealed recently that Simon will have a further large arc in the final book, and as Sarah Rees Brennan mischievously added, someone will rip his shirt off (*Cassandra Clare's Clockwork Princess Bus Tour*). Raphael has sworn revenge on Simon, and Maureen, too, is waiting. Combining vampire powers and everyday wisdom, he will complete his journey from darkness into salvation.

Jace's Hero Journey

Jace's struggle through the series is with morality. His first family, Valentine, was evil, deceptive, and loving. His second family is more moral but less accepting: When Maryse Lightwood rejects him, Jace finds himself turning to Valentine. Clare notes that Valentine is a strong character, with powerful shadow traits to offer the hero:

> Valentine is someone who has total conviction and dedication. He would sacrifice anything for what he thinks is the greater good. He would die for it. That would be a wonderful quality, if he was right about what the greater good was. ("Cassandra Clare's Interview with German Magazine, Daisuki")

At the end of book one, Jace's struggle begins. He had sworn to take revenge on evil Valentine who killed his good father, Michael Wayland. But Jace discovers Valentine is that father. His loyalty is split. In his confusion, Clary becomes his spiritual guide, reminding him that the Lightwoods are his family. At the climax of the first book, Jace saves Luke and renames himself as Jace Wayland, not Jonathan Morgenstern. He decides at that moment that he doesn't want to follow his father's path but his own.

Valentine tempts him with the safety of childhood: to return to Idris. Jace, now an adult, rejects the offer. Idris may be alluring, but Jace now has the moral strength to understand Valentine is a monster. Gazing at him, Jace feels "a persistent familial affection corroded through with bleakness, disappointment, and mistrust" (*Glass* 430). Valentine even hands him the sword of patriarchal power, offering him the truth at the same time: Jace's only way to guarantee his family's safety is to ally himself with Valentine. Still, Jace refuses.

After Maryse's rejection, Jace tries several other mothers – the comatose good mother Jocelyn and the cruel disciplinarian who is the Inquisitor. He cannot bond with either, and his lack of connection drives him to Valentine and to Clary, the sister-girlfriend who is forbidden to him. Only at the end of *City of Ashes* does he make peace with Maryse, who looks like "the only mother he'd ever known" (*Ashes* 434). This is a reconciliation that leaves him strong enough to accept Clary's limits.

In the issue of romance, Jace is torn between the examples of his good brother Alec Lightwood and the bad brother Sebastian. Jace struggles to make the right decision – he is tempted by shallow relationships by the beautiful girls who always flirt with him and tormented by Clary, the sister (as he thinks) who is forbidden to him. As such, chaste Alec – who stays out of touch with the world and filled with guilt for his sexuality – represents one option Jace can choose for himself. Alec begins the series obsessed with Jace, while Jace only feels a "brotherly affection." Alec gives up his feeling and moves on in time. Sebastian and Valentine, however, urge Jace to be closer to Clary and show by example that they kidnap any woman they want, from Jocelyn to her daughter, without worrying about morality.

Tempted desperately by Clary, Jace finds it increasingly difficult to be good. Once he knows he's Valentine's son, corrupted with demon blood, he feels that all his evil impulses have a reason. In *City of Ashes*, Jace knows that he's acting badly because he's part demon. Like the other characters, he's slipping into his Shadow side. Valentine tells him that they are the same: Jace has inherited his own arrogance and courage, along with the quality that makes others die for him (*Ashes* 409).

However, none of this is true: Jace is neither Valentine's biological son nor part demon – his angry, cruel impulses are merely the human condition, and by accepting that they are part of him, he can grow strong enough to overcome them. Jace proves Valentine wrong when he kills Agramon, the fear demon, who wears his father's face. By striking down the demon as it preaches Valentine's philosophies, Jace rejects his father's teachings forever. Just after, he offers his blood to Simon, willingly sacrificing to bring his own romantic rival back to life. Jace nearly dies at Simon's hands, and revives with a new sense of purpose. With Simon, a Downworlder, by his side, he confronts Valentine and saves Clary.

Jace learns to tolerate Simon. However, he must face the evil part of himself as it comes to life before his eyes as Jonathan Morgenstern, the demon-blooded son of Valentine. This is the part of himself he's always feared and loathed, just as everyone else has. Jonathan, sometimes called Sebastian, is the failed, rejected creation. His mother wanted to kill him at birth. Even Valentine loved Jace enough to have given him to caring parents, but only tolerated the unloving Sebastian.

However, he is unloving completely because of his father's actions. In the story of Frankenstein, the monster protests to his creator: "I am thy creature: I ought to be thy Adam, but I am rather the fallen angel, whom thou drivest from joy for no misdeed" (116). Jonathan has done nothing but support his father and act according to the demon nature his father gave him – for this he is unloved. Jonathan feels this unfairness clearly and poignantly. He lashes out at Jocelyn during their single meeting, for he feels, justifiably, that she was wrong to abandon him without trying to love him. However, he sees Clary and Jace as the two people in the world who share his birth – the only two people who can be his loved ones, as much as he's capable of such a thing. In *City of Lost Souls*, Jonathan tries to bond with his adopted brother and full sister. Though he seeks a revolting relationship with Clary, he doesn't appear to know it's wrong as he lovingly quotes the *Song of Songs* to her.

As such, Jonathan is the needy, unloved Shadow inside Jace himself. He kills the childlike innocence in the Lightwood family, young Max, and tries to destroy all of Idris. He offers Clary a deceptive, immoral, creepy affection. In short, he is Jace's evil impulses brought to life, and Jace must experience these impulses, accept them, and take charge of them, then kill Jonathan and thus banish his inner Jonathan – the voice that calls for him to act like Valentine's son and burn the world.

Jace and Jonathan are opposites in every way: one is angel, one demon. One has a loving family, the other has no one. One fears loving Clary, his sister and romantic interest, the other pursues both relationships without a thought of morality. But Jace, who considered running away with Clary, who believed he had demon blood and lusted after his own sister, who loved Valentine as a father, understands Jonathan's motivations much more than he'd like.

Having Jonathan facing him in the flesh forces Jace to deal with his feelings for Valentine, Clary, and the Lightwoods, to decide whether he wants to be Jonathan Morgenstern (as this "other self" is named) or Jace Lightwood.

Jace masters his own dark side by using his father's vicious lessons as a tool. He meets Sebastian in the dark tunnels his father once built, a cave of darkness like the underworld or like "crawling through the entrails of an enormous monster" (*Glass* 426). There he faces certain death as Sebastian toys with him, tortures him, and knocks him out. Struggling to save his own life, Jace persuades Sebastian to let them fight. As he does, he "heard his own voice drop into his father's cadences, the way Valentine spoke when he wanted something: soft and persuasive" (*Glass* 455). He accepts his father's skills, and so allows a fragment of the dark side into himself, using its power to beat Sebastian. In fact, he kills Sebastian with his father's move, piercing the heart and severing the spine as he's been taught. Finally, Jace slays Sebastian and takes the Morgenstern sword.

Jace nearly dies at Sebastian's hands, and then is killed by Valentine. Like Luke Skywalker, Jace is offered the choice to come to the dark side, and he refuses. In the tradition of ancient heroes, he dies heroically, only to return stronger than before. Initiation ceremonies, like the hero's journey myths, use this death and rebirth or separation and return pattern as a way of "killing the infantile ego and bringing forth an adult" (Campbell 138). By dying and returning, Jace is reborn as the self he wants to be: righteous Shadowhunter, Clary's boyfriend, and Jace Lightwood.

Jace is also on a quest to find faith – in book one, he mentions he has no reason to believe in angels, as he's never seen one. His father's apparent death took his faith as a child. In *City of Glass*, he meets one angel, then another saves his life. He discovers he's had angel blood and an angel's mark his entire life. After Simon pleads for aid, the Angel Raziel offers the sword of Michael, which cuts Jace free from Sebastian and fills him with holy fire. From having no faith, Jace is resurrected by the angels twice and thus grows into a more powerful warrior of the light.

Second Trilogy

In *City of Fallen Angels*, Jace struggles with his identity, reading his birth father's letters, but worrying that he's demonic because of Valentine's influence. "Maybe Jace Lightwood deserves to get everything he wants. But Jace Morgenstern doesn't," he complains (*Fallen Angels* 257). On a subconscious level, he knows this, and he distances himself from Clary, ruining their relationship. At the same time, he considers her his source of salvation: "I see who I am in your eyes and I try to be that person because you have faith in that person," he tells her (*Fallen Angels* 304).

He soon discovers that his insistence on exploring his guilt has left him open to spiritual corruption: he dreams nightly of killing Clary in dreams sent by Lilith. As he explains to Clary, he's been worried that she's training to be a Shadowhunter and die young, but "It isn't my job to tell you what to do with your life" (*Fallen Angels* 255). On a deep level below consciousness, he wants to control her and keep her eternally safe. So Evil Jace is born.

Myths and Motifs in *The Mortal Instruments*

Under Lilith's control, Jace Marks Clary into unconsciousness, picks her up and carries her to Lilith's demonic temple. There, he holds her prisoner for, as he thinks, the greater good. This is a manifestation of all he's been avoiding: since he refuses to discuss his shadowy dreams or seek help for them, the Shadow takes over his entire personality. Clary saves him with a dagger slash. As before, the silver dagger with his true father's name cuts through the illusion and lets Jace and Clary see each other honestly. Jace battles Lilith and then confronts his own guilt about what he's done.

However, the worst still comes as Sebastian, now tied to Jace's very lifeforce, rises again. He marks his adoptive brother, and Evil Jace, the true Shadow, is born. On some level, being Evil Jace is what Jace has always wanted. He has the paradise of his childhood, with his father's replacement, Sebastian, watching over him. He has Clary. And all the morals and doubts of the past few years, all the struggle to reconcile Valentine and the Lightwoods has vanished. Ending the conflict at last and having all choice taken from him is actually makes him happy. Discovering he had demon blood and wasn't responsible for his worse impulses was "a relief in a way" since he doesn't consider himself angelic (*Lost Souls* 384). Before Sebastian's new Shadowhunters, Jace complains of all the sacrifices the Shadowhunters have made for mundanes and cries, "We are the saviors of this earth *and we should be ruling it*" (*Lost Souls* 467) He has always felt superior, and Sebastian is giving him a chance to explore these suppressed desires in the ultimate temptation.

At the same time, Jace describes being jealous of "*Him*. That other me. The one Sebastian controls" (*Lost Souls* 400). After discovering what it feels like to lose his ethics and sense of purpose, he realizes he was happier before and would do anything to regain his real self. If the other side is "Evil Jace," then he is Good Jace, the one willing to offer his life to stop Sebastian. This helps him overcome his mental conflict. He realizes he wants his family and his life as Jace Lightwood back.

Clary's stabbing him is a test offered by heaven: If he isn't "more Heaven's than Hell's" he will die (*Lost Souls* 494). At last, he has physical, incontrovertible proof that he is on the side of angels, not demons. When Jace wakes, he describes having been "scorched, melted, and recreated like gold in a crucible" (*Lost Souls* 498). He acknowledges that what he truly missed was the Lightwoods – his true family. He's learned "the fragility of will and the difficulty of goodness" (*Lost Souls* 499). He's also learned that trying to control Clary and keep her safe was wrong, the Evil Jace side of himself determined to force her to do things for her own good.

Coming through the crisis, he's learned to understand Sebastian and also Stephen Herondale. He also chooses his purpose: As God's chosen warrior, he will kill Sebastian for all he's done to Jace, Clary, Max, and the Shadowhunters.

Tessa's Heroine Journey

Tessa begins her tale on a quest to save her brother – the classic heroine's journey. Like Clary, she loses the story's good mother with Aunt Harriet's recent death. Upon her arrival in London, she's kidnapped by the Dark Sisters, who force her to learn her untapped ability. They, like Dorothea, are the Deceivers – they lie to entrap her and then tutor her in the art of deception – changing her face. They are the wicked stepmothers of the tale…frequently, the only mentors the heroine receives.

The Little Mermaid, Cinderella, and Snow White have only cruel stepmothers to guide them. But as they, like Gretel or Psyche, enter servitude and do tasks for the cruel feminine, they learn valuable life skills.

> Snow White's stepmother laces her so tightly she can't breathe, and Venus beats Psyche and makes her labor to the edge of her sanity. Despite their cruelty, these evil stepmothers teach valuable lessons. Cannibalistic witches teach Gretel to clean house and Vasilisa the Beautiful to cook. (Frankel, *Girl to Goddess* 43)

Tessa, of course, learns to change shape and discovers she's more than human. On a deeper level, she comes to understand the nature of death and understand people's thoughts through her transformations. These are skills the heroine must absorb to grow from child to woman. Moments after Tessa loathingly dismisses them as "useless," she transforms into a young girl and slips out of her bonds. By the book's end, she's learned to use her powers cleverly to save herself, even without training in arms.

> The period when one begins to realize that one isn't running the show is called adolescence, when a whole new system of requirements begins announcing itself from the body. The adolescent hasn't the slightest idea how to handle all this, and cannot but wonder what it is that's pushing him – or even more mysteriously, pushing her. (Campbell 142)

This emotional change is represented by supernatural powers – the heroine is developing new impulses, new skills, new ways of interacting with the world. Her task is discovering how to use them. "In writing about Tessa, I can make literal the experience, which is often strong in adolescence, of feeling that your identity is fluid and shifting, that you're not sure who you are yet – that you're someone different every time you look in the mirror," Clare explains (*Enchanted Inkpot*).

Angels symbolize an ascending spiritual principle, and Tessa's is doubly strong, as it's on a protective amulet. It reflects her quest for identity and purpose. The angel is her dying mother's gift, like the gifts of many saintly dying mothers in fairytales. Like those gifts, its powers provide a kind of protection from beyond the grave, like a true guardian angel. The clockwork angel is Tessa's talisman, but her powers aid her as well.

When Tessa escapes her evil mentors, the Institute is like the normal world by comparison. The Institute is surprisingly prosaic, with dinner at seven. "Everything was tasteful and very ordinary" (*Clockwork Angel* 67). The Shadowhunters are amazed by Tessa's powers. In fact, Tessa's origins and abilities are a mystery to them.

In the Institute, Tessa begins to discover who she wants to be and learns about the magical world. Will gives her the *Shadowhunter's Codex* to further this, a magical book for the questing heroine. (Clare mentioned on her tour that this is the book Tessa holds on the cover of *Clockwork Princess*.) Indeed, she and Will quote a library of books to each other, and Will advises her that he gains courage by pretending to be a character in a book – an amusing thing for a fictional character to say. In *Clockwork Prince*, he tells her that their shared love of books is what has turned to real love between them. Reading her letters enabled him to feel with her. "I dreamed what you dreamed, wanted what you wanted – and then I realized that truly I just wanted you. The girl behind the scrawled letters" (468). Tess is enraptured – she had always dreamed of someone truly knowing, understanding, and loving her.

Facing Shadows

Tessa's trapped between conflicting examples: Jessamine who's all lady, and Charlotte, who's a Shadowhunter first, a warrior and capable administrator in a man's world. Charlotte works only for others, Jessamine only for herself. As she watches, Tessa decides what kind of woman she wishes to be: a pretty, dependent wife or a capable adult. Charlotte tells her, "You have a power of incalculable value. You need ask nothing of anyone. You need depend on no one" (*Clockwork Angel* 197). When Tessa tries to be brave and competent, she holds Charlotte in her thoughts. When Tessa tries on Jessamine's form, she also gets to experience her hatred and resentment. Both women are like Tessa's internal voices that urge her down various paths: They are the stepsisters seen in every fairytale:

"Inside our heads we hear their voices, telling us where we fall short, but only in matters that concern us as women, and only the external aspects" (Gould 56). Jessamine buys Tessa proper clothes, counsels her on which colors look best, takes her for a walk in Hyde Park and tells her who's who in society. However, Jessamine's gifts are judgmental, cold, and self-serving. She parades Tessa through town as a poor country cousin, and that's how Tessa feels beside the sophisticated rich girl. Charlotte's gowns, offered at the end of *Clockwork Prince*, are gifts of love from her own trousseau, which make Tessa feel like family. She parades a gown before Will, her prince, and he admires her in it. As Jessamine refuses to do her part as Shadowhunter and coaxes Tessa to leave, Charlotte begs her to stay and utterly accepts her. When Tessa sees Jessamine let the men sacrifice themselves for her because "It is expected that a man sacrifice himself for a lady's safety" (*Clockwork Angel* 427), she is repelled.

Shadow moments can occur when facing one's opposite – when Tessa and Jessamine speak in the park, for instance. However, to truly have the ultimate Shadow experience in fantasy, one puts on another's guise – the real way to walk in his or her shoes. Camille is everything Tessa is not – ancient and wise, sensual, and also comfortable with her magical powers. Tessa takes Camille's ruby pendant and transforms into the vampire. At least momentarily, she experiences the chill of death. However, she also discovers what it is to be an ancient, titled, sophisticated Downworlder – all she's not but one day must become. Camille is a worldly political adversary. She's sexually forward and boasts that Magnus is her lover. She carries herself proudly like a queen. Pretending to be her, Tessa gets to lead Will around on a leash and experience dominant sexuality. In the raid, she feels Camille's sensual memories of Magnus and channels her imperiousness for the first time. Finally, she fires a pistol at the vampire patriarch De Quincey. When she sees Nate in chains, she feels the most rage. As she reflects later, however, the rage was like a gift from Camille, not from herself.

After, she seeks out Will and experiences her first kiss. At the end of the day, she reflects it was a day of firsts, the first time she used her power as a valuable tool, the first time she fired a pistol, the first time she kissed anyone. Camille, like the Dark Sisters, has taught her much about female power.

At book's end, she uses her shapeshifting to trick Mortmain into believing she's dead. Of course, she faints from the shock of near-death and has an descent into death and return. Like Snow White or Sleeping Beauty, she returns ready to find her true love, only to see Will holding her and pleading that she live. "Sleep is the refuge in which an adolescent girl can absorb the new sense of herself that she gains from the prick of the spindle, and changes from girl to woman: a transformation more radical than from boy to man," explains Gould (108). Tessa awakens more confident, to discover she's a powerful woman in charge of her own destiny.

Tessa's gift is shapeshifting, and she uses it to discover who she is, trying on different roles as she wonders who the Tessa underneath really is – the mystery of her origins and uncertainty about her parents casts all into confusion. Mortmain's comment that there is no Tessa Grey continues to haunt her. Gould comments, "We use clothes, like words, to reveal our natures or disguise them, as we choose" (45). This is Tessa's power as she acts calm and capable or weak and stereotypically feminine to achieve her goals. In Yorkshire, Tessa finds herself playing a role but with her own face, a situation that terrifies her. Her clockwork angel, a powerful protector of mysterious origin, is a clear symbol for the strongest part of herself.

Perception and appearance are key in the heroine's journey – Cinderella heroines wear glittering gowns to the ball or hide themselves below tattercoats and donkeyskins to determine their own destinies. Cinderella's costume changes signal "a change of state, as if she were continually changing one skin for another" (Gould 44). Clary's clothes in Idris, from the velvet coat like Isabelle's to her first Shadowhunter gear to the silvery gown, all indicate that she's becoming a real Shadowhunter, like Isabelle, her mother, and Amatis. Like Tessa, Clary too tries on a glamour to show the Council that she has powers beyond anything they've seen. In fact she combines the glamour with feminine emotion, letting the Shadowhunters see whoever they love most as she stands proudly on the podium.

As *Clockwork Prince* continues, Tessa tries on Jessamine's persona, a girl she regards as a delicate fairy princess (260). Underneath the lovely surface, however, she feels her "rage and longing and bitterness," dark emotions cheerful Tessa rarely experiences (*Clockwork Prince* 262). Jessamine, as she soon discovers, is married, while Tessa is struggling with her feelings for Jem and Will. Though Tessa has behaved scandalously, as she fears, Jessamine's secret marriage to an enemy of the Clave is far worse. As Jessamine, she finds herself at a ball straight out of her novels. However, like the vampire ball, this one is corrupted – evil and filled with enemies. In this way, she has entered the patriarchal stronghold. She must charm Nate, much as she charmed De Quincey at the previous ball. After playing the part, she finds herself mesmerized by Will and kisses him passionately, forgetting her loyalties. It's heady and delightful to cast off responsibility and be another Jessamine.

In the battle of *Clockwork Prince*, Nate grabs Tess. She thinks to herself that he's bigger and faster "but there is one thing I can do that he cannot" (383). She transforms into him and orders the automatons to seize her brother. By transforming into him, Tess takes his power over the machines and uses it to save her friends. Nate is killed by his own automaton, in a blast that hurts Tessa in a reflection of her painful emotional devastation.

Caught between these roles – spoiled feminine and spoiled masculine, Tessa realizes she doesn't want to imitate Jessamine or Nate. However, she is becoming more confident in her shapechanging power, eager to experience others' emotions as a way of discovering herself. In *Clockwork Princess*, Tessa transforms into the warlock John Shade. This transformation affects her more than any, trapping her inside. With her new knowledge of her demon father's powers, she at last faces her warlock nature.

After she loses Nate, her Aunt Harriet, another good mother, visits her in a dream and forgives her for Nate's death. She tells Tessa that lies "are like a cancer in the soul. They eat away what is good and leave only destruction behind" (*Clockwork Prince* 395). She also tells Tessa she still has family – a suggestion that she let the Shadowhunters into her heart. This, like the clockwork angel itself, is a momentary blessing from the perished good mother, a moment of protection and hope on the heroine's tumultuous journey.

The love triangle is also central to the story. Tessa sees Will as a shapechanger just as she is – kind and thoughtful one moment, vicious in the next. Frequently, the protagonist sees his or her love as a shapechanger, reflecting the mystifying mood changes the other person undergoes. From here come all the tales of frog princes, beasts, and swan maidens. The reasons behind Will's inconsistency are only explained to Tessa at the end of *Clockwork Prince*, after she's committed to Jem: He gives her his family ring when they pretend to be engaged, then later gives her his mother's jade pendant when they begin a real engagement.

These too are talismans: a ring symbolizes commitment, though there are deeper meanings as well. Jung said that a circle symbolizes the totality of the psyche, while a square suggests terrestrial matter and reality. A protective circle for a person can take the form of a ting, bracelet, necklace, or crown (Chevalier 200). As such, the round jade pendent, like Will's anniversary bracelet much later, is a token of protection and personal power along with commitment. Tessa's angel necklace too, adds to her protective circle.

A jade ring symbolizes heaven, and was a symbol worn by royalty. The symbol also calls for austerity and restraint – strong symbols of Jem himself. With a pair of dragons, it symbolizes yin-yang, echoed in the inscription on Jem's pendant that two are stronger than one. The hole in the middle is a channel for celestial influence (Chevalier 806). Significantly, Tessa wears it with her angel, strengthening her divine connection just as she's strengthened through Jem's love and faith.

The Ouroboros

Tessa's main enemy is the Magister, who represents all the evil strength of patriarchy – he calls himself her "creator," and wants to marry her and use her power for his own aims. Further, he is the corrupter of Nate, wielder of the cruel Dark Sisters.

At the same time, he is the child of warlocks, one who knows everything about the magical world Tessa must discover. He reveals her powers to her and forces her to train in them. Without him, she would never discover who she is or meet the Shadowhunters.

The Magister himself is a masculine force, but he wields a number of feminine ones. The cruel Dark Sisters are in his employ. Like Lilith, he has given birth to a "monstrous creature" with Shadowhunter runes and skin over a metal body (*Clockwork Princess* 403). Further, his symbol is the Ouroboros, an ancient symbol depicting a serpent or dragon eating its own tail.

Snakes are a feminine symbol, associated as they are with regeneration as they shed their skins. The python priestesses originally belonged to Gaia, Mother Earth, while India and Mesopotamia had powerful snake creator goddesses. Only later did the snake become an androgynous figure. The name Ouroboros originates from the Greek *oura* meaning "tail" and *boros* meaning "eating," for this tail-eating serpent. The symbol is first seen as early as 1600 BC in Egypt, followed by the Norse Jörmungandr and the Hindu dragon circling the tortoise which supports the world. The West African god Aidophedo or Oshunmare of the Yoruba. Aztec Quetzalcoatl is sometimes portrayed as an ouroboros, as is the Chinese yin-yang symbol. It was used in Native American symbols as well as medieval Europe.

Will describes it as an alchemical symbol for the different dimensions: "Our world, inside the serpent, and the rest of existence, outside" (*Clockwork Angel* 85). The Ouroboros represents the perpetual cycle of renewal and infinity, the concept of eternity and the eternal return, and suggests life, death and rebirth, leading to immortality. It has become the modern symbol for infinity. This immortality is what Tessa is on a quest to discover within herself – she is questing from the girl who believes she's human to the warlock who will live forever and astound the world with her shapechanging magic. This quest takes her into her origins as well as her future – the ever-cycling circle indeed. Jung notes:

> The alchemists, who in their own way knew more about the nature of the individuation process than we moderns do, expressed this paradox through the symbol of the ouroboros, the snake that eats its own tail. In the age-old image of the ouroboros lies the thought of devouring oneself and turning oneself into a circulatory process, for it was clear to the more astute alchemists that the prima materia of the art was man himself.
>
> The ouroboros is a dramatic symbol for the integration and assimilation of the opposite, i.e. of the shadow. This "feed-back" process is at the same time a symbol of immortality, since it is said of the ouroboros that he slays himself and brings himself to life, fertilizes himself and gives birth to himself. He symbolizes the One, who proceeds from the clash of opposites, and he therefore constitutes the secret of the prima materia which [...] unquestionably stems from man's unconscious. (*Collected Works*, Vol. 14, 513)

Inside the clockwork men are ouroboros boxes – while their outer forms are men, a monstrous mechanical army and symbol of male power, inside they conceal boxes like Pandora's – the dark, hidden feminine force. Likewise, the Magister's stronghold, under a towering mountain (a masculine symbol) contains a dark lake, a domed ceiling, and mirrorlike walls of glittering quartz – feminine symbols. Here is where Tessa learns the truth of her origins and falls for Will.

While Mortmain is one enemy, the Council becomes a different kind of adversary – a force of hidebound stagnation. Members include Benedict Lightwood, who consorts with demons, and Starkweather, who hordes illegal spoils and boasts of killing Downworlders. Both foreshadow Valentine, indicating where the Council is heading.

In *Clockwork Princess*, Lightwood's evil becomes more apparent, as he transforms into a monster and attempts to eat his own family. The Consul is revealed as treacherous as well, only allowing Charlotte power because he believes he can control her. Worst of all are the Council members. When Charlotte calls in the cavalry and rushes to stop Mortmain, the Council only holds a meeting. Shockingly, none of them come to help Charlotte – only the Silent Brothers take arms to save their race.

This force of stagnation and useless power, like the Old Republic in *Star Wars*, must be dismantled to make way for a better world. The Destroyer accomplishes one good thing in his rampage through London – Mortmain attacks the Council while they're foolishly arguing over Charlotte's replacement, and points out how imprudent they were to all assemble together. By slaughtering them, he paves the way for a newer, better government to replace them.

Facing the Magister

Mortmain is the Destroyer – he sets his automatons on a village just because he can and tells Tessa he has no better self to appeal to.

The Magister, Mortmain, is Tessa's enemy, and she is on a quest to conquer the patriarchy, to become dark and powerful like Camille, magical like the Dark Sisters. Thus the ouroboros becomes the symbol of her quest. Mortmain calls his demonic automatons "What we have created together" – Tessa's spark is needed to solve the puzzle and show Mortmain how to animate his demons, just like the ouroboros symbol blends male and female (*Clockwork Princess* 384). As with Clary, Tessa's female allies grow in strength as she does- -the weaker cook of *Clockwork Angel* is replaced by the skilled fighter Bridget. Sophie too grows in fighting skill and finally becomes a Shadowhunter. Cecily joins the team, replacing the frail Jessamine.

Before battling, Tessa has a respite as she dreams of the angel Ithuriel and receives his blessing. Following this, Will finds her and they begin their romance. This brief pause before the battle allows Tessa to regroup and decide who she wants to become. With the closest males to her, Will and her angel, offering their love, Tessa is strengthened for the coming battle.

The heroine must come to understand the power of death as well as life – frequently in the dark stronghold, she encounters the death-dealing mother (like Mrs. Black) and learns from her. Instead, Tessa faces Mortmain and turns into the avenging angel of the Lord. In this scene, her power is shapechanging and saving her friends, but it's also wielding the power of death.

Mortmain and Valentine both trap the angel Ithuriel and try to create new beings. Like Valentine, Mortmain is trying to subvert the natural order and take the power of birth and creation for himself. As Tessa says, "Life is the province of heaven. And Heaven does not take kindly to usurpers" (*Clockwork Princess* 461). Life is also the province of the feminine – she like Charlotte is a future mother and creator of life. Mortmain has trespassed on that right, and she is taking it back.

Tessa reaches into the angel pendant and changes into a towering figure of light and power. Mortmain the patriarch has no chance against her: She slays him, and his unnatural automatons die. In this one gesture, all of her friends are saved. Further, Tessa has always had this power – she has had the guardian angel and shapechanging magic since before her birth. Only through adversity and facing the enemy has she come to know it, and grown so powerful that the patriarchy cannot stand against her. She crushes Mortmain in her fist, and he and his army crumple to nothing.

Like Psyche, who journeyed to the underworld and sampled the power of death, Tessa cannot bear the dark power she's harnessed and collapses. Will tells the others that she cannot awaken until she resolves matters with Jem – her collapse is psychological rather than physical.

The story ends with the world shifting forever, much as it goes in *City of Glass* and *City of Heavenly Fire*: The old ways, with the power-mad Consul and savage Starkweather, die along with them. There is a beautiful Christmas celebration with golden candles everywhere, as Charlotte, the proud new Consul, presides over Sophie's Ascension. The first female Consul takes charge; Tessa and Will find a way to be together. Gideon breaks out of his father's legacy by wedding a servant, even as Charlotte elevates that servant to the rank of Shadowhunter. Under Charlotte's compassionate rule, Cecily and Will can even see their parents, because it's Christmas, season of hope and renewal.

Charlotte tells her husband she doesn't want to be the one to send Shadowhunters to their deaths. But she knows that by ruling she can also save lives. This balance is something the questing heroine must reach in order to reach enlightenment. Charlotte and Tessa end the story by having children though they must also care for their injured or dying husbands, as the circle of life spins ever onward.

CHAPTER 2
THE BIBLE REIMAGINED

With Dante and the Bible – and Paradise Lost, which is another big influence on these particular books – these are all works of (for want of a better term) Christian mythology, specifically the myth of the Nephilim, and of the war in Heaven, angels vs. demons, the fall of Lucifer, all of that. And when you're dealing with a magic system dependent on the idea of angels and demons, you have to draw on all that, that's your canon. ("Interview: Cassandra Clare")

Indeed, all of these make up the mythology behind the series. Shadowhunters are tied with religion so completely that the two cannot be clearly separated – every religious institution supports them with caches of weapons. Jace quotes "Mea Culpa" out of the Mass, and says honor, fault and penance are required for Shadowhunters. It's deeper than belief – it's the code they live by. Learning about some of these concepts aids a deeper understanding of what Jace, Clary and their friends are fighting for.

Jem describes religious texts as "instruction manuals" for the Shadowhunters (*Clockwork Prince* 91). Certainly, they contain the source material for angels, demons, and other supernatural forces. All Shadowhunter lifecycle events: births, deaths, marriages, are surrounded by ritual, and much of that ritual is Biblical in nature, whatever the individual Shadowhunters believe (granted, we've only seen Britain and America – cultures in the far East, for instance, might be different). Jem quotes the Biblical Song of Songs, sometimes called the Song of Solomon, when describing the runes from a Shadowhunter wedding: "Set me as a seal upon thine heart, as a seal upon thine arm; for love is strong as death; jealousy is cruel as the grave" (8:6). Shadowhunters part with the word *Mizpah*, from the story of Laban, quoting the Bible passage: "And Mizpah; for he said, The Lord watch between me and thee, when we are absent one from another" (King James Bible, Genesis 31:49).

The Parabatai ritual likewise originates in the stories of the Old Testament.

Most of Clare's sources come directly from the Bible, together with its Apocrypha and the Jewish books that followed, such as the mystical Zohar. Related works such as Dante's *Inferno* and *Paradise Lost* are quoted often, along with other classics. At the same time, Japanese kitsune and oni lurk between the pages alongside Judeo-Christian demons. Jordan's tattoos, *shaantih shaantih shaantih*, are a Hindu mantra for peace from the Upanishads, traditionally recited at the beginning and end of religious study. Shadowhunters evoke the Muslim angels Malik, Nakir, and Munkir, emphasizing that all religions fight on the same side in this war. Clare adds:

> I wanted to make sure the mythology of the series was rooted in world mythology – not just Western religious mythology, though there is a lot of that, given the books' partial basing on Paradise Lost and The Inferno – so I did a lot of reading up on world mythology, especially anything having to do with good and evil spirits. I wanted to make sure multiple types of demonic myth were present, so you'll find Japanese, Indian, Tibetan, and other kinds of demons represented (plus the kind I've made up.) I read a lot of old "demonologies" – there was a whole time period where scholars were obsessed with listing every kind of demon and mapping Hell. I read up on the mythology of angels and fallen angels. (FAQ)

The Book of Raziel

The Jewish religion begins with the Jewish Bible (basically the Old Testament, though there are differences in translation). However, it continues with centuries of additional interpretation and even folklore concerning the Bible's teachings. This story is one example, which explains the powers of the Book of the Angel Raziel: "Each day the angel Raziel makes proclamations on Mount Horeb, from heaven, of the secrets of men to all that dwell upon the earth, and his voice resounds throughout the world," explains *Targum Ecclesiastes*, a collection of explanatory stories about the Book of Ecclesiastes (10:20).

Clare notes:

> Raziel, for instance, is an angel from the Jewish kabbalistic tradition, who is supposed to have given Adam, in the Garden of Eden, a book of wisdom – he is sometimes called the Angel of Secrets, or Angel of Knowledge. Therefore he seemed the right angel to have given the Gray Book to the first Shadowhunter. (FAQ)

The Book of Raziel, or at least a book by this name, appeared in the thirteenth century. It was a Jewish grimoire, or spellbook of a sort, drawing heavily on Kabbalah, the teachings of Jewish mysticism. It contains a detailed angelology, instructions for creating protective amulets with the runes of God's name, and other ancient lore. Its origins appear in the oldest of myths.

After Adam's expulsion from the Garden of Eden, Adam remembered the letters of the Holy Name. As he told his family, "By the light of all luminaries, rule in righteousness and in reverence of Elohim [God]. Also, hold dominion over the spirit and over violence and over misfortune and adversaries rising up over men and women. It is written, be summoned as you wish and desire" (*Sefer Rezial* 3). Using the name of God, he and his descendants performed miracles. As he was dying, he prayed to God for compassion and grace. He added:

> "Grant me knowledge and understanding, that I may know what shall befall me, and my posterity, and all the generations that come after me, and what shall befall me on every day and in every month, and mayest Thou not withhold from me the help of Thy servants and of Thy angels." (Ginzberg)

Three days later, the angel Raziel came with a book in his hand. The angel addressed Adam thus:

> O Adam, why art thou so fainthearted? Why art thou distressed and anxious? Thy words were heard at the moment when thou didst utter thy supplication and entreaties, and I have received the charge to teach thee pure words and deep understanding, to make thee wise through the contents of the sacred book in my hand, to know what will happen to thee until the day of thy death. And all thy descendants and all the later generations, if they will but read this book in purity, with a devout heart and a humble mind, and obey its precepts, will become like unto thee. They, too, will foreknow what things shall happen, and in what month and on what day or in what night. All will be manifest to them – they will know and understand whether a calamity will come, a famine or wild beasts, floods or drought; whether there will be abundance of grain or dearth; whether the wicked will rule the world; whether locusts will devastate the land; whether the fruits will drop from the trees unripe; whether boils will afflict men; whether wars will prevail, or diseases or plagues among men and cattle; whether good is resolved upon in heaven, or evil; whether blood will flow, and the death-rattle of the slain be heard in the city. And now, Adam, come and give heed unto what I shall tell thee regarding the manner of this book and its holiness." (Ginzberg)

As the legend tells:

> It is the book out of which all things worth knowing can be learnt, and all mysteries, and it teaches also how to call upon the angels and

make them appear before men, and answer all their questions. But not all alike can use the book, only he who is wise and God-fearing, and resorts to it in holiness. Such a one is secure against all wicked counsels, his life is serene, and when death takes him from this world, he finds repose in a place where there are neither demons nor evil spirits, and out of the hands of the wicked he is quickly rescued. (Ginzberg)

Raziel's name means "the Secrets of God," and he is said to stand beside God's throne and hear many of his secrets. The legend goes on to tell that the other angels grew jealous of Adam and threw the Book of Raziel into the ocean, though God took pity on mankind and sent it back to them. Enoch, Noah, and Solomon eventually inherited it and used its secrets in turn.

The Book of Raziel has a section of gematria, a mystical math applied to the Bible. In Hebrew, each of the 22 letters has a numeric value, so each word likewise has a value. For instance, eighteen is lucky in Judaism, because it is the numeric value of the word *chai*, meaning life. (ch has a value of eight, ay has a value of ten). This word magic is an ancient part of Judaism, used to interpret some of the Bible's hidden meanings. At the same time, it's linked to rune magic, the individual magic and meaning of letters. It is written: "The letters are prominent, illuminated by shining lights and complete. Thus, before the creation of the universe, letters are prominent" (*Sefer Rezial* 55). They are the building blocks of the universe, tools for invoking miracles. In itself, this is quite similar to Clare's rune magic: the letter has a meaning, power, and story. With the letter shin, one can "create fire."

Mene Mene Tekel Upharsin

Belshazzar the king made a great feast to a thousand of his lords, and drank wine before the thousand… Then they brought the golden vessels that were taken out of the temple of the house of God which was at Jerusalem; and the king, and his princes, his wives, and his concubines, drank in them. They drank wine, and praised the gods of gold, and of silver, of brass, of iron, of wood, and of stone. In the same hour came forth fingers of a man's hand, and wrote over against the candlestick upon the plaister of the wall of the king's palace: and the king saw the part of the hand that wrote. Then the king's countenance was changed, and his thoughts troubled him, so that the joints of his loins were loosed, and his knees smote one against another. The king cried aloud to bring in the astrologers, the Chaldeans, and the soothsayers. And the king spake, and said to the wise men of Babylon, Whosoever shall read this writing, and shew me the interpretation thereof, shall be clothed with scarlet, and have a chain of gold about his neck, and shall be the third ruler in the kingdom.

Though the wise men of the kingdom tried, only Daniel, a Jew, succeeded. He told the king:

> "This is the inscription that was written: mene, mene, tekel, parsin.
> "Here is what these words mean: Mene: God has numbered the days of your reign and brought it to an end. Tekel: You have been weighed on the scales and found wanting. Peres: Your kingdom is divided and given to the Medes and Persians" (Daniel 5: 1-28).

This story is famous for Daniel, a wise man blessed by God, being the only one able to interpret the signs. Of course, Belshazzar, King of Babylon, was the enemy of the Jewish people, as the Babylonians had taken them into exile. Valentine too is the enemy of all that is holy, as he uses demons against the Shadowhunters and tries to corrupt the Mortal Instruments. A point is made at the Bible chapter's beginning that Belshazzar and his family had looted the Temple, and uses God's sacred vessels to toast and worship idols. Thus, as an enemy of God, he will be punished. Valentine, of course, is a murderer of innocents. Even Raziel, confronting him, tells him vampires and werewolves have souls and Valentine has only been acting for his own power and hatred, not God's will.

Basically, the four words mean "God has decided your reign of tyranny is over and God will send other nations to bring you down." When Clary tears open the ship in *City of Ashes*, Valentine interprets her rune this way – his tyranny is ending because Clary has come, sent by God to tear him apart. Clary also writes this message in the sand when she defeats Valentine by rewriting his circle. Again, his time as tyrant is over.

In the third book, Jace tells Simon that Clary's amazing rune gifts are a portent – "The Laws are changing. The old ways may never be the right ways again" (*Glass* 60). This could mean the end of the Nephilim's current way of life – which in fact happens, as Clary and Luke revolutionize the Accords. Ironically, it is Valentine who has brought about his own destruction and cemented the bond between Downworlders and Nephilim, all by creating Clary.

Nephilim

What are nephilim? It's been widely debated. The Bible tells us this:

> There were giants in the earth in those days; and also after that, when the sons of God came in unto the daughters of men, and they bare children to them, the same became mighty men which were of old, men of renown. (Genesis 6:4)

The Hebrew word for "sons of God," Nephilim, has sparked a great deal of debate through history – are they angels who had children with human women? The descendants of Seth (Adam and Eve's third son) meeting the descendants of another tribe? Lore is uncertain, though many of the more romantic and fantastical modern works label them as "fallen angels."

The puzzling word also appears when Joshua and his followers consider Canaan a place of "giants." The Hebrew word *gibbowr* was used often to describe descendants of various nephilim, literally meaning "powerful, warrior, tyrant, giant or mighty man." Were nephilim mighty warriors, supernatural heroes, or fallen angels? Accounts differ.

As Henry Branwell points out in *The Infernal Devices* trilogy, Nephilim in the Bible may not be monsters, as there's "an issue of translation from the original Aramaic" (*Clockwork Angel* 140). Some tales in fact call them mighty wielders of magic, who called on God to give them power. The source of this magic was Enoch, a Biblical figure so righteous that God carried him straight to heaven. As the Zohar, the book of Jewish mysticism states:

> All the just men who lived subsequent to Enos [Enoch], as Jared, Methusalah and Henoch, did all in their power to restrain the practice of magical arts, but their efforts proved futile and ineffectual; so that the professors of them, proud of their occult knowledge, became rebellious and disobedient to their Lord, saying, 'Who is Shaddai [one of God's many names], the almighty, that we should serve him and what profit should we have in praying unto Him'?' Thus spake they and foolishly imagined that by their occultism and magic they would be able to nullify and turn away the oncoming judgment that was to sweep them wholly out of existence. Beholding their wicked deeds and practices, the Holy One caused the earth to revert back to its former condition and become immersed in water. After the deluge, however, He gave the earth again to mankind, promising, in His mercy, it should never again and in like manner be destroyed. It is written, 'The Lord caused the earth to be covered with the deluge' (Psalms xxix:10). The word for Lord, here, is Jehovah and not Alhim; the first representing mercy, the other severity and judgment. In the time of Enos, even young children became students and trained in the higher mysteries and knowledge of the secret doctrine." (de Manhar 238)

These practitioners of magic were the Nephilim, the ones God sent Noah's flood to destroy. In the *Book of Enoch*, the Angel Uriel condemns them, calling them, "the angels who have connected themselves with women, and their spirits assuming many different forms are defiling mankind and shall lead them astray into sacrificing to demons [and worshipping them]" (19:1). In Jewish and Christian lore, and in Clare's series, the demons and fallen angels are the enemy of God – their vulnerability to religious symbols and holy water emphasizes this.

Likewise, Shadowhunters use the holy water and religious symbols, which they are freely given by the caretakers of temples, synagogues, and churches. When Jace asks entry to a church "in the name of the Battle the Never Ends" and beseeches its blessing, the locked doors open for him (*Bones* 253). Within, he finds a cache of weapons under the altar, left because "all religions assist us in battle" (*Bones* 255). Jace mentions "tests, ordeals, levels of training," which certainly involve reading holy books from around the world (*Bones* 101). Shadowhunters fight in God's service, and each naming of a seraph blade is a prayer for that angel to provide aid.

Lucifer and Paradise Lost

And there was war in heaven: Michael and his angels fought against the dragon; and the dragon fought and his angels, And prevailed not; neither was their place found any more in heaven. And the great dragon was cast out, that old serpent, called the Devil, and Satan, which deceiveth the whole world: he was cast out into the earth, and his angels were cast out with him. (Revelations 12:7-9)

Valentine brags of his falling star crest and his name Morgan-stern, morning star (Lucifer's star) and then quotes the Bible: "How art thou fallen from heaven, O Lucifer, son of the morning! How art thou cut down to the ground, which didst weaken the nations!" (Isaiah 14:12). Lucifer was known for being the light-bearer, brightest angel of the heavens. He's associated with the morning star, the shining planet Venus. However, he rebelled against God and was finally cast from the sky. Valentine, of course, grew up among the richest and most privileged of the Shadowhunters before they cast him out.

Descended from angels, Valentine, like the angels, was given the mission to protect humanity. He even insists that the Shadowhunters are "the closest thing that exists in this world to gods" (*Ashes* 262). He is a type of angel himself. Young Jace sees him as an angel, white hair lit by the sun. To Clary, Valentine's face is "a restrained, closed, interior face, the face of a priest, with sorrowful eyes" (*Bones* 367). Jocelyn notes that Valentine "seemed to give off light" in school (*Glass* 387). Everyone wanted to be close to him and share his specialness. However, he became convinced of his own superiority and led a great rebellion against the Shadowhunters. They cast him away, but like Lucifer, he waited in the shadows, plotting his revenge. It's said in 2 Corinthians 11:14 that "Satan himself masquerades as an angel of light," and Valentine indeed maintains an unearthly beauty.

Paradise Lost is Milton's epic poem of the war in heaven: war between the angels of God and the fallen angels who follow Lucifer. The following lines from the poem begin *City of Bones*, setting the scene of the fallen angel's rebellion against heaven:

> I sung of Chaos and eternal Night;
> Taught by the heavenly Muse to venture down
> The dark descent, and up to re-ascend,
> (3:18-20)

As such, Valentine Morgenstern's rebellion against the angel-blooded Nephilim echoes this story. As the poem introduces Lucifer:

> Th' infernal Serpent; he it was, whose guile
> Stird up with Envy and Revenge, deceiv'd
> The Mother of Mankind, what time his Pride
> Had cast him out from Heav'n, with all his Host
> Of Rebel Angels, by whose aid aspiring
> To set himself in Glory above his Peers,
> He trusted to have equal'd the most High,
> If he oppos'd; and with ambitious aim
> Against the Throne and Monarchy of God
> Rais'd impious War in Heav'n and Battel proud
> With vain attempt. Him the Almighty Power
> Hurld headlong flaming from th' Ethereal Skie
> With hideous ruine and combustion down
> To bottomless perdition, there to dwell
> In Adamantine Chains and penal Fire,
> Who durst defie th' Omnipotent to Arms.
> (1:34-49)

So too does his demonic son Sebastian's rebellion against the Nephilim and his creation of a race of demonic Shadowhunters. Both lead a group of followers and are cast down in the struggle. In fact, Sebastian "looked like the sort of bad angel who might have followed Lucifer out of heaven" (*Glass* 452). Idris with its City of Glass is portrayed as a type of heaven – only those who are special can enter, and a common punishment is banishment. Similarly, Lucifer is famous for falling – being cast out of heaven and torn from God's light. Lucifer commands a great host of fallen angels, like Valentine's Circle and Sebastian's evil Shadowhunters.

Valentine made Jace read *Paradise Lost* over and over and comments that Milton's devil is far more interesting than his God (*Ashes* 258). Valentine was likely grooming Jace for a special place in his army. Satan describes how Lucifer has fallen:

> But O how fall'n! how chang'd

> From him, who in the happy Realms of Light
> Cloth'd with transcendent brightness didst out-shine
> Myriads though bright
> (1:84-88)

Valentine too lost much of his glory. He explains that he rebelled against a "corrupt government" as he puts it, which was willing to compromise with Downworlders. For his rebellion, he was cast out and stripped of his home and fortune (*Bones* 438). His pregnant wife left him and he lost half his family as well.

Of course, this is the story of Valentine after his fall – every time he's mentioned in the series it's as a monster – the murderer of the innocent who tried to start a genocidal war. Clare's first trilogy is the story of Valentine's quest to climb back from hiding and claim the power of the angel Raziel in a second rebellion against the Clave. *Paradise Lost* is a similar story – Lucifer begins it cast down to hell, surrounded by his defeated followers. However, pride and hate fill him until he's determined to take power.

> But his doom
> Reserv'd him to more wrath; for now the thought
> Both of lost happiness and lasting pain
> Torments him; round he throws his baleful eyes
> That witness'd huge affliction and dismay
> Mixt with obdurate pride and stedfast hate
> (1:50-55)

When Satan sees how they've fallen, he proposes they destroy the gloating foe, either by strength or guile.

> In Arms not worse, in foresight much advanc't,
> We may with more successful hope resolve
> To wage by force or guile eternal Warr
> Irreconcileable, to our grand Foe,
> Who now triumphs, and in th' excess of joy
> Sole reigning holds the Tyranny of Heav'n.
> (1:119-124)

This of course is Valentine's plan, to win by guile as he sends Sebastian in to charm the Shadowhunters and destroy the wards while he sets himself up as the Clave's focus. As the Clave gathers in endless meetings and alienates the Downworlders, they are poised for a takeover.

Jace, like the Archangel Michael, is the greatest of the angelic warriors and thus their leader. In fact, when Jace names his blade after Michael, it glows the brightest Clary's ever seen. The poem identifies Michael as heaven's commander:

> Go Michael of Celestial Armies Prince,
> And thou in Military prowess next
> Gabriel, lead forth to Battel these my Sons
> Invincible, lead forth my armed Saints
> (6.44-47)

Mi-cha-el means "Who is like God?" so it's no surprise those words are written on his sword. His holy weapon is called Sword of Discrimination, which cuts through illusion and lays the truth bare. In alchemy, the sword represents purifying fire (Cirlot 324). In fact, Michael's sword, seen in *City of Lost Souls*, fills Jace with this very quality as it burns the evil Sebastian out of him.

By contrast, the name "Sebastian" means awe and dread, similar to the Roman Emperors' title "Augustus." Valentine's name means strength and worthiness, perhaps with some irony, for his love is selfish and poisonous, as is his worthiness. Of course, he came from the best of Shadowhunter lineages before he fell into evil and rebellion. Both names were also the names of saints, emphasizing the fallen angel connection. As Valentine and his son rage against the heavenly authority that cast them from Idris and plot a rebellion against their former allies, they reenact the epic in modern times.

Ithuriel

Ithuriel, "Discovery of God," carries a spear that burns away false images. His gift is revealing the truth to those who seek it. "I know he's an angel with the worst luck in the world….Angels have different dominions of power, and his is protection," Clare notes, explaining how she came to use him in *Clockwork Princess* as well as *City of Glass* (Cassandra Clare's *Clockwork Princess* Bus Tour). In *Paradise Lost*, Ithuriel acts as Eve's guardian and wakes her with a gentle touch of his spear before Satan can whisper lies to her:

> Ithuriel and Zephon, with winged speed
> Search through this garden; leave unsearched no nook;
> But chiefly where those two fair creatures lodge,
> Now laid perhaps asleep, secure of harin.
> …
> Him [*i.e.* Satan], thus intent Ithuriel with his spear
> Touched lightly; for no falsehood can endure
> Touch of celestial temper, but returns
> Of force to its own likeness.
> (IV:788-791,.810-813)

MYTHS AND MOTIFS IN *THE MORTAL INSTRUMENTS*

Ithuriel is a very quiet angel. Since he's not a fierce Warrior of Light like Michael or Uriel, he carries no sword, only a spear for fighting at a distance. His true, angelic form is that of a bright, golden light resembling a crown. However, this form is hardly ever visible, because Ithuriel prefers subtlety. Ithuriel is invoked to reveal hidden characteristics. He helps people change bit by bit and harness their dreams, intuition, and innate talents: As such he's an ideal source of inspiration and visions for Clary. Ithuriel also inspires people to discover God within themselves, as Tessa does at the climax of *Clockwork Princess*. He removes the masks from people's faces and forces them to look into the mirror of their Soul - to see who or what they truly are – a power that's important for both heroines (Davidson).

Ithuriel is also mentioned in the poem "The Hour of the Angel" by Rudyard Kipling, which describes the final judgment as "Ithuriel's Hour." Tessa and Clary both encounter moments of judgment when their lives and the entire world of Shadowhunters are in mortal peril. Both of them, inspired by Ithuriel, find the courage and inspiration to use their innate magic and save everyone. Using "the sum of all [their] past" – their experiences and lessons – they do indeed find "victory at the last."

> **The Hour of the Angel**
> Sooner or late – in earnest or in jest –
> (But the stakes are no jest) Ithuriel's Hour
> Will spring on us, for the first time, the test
> Of our sole unbacked competence and power
> Up to the limit of our years and dower
> Of judgment – or beyond. But here we have
> Prepared long since our garland or our grave.
>
> For, at that hour, the sum of all our past,
> Act, habit, thought, and passion, shall be cast
> In one addition, be it more or less,
> And as that reading runs so shall we do;
> Meeting, astounded, victory at the last,
> Or, first and last, our own unworthiness.
> And none can change us though they die to save!
> (743)

PARABATAI

Jem explains that Greek Parabatai are soldiers paired with chariot drivers but for Nephilim, they are "a matched team of warriors – two men who swear to protect each other and guard each other's backs" (*Clockwork Angel* 209). It's mentioned that David and Jonathan in the Bible had such a relationship. David and Jonathan's love is famous – best friends who would protect each other with their lives. Jonathan's father, King Saul, schemed against David, but Jonathan stood by him nonetheless.

> And it came to pass, when he had made an end of speaking unto Saul, that the soul of Jonathan was knit with the soul of David, and Jonathan loved him as his own soul. And Saul took him that day, and would let him go no more home to his father's house. Then Jonathan and David made a covenant, because he loved him as his own soul. (1 Samuel 18: 1-3)

They are held up as a famous example of perfect platonic love. As Jem notes, "Their souls were knit together by Heaven, and out of that Jonathan Shadowhunter took the idea of parabatai" (*Clockwork Princess* 325). The Parabatai oath also comes from the Bible: Naomi, an Israelite, was returning to her homeland after the death of her husband and sons. Her daughter-in-law, Ruth, wanted to follow her to that land for love of her, but Naomi refused.

> And Ruth said, Entreat me not to leave thee, and to return from following after thee, for whither thou goest, I will go; and where thou lodgest, I will lodge; thy people shall be my people, and thy God my God; where thou diest, will I die, and there will I be buried: Jehovah do so to me, and more also, if aught but death part thee and me. (Ruth 1:16-17)

With "the angel" substituted for God, this is the Parabatai oath, shown at the end of *Clockwork Prince*. Will references the story of Ruth as he insists he will stay with a dying Jem no matter what. Ruth's story is one of love and loyalty so great that she left her home, her parents, and all she knew to care for her mother-in-law. For this she was honored with being the ancestress of King David, and through him, the Messiah. This quote also frequently appears in wedding vows.

Of course, a poignant part of the parabatai relationship is the trust, which may lead to betrayal. Will resolves to let his beloved marry his parabatai rather than destroy Jem's happiness. By contrast, Valentine betrays Luke to the werewolves then orders him to kill himself. The half a pair of ancient kindjal daggers he tosses represents their partnership, which like the paired daggers splits for many years.

Being Parabatai apparently means different things in different relationships: Alec and Jace are adoptive brothers and fighting partners, but don't define each other the way Will and Jem do. Will and Jem watch each other obsessively and act like two halves of a whole. "I tend to think with every pair of parabatai there's one that grounds the other – Jem grounds Will, Alec grounds Jace, and Julian grounds Emma," Clare comments ("Blackthorns and Co").

Myths and Motifs in *The Mortal Instruments*

Coming soon is Clare's third series in this universe, with a pair of parabatai who are falling into a forbidden love. This story will reveal much more about the parabatai relationship.

The Mark of Cain

In the Bible, Cain killed his brother Abel out of jealousy and was cursed forever. Cain is generally seen as the world's first murderer, and his heritage is monstrous. For instance, Grendel, in *Beowulf*, is described as an evil creature because he's descended from Cain, the kinslayer. In popular culture, "the mark of Cain" is known as a sign of sin or shame. In several series, vampires are descended from Cain or bear the mark of Cain, providing an interesting link between concepts. Genesis 4:11-16 depicts Cain's punishment when the Lord discovers that he murdered his brother Abel.

> And now art thou cursed from the earth, which hath opened her mouth to receive thy brother's blood from thy hand; When thou tillest the ground, it shall not henceforth yield unto thee her strength; a fugitive and a vagabond shalt thou be in the earth. And Cain said unto the Lord, My punishment is greater than I can bear. Behold, thou hast driven me out this day from the face of the earth; and from thy face shall I be hid; and I shall be a fugitive and a vagabond in the earth; and it shall come to pass, that every one that findeth me shall slay me. And the LORD said unto him, Therefore whosoever slayeth Cain, vengeance shall be taken on him sevenfold. And the LORD set a mark upon Cain, lest any finding him should kill him.

Cain is banished from his family, cursed to be a "fugitive" and "vagabond" or "wanderer," words only linked here in the entire Bible. Various interpretations suggest the mark pained him, denounced his crime to others, or even proclaimed him soulless. At the same time, in the Bible story, God gives Cain the mark as (apparently) a sign of mercy – Cain is banished from his family yet protected. This is a sign that Cain cannot be punished by man, only by a greater power.

Simon, as a vampire who can walk in the sun, has not sinned. He bit an angel, but only after the angel, Jace, offered his blood freely. Yet Raphael wants to kill him as an "abomination." In fact, thanks to the angel blood, he has become something new. Like Cain, he finds that everyone, from the Shadowhunters of Idris to the vampires, wants to kill him. He is no longer part of human society, and Raphael reminds him that Simon cannot pretend to be a human teen and continue to live with his mother. He, like Cain, has become set apart. Clary gives him the protection and curse that God gave Cain – a warning for others to leave his punishment to a higher power.

Ironically, Simon's curse makes him the only one able to summon Raziel. Notably, he offers his life not for true love as Jace and Clary repeatedly do, but for the side of goodness. Though he hesitantly claims he's not offering his life exactly for Jace (whom he doesn't appear to like much) saving Jace will preserve Clary and Isabelle's happiness and preserve a warrior for the side of good. Simon is not cursed but gifted, and as such, he becomes the power of his friends' salvation.

Once the angel arrives, Simon argues with him, much as Biblical Jacob wrestles with an angel. Genesis 32 has the tale:

> And Jacob was left alone; and there wrestled a man with him until the breaking of the day. And when he saw that he prevailed not against him, he touched the hollow of his thigh; and the hollow of Jacob's thigh was out of joint, as he wrestled with him. And he said, Let me go, for the day breaketh. And he said, I will not let thee go, except thou bless me. And he said unto him, What is thy name? And he said, Jacob. And he said, Thy name shall be called no more Jacob, but Israel: for as a prince hast thou power with God and with men, and hast prevailed. And Jacob asked him, and said, Tell me, I pray thee, thy name. And he said, Wherefore is it that thou dost ask after my name? And he blessed him there. And Jacob called the name of the place Peniel: for I have seen God face to face, and my life is preserved. And as he passed over Penuel the sun rose upon him, and he halted upon his thigh. [as in, his thigh was injured] (24-31)

Some interpret Jacob's story as one of wrestling with God (echoing his new name, Isra-el), but as the figure has a physical form, most traditions consider him an angel. His refusal to reveal his name, like Abraham's angelic visitors, also points toward this. Some believe this angel that fears the light of day is the Angel of Death, or perhaps the Metatron. Interestingly, Jacob is crippled from the fight. Simon too is crippled, separated from the Mark of Cain that has defended him. Jacob walks from the fight knowing he has God's blessing. Simon, with the sword of the angels, knows that he has been blessed as well. Both go on to fulfill God's mission on earth and help the righteous.

Magic

Many consider magic anti-religious: Either one believes in God or in witches and wizards: one cannot have both. In fact, Cassandra Clare incorporates both traditions, giving her Shadowhunters the magic only of prayer. Various Bible passages condemn sorcery, it's true:

> There shall not be found among you any one that maketh his son or his daughter to pass through the fire, or that useth divination, or an

Myths and Motifs in *THE MORTAL INSTRUMENTS*

> observer of times, or an enchanter, or a witch. Or a charmer, or a consulter with familiar spirits, or a wizard, or a necromancer. For all that do these things are an abomination unto the Lord: and because of these abominations the Lord thy God doth drive them out from before thee. (Deuteronomy 18:10-12)

However, the term "sorcerer" referred to God's opponents, like the sorcerers of Pharaoh's court in the Exodus story. Worse were the "practices of the nations," specifically those who followed the Canaanite deity Moloch and sacrificed babies to him.

> Throughout the text of the Pentateuch, "magic" and "sorcery" are seen as forces in direct opposition to the God of the Bible. This opposition is manifested in form of giving tribute or worship to any other supernatural forces other than that of God Himself. (Stewart 44)

In the Bible and the Christian tradition, "sorcery" always meant being "aligned with forces that prevented whole-hearted devotion to the faith, this time to the Church and the message of Jesus of Nazareth" (Stewart 44). "Magic" likewise meant false or idolatrous worship of other deities. Magic that relied on beseeching God and his angels for intercession and mercy, however, was considered acceptable. This type of magic exists in the oldest of Jewish spiritual texts:

> Said Rabbi Eleazar: "In the days of Enos [Enoch], men were deeply versed in occult knowledge and magical science and the manipulation of natural forces, in which no one was more skilled than he, since the time of Adam whose chief study was on the occult properties of the leaves of the Tree of Knowledge of good and evil. It was Enos that taught and imparted this occult lore to his contemporaries…Whilst Enos lived, men became initiated into the higher life, as scripture states. 'Then began men to make invocations in the name of Jehovah.'" (de Manhar 238)

As with Narnia, the Shadowhunters fight for God's glory, battling evil forces of demonic magic and the children of Lilith.

Runes

As Jace points out, he and his friends don't use magic, they use runes, which are an ancient and godly Jewish and Christian tradition. Both religions used God's name and angels' and saints' names on protective amulets to ward off evil.

Letters are sacred in Judaism, as they are believed to be crafted by God. There's a tradition of magic using Hebrew letters: Golems are brought to life (in folklore) by inscribing Hebrew letters on them. In the tradition of the Kabbalah, the Mark of Cain was likely a Hebrew letter written by God. In fact, the Zohar, mystical book of Kabbalah, describes major significances of each Hebrew letter, from God creating the world with a Bet (for Berisheet, in the beginning, the first world of the Bible and of creation) to Alef, the silent letter that begins the Hebrew alphabet and encompasses everything.

In the Zohar, each letter corresponds to God creating a part of the body and an attribute: The letter Zayin represents movement and corresponds with the left foot, and so forth. Given this mysticism in one of Judaism's most sacred books, it's easy to take this a step further and hypothesize a Zayin mark of swiftness, with the left foot its traditional place of inscription.

Clare's runes, available on her website at http://www.cassandraclare.com/my-writing/excerpts-extras/runes are Arabic in appearance, curly and vaguely reminiscent of both pictographs and Hebrew or English letters.

The word rune derives from the Indo-European root *ru*, mystery or secret. Runes today are used for divination spell casting and meditation. They have alphabetic meanings as well as magical ones. Runes in rune sets are traditionally made from bark or leather, but today may be glass or stone. The runes most commonly seen today come from the Norse tradition, appearing in fantasy works by Tolkien as well as numerous classics. The Ultima computer game series uses the same Norse runes for spellcasting. The Norse god Odin was said to have traded his eye for the runic language along with other wisdom.

Judaism has always likewise relied on protective magic, especially that of letters and drawn symbols. In medieval Judaism, amulets were used to ward off the evil eye. Most commonly, they were shaped like an eye, or an eye on the palm of a hand. This corresponds to a Shadowhunter's first rune, which offers them sight into the mystic world. This "Kemi," or written amulet, was used by Jews in the Middle East:

> Prosper me in the writing of this parchment, that it be a preservative, deliverance, protection and a perfect cure to the wearer of this Charm from sundry and divers evil diseases existing in the world, from an evil eye and an evil tongue. I adjure you all ye kinds of evil eyes, a black eye, a hazel eye, blue eye, yellow eye, short eye, broad eye, straight eye, narrow eye, deep eye, protruding eye, eye of a male, eye of a female, the eye of a wife and the eye of a husband, eye of a woman and her daughter, eye of a woman and her kinsfolk, eye of an unmarried man, eye of an old man, eye of an old woman, eye of a virgin, eye of one not a virgin, eye of a widow, eye of a married wife, eye of a divorced wife, all kinds of evil eyes in the world which looked and spoke with an evil eye concerning or against the wearer of this charm, I command and adjure you by the Most Holy and Mighty and Exalted Eye, the Only Eye,

the White Eye, the Right Eye, the Compassionate the Ever Watchful and Open Eye, the Eye that never slumbereth nor sleepeth, the Eye to Which all eyes are subject, the Wakeful Eye that preserveth Israel, as it is written, " The Eye of the Lord is upon them that fear Him, and upon them that trust in His Goodness."

By this Most High Eye, I adjure you all evil eyes to depart and be eradicated and to flee away to a distance from the Wearer of this Amulet, and that you are to have no power whatever over her who wears this Charm. And by the power of this most Holy Seal, you shall have no authority to hurt either by day or by night, when asleep or when awake: nor over any of her two hundred and forty-eight limbs, nor over any of her three hundred and sixty-five veins henceforth and for ever.
A.N.S.V. [Abbreviation for 'Amen, Netzach, Tsilol, Ve'ad]
UZAH. ADIAH. LEHABIEL
PI. JH. VH. JHVH. EHYEH. AH. ASHER. HV. GH. VH.
Kinbijah. Baduomfiel. Beduftiel. (Hanauer 319)

Note the angel names at the end, similar to the Shadowhunters' invocation of a particular angel when they draw an angelic blade. The letter combinations before this, often formed from the names of angels, were added to these amulets and scrolls. The position of the letters was said to power the charms and protect the wearer (Hanauer 320).

THE HERO SWORD

The heavy-bladed silver sword Maellartach has a hilt shaped like outspread wings. It hangs above the Speaking Stars in the Silent Brothers' Council Room for use in trials. As such, it echoes the great hero-swords seen in many epics. Clare adds:

> The Mortal Sword is one in a long line of fictional, historical and mythological swords. There are swords so famous we all know their names – Arthur had Excalibur, Roland had Durendal, Caesar had Crocea Mors, and Siegfried had Balmung (made by Wayland Smith), etc. I wanted the Mortal Sword to be one of history's famous swords, so, since the MI series draws on a lot of Biblical myth, Maellartach is supposed to be the sword in Genesis – "So God placed at the east of the garden of Eden Cherubims, and a flaming sword which turned every way, to keep the way of the tree of life." So it's the sword that separates man from Paradise, in theory. It's also why I named one of the chapters in Ashes East of Eden. (*Reader's Quill*)

When Adam and Eve were forced to leave the garden, cherubim, one wielding a "flaming sword," kept them from returning:

> So he droue out the man: and he placed at the East of the garden of Eden, Cherubims, and a flaming sword, which turned every way, to keep the way of the tree of life. (Genesis 3:24)

The sword is a masculine symbol of war and law. It's no surprise the rather patriarchal Clave wields it. "Mortal Sword" is actually a phrase in Shakespeare's *Macbeth*: Macduff cries, "Let us rather/Hold fast the mortal sword and, like good men/Bestride our downfall'n birthdom." In other words, he demands his people take their swords and defend their fallen homeland like honorable men (IV:iii:2-4). This of course is the mission Jace and his friends face in the first series as Idris crumbles.

A second sword that appears in *City of Lost Souls* is Glorious, the sword of Joshua. The series describes the sword as the one given to Joshua in the following moment of the Bible:

> And it came to pass, when Joshua was by Jericho, that he lifted up his eyes and looked, and, behold, there stood a man over against him with his sword drawn in his hand: and Joshua went unto him, and said unto him, Art thou for us, or for our adversaries? And he said, Nay; but as captain of the host of the LORD am I now come. And Joshua fell on his face to the earth, and did worship, and said unto him, What saith my lord unto his servant? And the captain of the LORD'S host said unto Joshua, Loose thy shoe from off thy foot; for the place whereon thou standest is holy. And Joshua did so. (Joshua 5: 13-15)

As captain of the host, this is assumed to be the Archangel Michael. He gave Joshua his own sword, and with it, Joshua led his army against Jericho. By God's blessing, the walls fell, and Joshua captured the city. Simon receives this sword from the Angel Raziel and gives it to Clary, demonstrating that they are both in heaven's favor and have been given the power to strike down their enemies. Simon gives Clary the sword "and in that moment, she was no longer Clary, his friend since childhood, but a Shadowhunter, an avenging angel who belonged with that sword in her hand" (*Lost Souls* 485-486).

Elias Carstairs, Jem's uncle, possesses the sword Cortana forged from the same steel as Joyeuse and Durendal: Durendal is the hero's sword in *The Song of Roland*, while Joyeuse belonged to Charlemagne. Cortana, of course, will be the destined weapon for the children of *The Dark Artifices*.

According to legend, Cortana was the sword of Ogier the Dane; it bore the inscription "My name is Cortana, of the same steel and temper as Joyeuse and Durendal." It is supposed to have originally been the hero Tristan's sword, and gained the name "Cortana" when it was "cut down" to fit Ogier. It comes from the Latin curtus, used to refer to a type of ceremonial sword. Edward the

Myths and Motifs in *The Mortal Instruments*

Confessor's sword, the "Sword of Mercy" was such a blade. All stories are true, and with a blade of such stature, a new generation of warriors will emerge.

Angels

The first thing angels say is "fear not," suggesting that they're quite terrifying. According to tradition, angels do not have free will like man; they are only messengers passing on God's word. In fact, they can only each do a single act, which is why three angels often appear, to bring three different messages. "Angelus" is Latin for messenger.

The three books of Enoch are the best source for Judeo-Christian angels and fallen angels. Another strong source is *The Celestial Hierarchy* by Dionysus the Aeorpagite written in the fifth century. This contains the best-known hierarchy of angels, used in St. Thomas Aquinas's thirteenth century work, *Summa Theologiae*. In his time, Angelology was popular, and Aquinas created a great deal of educational material. Medieval grimoires such as *The Lesser Key of Solomon* contain much on angels and demons as well. Dr. John Dee and Emmanuel Swedenborg communicated with angels regularly and wrote books about their experiences.

The Celestial Hierarchy sorts angels thus:

First Choir	**Second Choir**	**Third Choir**
1). Seraphim	4). Dominations	7). Principalities
2). Cherubim	5). Virtues	8). Archangels
3). Thrones	6). Powers	9). Angels

Paradise Lost adds:

> Hear all ye Angels, Progenie of Light,
> Thrones, Dominations, Princedoms, Vertues, Powers,
> Hear my Decree, which unrevok't shall stand. (5:600-602)

The third choir is the one closest to mankind. Angels are the closest to humanity and thus beings we can relate best to. The more powerful of the angels, their chiefs, are called archangels. Michael and Gabriel, some of the few named angels in the Bible, are on all the lists of archangels, though the identities of some of the others vary slightly. Here is the list from the *Book of Enoch*, one of the earliest:

> And these are the names of the holy angels who watch. Uriel, one of

the holy angels, who is over the world and over Tartarus. Raphael, one of the holy angels, who is over the spirits of men. Raguel, one of the holy angels who takes vengeance on the world of the luminaries. Michael, one of the holy angels, to wit, he that is set over the best part of mankind [and] over chaos. Saraqâêl, one of the holy angels, who is set over the spirits, who sin in the spirit. Gabriel, one of the holy angels, who is over Paradise and the serpents and the Cherubim. Remiel, one of the holy angels, whom God set over those who rise. (20:1-8)

Greater Demons

Judaism has no devil, but is has long been aware of another presence besides God and his angels:

> I blessed always the Lord of Glory, and I continued to bless the Lord of Glory who has wrought great and glorious wonders, to show the greatness of His work to the angels and to *spirits* and to men, that they might praise His work and all His creation: that they might see the work of His might and praise the great work of His hands and bless Him for ever. (italics added, Enoch 36:1)

The ancient book the *Lesser Key of Solomon* describes the ranks of demons and instructions to summon them. It also includes complex rune markings for each of the demons. It also shows the protective pentagram and Seal of Solomon that must be used – In alchemy, the seal of Solomon represents the conscious and unconscious realms, as three points of the star point to the upper world and three to the lower (Cirlot 281). It is frequently circled with a ring of protection. Similar protective circles were used across the world, from Vodou véves to Pennsylvania Dutch hex signs. Words of conjuration also appear in the book, for in the Bible it's said that Solomon conjured a host of demons to build his temple:

> Beralanensis, Baldachiensis, Paumachia, and Apologia Sedes, by the most mighty kings and powers, and the most powerful princes, genii, Liachidæ, ministers of the Tartarean seat, chief prince of the seat of Apologia, in the ninth legion, I invoke you, and by invocating, conjure you; and being armed with power from the supreme Majesty, I strongly command you, by Him who spoke and it was done, and to whom all creatures are obedient; and by this ineffable name, Tetragrammaton Jehovah, which being heard the elements are overthrown, the air is shaken, the sea runneth back, the fire is quenched, the earth trembles, and all the host of the celestials, and terrestrials, and infernals do tremble together, and are troubled and confounded: wherefore, forthwith and without delay, do you come from all parts of the world,

and make rational answers unto all things I shall ask of you; and come ye peaceably, visibly and affably now, without delay, manifesting what we desire, being conjured by the name of the living and true God, Helioren, and fulfill our commands, and persist unto the end, and according to our intentions, visibly and affably speaking unto us with a clear voice, intelligible, and without any ambiguity. ("Of the Art Goetia")

In Catholic theology "demon" has come to be a synonym for devil or fallen angel. The Fourth Lateran Council issued the decree: "Diabolus enim et alii daemones" (the devil and the other demons), i.e. all are demons, and the chief of the demons is called the devil. The Vulgate New Testament echoes this system of naming. Satan is clearly included among the daemons in James 2:19 and in Luke 11:15-18. "For our wrestling is not against flesh and blood; but against principalities and powers, against the rulers of the world of this darkness, against the spirits of wickedness in the high places" (Ephesians 6:12). Instances of possession have also been recorded: Saint Augustine attests that while the soul cannot be corrupted, the body may be taken over (Kent).

Clare notes:

> I wanted to make sure multiple types of demonic myth were present, not just the Christian view of them, so you'll find Japanese, Indian, Tibetan, and other kinds of demons represented (plus the kind I've made up.) I read a lot of old "demonologies" – there was a whole time period where scholars were obsessed with listing every kind of demon and mapping Hell. ("Interview: Cassandra Clare")

In Jewish legend, demons were forces opposed to mankind, most likely the children of Lilith (whose legend is recounted below). Some scholars believed they were instead a response to man's sin – uncleanliness, lust, straying from prayer, and so forth. Thus leading a righteous life would banish them.

Lilith

> After God created Adam, who was alone, He said, 'It is not good for man to be alone' (Genesis 2:18). He then created a woman for Adam, from the earth, as He had created Adam himself, and called her Lilith. Adam and Lilith immediately began to fight. She said, 'I will not lie below,' and he said, 'I will not lie beneath you, but only on top. For you are fit only to be in the bottom position, while I am to be the superior one.' Lilith responded, 'We are equal to each other inasmuch as we were both created from the earth.' But they would not listen to one another. When Lilith saw this, she pronounced the Ineffable Name and flew away into the air. Adam stood in prayer before his Creator: 'Sovereign

of the universe!' he said, 'the woman you gave me has run away.' At once, the Holy One, blessed be He, sent these three angels to bring her back.

"Said the Holy One to Adam, 'If she agrees to come back, fine. If not, she must permit one hundred of her children to die every day.' The angels left God and pursued Lilith, whom they overtook in the midst of the sea, in the mighty waters wherein the Egyptians were destined to drown. They told her God's word, but she did not wish to return. The angels said, 'We shall drown you in the sea.'

"'Leave me!' she said. 'I was created only to cause sickness to infants. If the infant is male, I have dominion over him for eight days after his birth, and if female, for twenty days.'

"When the angels heard Lilith's words, they insisted she go back. But she swore to them by the name of the living and eternal God: 'Whenever I see you or your names or your forms in an amulet, I will have no power over that infant.' She also agreed to have one hundred of her children die every day. Accordingly, every day one hundred demons perish, and for the same reason, we write the angels names on the amulets of young children. When Lilith sees their names, she remembers her oath, and the child recovers." (Stern and Mirsky 183- 184)

Lilith is first mentioned in *The Alphabet of Ben Sirah*, a book of Jewish magic and mysticism dating back to the first millennium. She derives from older sources: Mesopotamian mythology mentions a Liltu bird perched in the goddess Inanna's garden, and the Lilim, various she-demons. She appears in the ancient mythology of Samaria, Babylonia, Canaan, Persia, and Arabia.

Lilith entered Jewish folklore as a banished demon living in the deep caverns of the world, begetting monsters. She was a night demonness who would appear to strangle babies if she was not warded off. In fact, a medieval term for witches is "Daughters of Lilith." Many think of her as the original vampire or succubus, seducing men and strangling children to maintain her unholy existence. Babies had protections put on them to ward Lilith away – it is just these protections that Jace needs to keep her from influencing him in dreams.

Many protective amulets from medieval Jewish Europe contain the names of Lilith or another demon, supposedly in the belief that "the deterrent element which frightens the Evil Spirit away are the mysterious names of the Evil Spirit" (Gaster 149). One amulet, for instance, includes the following statement:

These are my names, Satrina, Lilith, Abito, Amizo, Izorpo, Kokos,

Myths and Motifs in *The Mortal Instruments*

Odam, Ita, Podo, Eilo, Patrota, Abeko, Kea, Kali, Batna, Talto, and Partash. Whoever knows these my names and writes them down causes me to run away from the new-born child. (Gaster 149)

It is the sight of their names which "terrifies her away, and protects those who invoke their aid against the attacks of the child-stealing witch" (Gaster 150). The names Satrina and Talto appear in Clare's books as Lilith makes her dreaded reappearance. Her desire to hide her name is likely linked with the concept that calling her by name can banish her. Angels' names were another defense. One Lilith incantation bowl contains the following inscription:

> You are bound and sealed,
>   all you demons and devils and liliths,
> by that hard and strong,
>   mighty and powerful bond with which are tied Sison and Sisin....
> The evil Lilith,
>   who causes the hearts of men to go astray
>   and appears in the dream of the night
>   and in the vision of hte day,
> Who burns and casts down with nightmare,
>   attacks and kills children,
>   boys and girls.
> She is conquered and sealed
>   away from the house
>   and from the threshold of Bahram-Gushnasp son of Ishtar-Nahid
> by the talisman of Metatron,
>   the great prince
>   who is called the Great Healer of Mercy....
> who vanquishes demons and devils,
>   black arts and mighty spells
>   and keeps them away from the house
>   and threshold of Bahram-Gushnasp, son of Ishtar-Nahid.
> Amen, Amen, Selah.
> Vanquished are the black arts and mighty spells.
> Vanquished the bewitching women,
>   they, their witchery and their spells,
>   their curses and their invocations,
>   and kept away from the four walls
>   of the house of Bahram-Gushnasp, the son of Ishtar-Hahid.
> Vanquished and trampled down are the bewitching women –
>   vanquished on earth and vanquished in heaven.
> Vanquished are their constellations and stars.

> Bound are the works of their hands.
> Amen, Amen, Selah.
> (qtd. in Patai 228f)

Adam was Lilith's first consort, but most legends give her a demon consort to follow, possibly Samael, the angel of death, whom Lilith mentions in the series.

Abbadon

Inside Madame Dorothea is "A Greater Demon. Abbadon – one of the Ancients. The Lord of the Fallen" (*Bones* 361). In Revelation 9:1-11, Abaddon is described as a star who falls to Earth from heaven and is given the key to open the bottomless pit. Abaddon opens the pit, releasing a swarm of locusts. "And they had a king over them, which is the angel of the bottomless pit, whose name in the Hebrew tongue is Abaddon, but in the Greek tongue hath his name Apollyon" (Revelation 9:11). In *The Greater Key of Solomon*, his is the name Moses invokes to bring a destructive rain down over Egypt. He is the one who lets out curses to plague mankind, much as he does in the most vicious battle of the first book. He represents a challenge for the teens and a chance to see how they all fight: Alec foolishly risks himself and is nearly killed, Jace can only think of Clary. Clary herself freezes. And Simon the Mundane, who's been told to wait in the car, saves the day with his archery training from camp.

Agramon

Agramon, the Demon of Fear, shapeshifts into a person's greatest fear and literally scares him or her to death. Agramon is fiendishly clever, and always uses his summoner's fear that he will escape to make that fear come true. When "formless" he is a black cloud with glowing eyes, an enormous, hideous shape with eyes the size of saucers. Of course, he is a metaphor for facing fear as the teens must do: Maia sees her abusive brother, Jace confronts both his love for Clary and his fear of his father, and beats the second with the help of a Fearless rune. This gives him the power to confront the other and promise to only be Clary's brother.

Asmodeus

The Book of Tobit from the Jewish Biblical Apocrypha describes the young woman Sara, who was married to seven husbands, all of whom Asmodeus the evil spirit had killed. Another righteous man, her cousin Tobit, was struck blind.

> And Raphael was sent to heal them both, that is, to scale away the

whiteness of Tobit's eyes, and to give Sara the daughter of Raguel for a wife to Tobias the son of Tobit; and to bind Asmodeus the evil spirit; because she belonged to Tobias by right of inheritance. (Tobit 3:17)

Asmodeus ("Creature of Judgment") may be the son of the human woman Naamah (sometimes called a demoness) and a fallen angel. He is the demon of lust and gambling. Originally, he was a Persian demon who provoked anger and revenge in his victims. It is said he tempted Noah into drunkenness in the Bible story.

Azazel

("God Strengthens") This is a greater demon who descended to earth to live with the humans and fell because of it. Azazel led the 200 angels who mated with mortal women, called grigori. He taught women to incite lust and men to make weapons.

> And Azazel taught the people (the art of) making swords and knives, and shields, and breastplates; and he showed to their chosen ones bracelets, decorations, (shadowing of the eye) with antimony, ornamentation, the beautifying of the eyelids, all kinds of precious stones, and all coloring tinctures and alchemy. (Enoch 8:1)

Magnus quotes the Book of Enoch, describing Azazel: "And the whole earth has been corrupted by the works that were taught by Azazel. To him ascribe all sin." Magnus calls him a "Greater Demon, Lieutenant of Hell and Forger of Weapons" (*Lost Souls* 207). He's still bound in eternal punishment to the jagged mountain of Duduael.

After Azazel and his fallen companions mated with humanity and taught them forbidden knowledge, the angels Michael, Uriel, Raphael, and Gabriel petitioned God to end it all. God told Noah to build an ark, and then issued the following command:

> And again the Lord said to Raphael: 'Bind Azâzêl hand and foot, and cast him into the darkness: and make an opening in the desert, which is in Dûdâêl, and cast him therein. And place upon him rough and jagged rocks, and cover him with darkness, and let him abide there for ever, and cover his face that he may not see light. And on the day of the great judgment he shall be cast into the fire. And heal the earth which the angels have corrupted, and proclaim the healing of the earth, that they may heal the plague, and that all the children of men may not perish through all the secret things that the Watchers have disclosed and have taught their sons. And the whole earth has been corrupted through the works that were taught by Azâzêl: to him ascribe all sin.' (Enoch 9:4-8)

Yanluo

Yanluo Wang, also called Yan Wang, is the demon who tortured Jem and addicted him to the yin fen. He's also the senior king of the ten courts of the Chinese underworld. He looks into the former lives of the dead and assigns them to the appropriate court for punishments fitting their sins. Many believe his name is related to that of the great death god, Yama. Men or women with merit will be rewarded, while others are sentenced to worse lives or torture. Will and Jem reflect a great deal on whether their lives balance as good or evil, and where their futures lie, on the great wheel of reincarnation. It seems more than coincidence that Yanluo has sealed Jem's fate.

CHAPTER 3
FANTASY TROPES AND GENRES

All Myths are True

> When I was a kid/teen I loved *The Dark is Rising* by Susan Cooper, the *Prydain Chronicles* by Lloyd Alexander, the *Lord of the Rings*, *War for the Oaks* by Emma Bull, anything by Robin McKinley, Diana Wynne Jones or Neil Gaiman, any of the Bordertown stories by Terri Windling, Ellen Kushner, Charles de Lint, and others. I love writing fantasy now because it works as an allegory for daily life and you can find powerful truths in fantastic literature and media if you are willing to look. In "Buffy the Vampire Slayer", high school wasn't just a hellish experience, it was actually hell. (*Enchanted Inkpot*)

In fantasy the concept that all myths are true appears in many series. The *Sandman* and *Fables* graphic novels are famous for it. The librarians of *Libriomancer* by Jim C. Hines can likewise bring any fictional object to life, and characters on television's *The Librarian* and *Warehouse 13* keep the items from all the legends safe. *Peter Pan* and *The Neverending Story* have characters enter the realm of dreams. In Jasper Fforde's *Thursday Next* and *Nursery Crime* series fictional characters take on lives of their own within the Bookworld. Marvel Comics say that all myths are real, thus Thor and Hercules appear and fight alongside superheroes. Neil Gaiman's *American Gods*, Robert A. Heinlein's *The Number of The Beast*, *Percy Jackson*, *The Dresden Files*, *The X-Files*, *Stargate*, *Supernatural*, *Charmed*, *The Secrets of the Immortal Nicholas Flamel*, and others rely on this trope.

It gives the author the opportunity to explore the best of literature – *Dracula* and *Carmilla* are true, as are fairytales, myths, and famous legends. The sword Cortana, out of *Tristan and Isolde*, shows up alongside the Sword of Joshua from the Bible. It's a delightful playground for any fantasy author, one that she can share with her more knowledgeable readers.

Valerie Estelle Frankel

Urban Fantasy and the City

Urban fantasy, in which demons and fairies roam the streets of the big city (often London or New York) has grown in popularity over the last few decades. Popular authors include Laurell K. Hamilton, Kim Harrison, Emma Bull, Charles De Lint, Neil Gaiman, Jim Butcher, Charlaine Harris, Melissa Marr, Tim Powers, and Laini Taylor. *The Dresden Files, Anita Blake. Young Wizards, Percy Jackson,* and *Spiderwick Chronicles* are a few popular series. Urban fantasy movies include everything from *Ghost* to *Ghostbusters*. Television offers shows like *The Vampire Diaries, Grimm, Lost Girl, Supernatural, Beauty and the Beast,* and *Being Human*. However, the genre also appears in much older works, such as *Dracula* and the works of H.P. Lovecraft.

Other genres such as fairytale retellings, paranormal romance, supernatural detective fiction, and thrillers often get crossed with this genre. There are elves who drive racecars, trolls under the bridges of Seattle, an alien entity in the Statue of Liberty. This is city fantasy, often the modern city but not always. As such, it provides a familiar setting from which to embark on the adventure.

Many readers prefer it because it takes place, not in some Tolkienesque pseudo-medieval setting, but in our world. As such, it often feels more accessible. Teens have cellphones and cars, and use the internet for research. Top series *Harry Potter* and *Twilight*, while both taking place in modern times, largely stay out of big cities. *The Mortal Instruments*, by contrast, is firmly set in New York, as are books by Clare's friends Delia Sherman and Holly Black. As Clare explains:

> When I sat down to sketch out the book, I wanted to write something that would combine elements of traditional high fantasy – an epic battle between good and evil, terrible monsters, brave heroes, enchanted swords – and recast it through a modern, urban lens. So you have the Shadowhunters, who are these very classic warriors following their millennia-old traditions, but in these urban, modern spaces: skyscrapers, warehouses, abandoned hotels, rock concerts. In fairy tales, it was the dark and mysterious forest outside the town that held the magic and danger. I wanted to create a world where the city has become the forest – where these urban spaces hold their own enchantments, danger, mysteries and strange beauty. It's just that only the Shadowhunters can see them as they really are. (FAQ)

New York

Clare revealed the Mortal Instruments series has its genesis in the 9/11 terror attacks: 'I had just moved to New York in September 2001 and

Myths and Motifs in *The Mortal Instruments*

> immediately 9/11 happened and of course it completely changed the city and everybody who lived there. I was in Brooklyn, coming down the bridge as everyone was walking over, covered in plaster dust and blood, and the shopkeepers opened up along the street to give out free water and we were running over to hand it out. People were very kind and brave in a crisis. It made me want to write a story set in New York, a kind of fantasy and a love letter to the city and the people who live there. There was this idea of monsters and demons and people were so afraid of the city being attacked. There were missing posters everywhere - it was a really a terrifying time to live in the city. I thought 'what if the city was really under attack by supernatural dark forces, who would protect it?' (Nathan)

The "City" titles on each book emphasize the urban nature of the writing. Likewise, the beginnings of the first two books are strongly linked to the city theme – Clary is dancing at a forbidden club filled with teens in exotic makeup and goth clothes...and one turns out to be an actual demon (this is an occasional staple in urban fantasy). *City of Ashes* begins with a poem about the magical city, then a description of the most luxurious and new downtown condo in Manhattan, blending the ideas.

Of course, Clary's world is a mixture of magic and mundane. Clary and Simon live in Brooklyn (in an apartment based on Clare's in the Brooklyn suburb of Park Slope), the Institute is in Manhattan. The teens spend their days shopping for comics at Forbidden Planet, hopping the subway, and traveling along other New York landmarks. Fairies live in Central Park and Nixies in the river. Renwick Smallpox Hospital on Roosevelt/Blackwell's Island was once the retreat of the Blackwell family, a Shadowhunter family in good standing. This clever melding of fantasy, history, and reality brings Clare's world to life in a special way for readers. Clare's life, along with the layout of New York, defines her magical world:

> Where Clary's stepfather Luke lives is where I lived when I first moved to New York and didn't have any money so I had to live in Williamsburg, while the Institute is on the Upper East Side where my grandparents lived. I like the idea that different neighbourhoods have different personalities and can lead to different kinds of magic. (Jewell)

London

The city of the *Infernal Devices* series is set in the 1870's London, far removed from our own. Steampunk series are often set there, blending the world of manners and Victorian culture with science-fiction technology and the supernatural. As with other Steampunk series, London with its landmarks becomes essential to the plot. First of all, the Institute is an amalgam of two famous London churches – St. Bride's and the no-longer-existent All-Hallows-the-Less. Jessamine and Tess encounter a goblin in Hyde Park, and Jem and Tessa are changed forever on Blackfriars Bridge. Though the city around it changes through the decades, the river remains, sweeping through it all. They later drive through the worst slums of London, seeking Will. In Whitechapel, they see starving beggars, even little children. There are "gambling hells" and fairy drug dens – the worst of the magical and mundane worlds.

The culture of 1878 is also highly evident: Even friends called each other Mister or Miss (Shadowhunters, it's explained, make an exception). A young woman like Jessamine was forbidden to live on her own. Hats, coats, and gloves were always worn outdoors. Men were expected to be chivalrous to ladies. Though the Shadowhunters are very progressive, especially in women's battle training, they remain aware of society's expectations. Jessamine, especially, is a product of her culture, as she wants to make a society marriage, like most wealthy women of her era. For her, the mundane world where women are admired for their beauty and frivolous accomplishments is far preferable to the magical one. When she chooses Nate, many of the flaws in this type of acquired helplessness are made evident. This world, too, is a product of Clare's life.

> Set in London in the Victorian era, *The Infernal Devices* is inspired by her childhood experiences living in the British capital for two years. "I fell in love with it," says Clare. "I didn't go to school so my parents would give me assignments to do all around the city. I would write up what I learned and I found out lots of fascinating details. So when I decided to do a corresponding series to the initial series that I had created, London was a natural fit. It has had a wonderful history for such a long time and it has a secret past that's no longer there but lives on in our imaginations."..."London is a much older city than New York, which is partly why it takes place 130 years in the past," she says. (Jewell)

Idris and Alicante

Idris is named for the Welsh Mountain of Caer Idris (Mount Idris). This enormous chair-shaped indentation in the mountains was said to be the seat of Idris the Giant. As the myth adds:

> Whoever dares to spend a night alone either upon the chair of the Giant Idris (the summit of Cader Idris, in Merionethshire), or under the haunted Black Stone of Arddu, upon the Llanberis side of Snowdon, will be found in the morning either inspired or mad. (Squire 305)

Myths and Motifs in *The Mortal Instruments*

Will thinks of the legend when he travels to the original Idris in Wales. There, the Magister has created an evil fortress on the site of Idris over the famed mirrorlike lake and is capitalizing on the legend. This myth is also used in several fantasy series, such as *The Fionavar Tapestry*, in which the dwarf king must spend a night in such a place. Idris is the name of a river in *The Chronicles of Prydain* by Lloyd Alexander (which Clary mentions she has read in *City of Bones*). Of course, in Clare's work, Idris is called the city of glass because its towers are made out of the same demon-repelling substance as steles. One assumes its magical associations are behind the choice of name – like journeying to Fairie or the Otherworld. Book four of *Paradise Lost* describes Eden with golden fruits and native perfumes in a woodland paradise, much like Idris.

Alicante is likewise a real place, with a name probably chosen for its meaning.

> A shot of Light... Like something hitting you straight between the eyes. This sensation is what the sailors of old must have felt on board their ships as the White Mountain came into view in the distance. Emerging from the sea horizon, intensely blue, what was to become a watchtower and founding reference of the city appeared before the eyes of Greeks, Phoenicians and other peoples who ventured into the unknown west, a flash in the distance, and a reason for respite, a place full of hope. (Serrano)

Alicante, the city of light, named for its "white hill, the powerful mass of white limestone on which the sunlight returns a blinding impression between the blue of the sky and the sea," is a real city in South Spain. At night, the city is intensely lit and frequently filled with outdoor festivals. The Romans named it "the City of Light," which may have inspired Clare's version. It's known for the white limestone hill it sits upon, which must have flashed like a white light in the eyes of incoming sailors. The pale stone city beneath Mount Benacantil looks Mediterranean but also Biblical, rising from the sands and overlooking the sea. It dates back to the Bronze Age, with medieval walls and castle. Like much of Spain, this city was embroiled in religious wars between Catholics and Muslims. The castle was owned at times by the Iberians, Carthaginians, Romans, Muslims, Castilians and Aragonese, and reflects their myriad of styles. The gothic cathedral was used as a fortress of defense as much as a place of worship, like the Shadowhunters' Institutes. As a watchtower and a beacon of hope, this city is a shining namesake for Clare's city. (Serrano)

In her series, it's the City of Glass, filled with light and spires. Glass also suggests the wall of glass Jocelyn built around her daughter, now vanished as Clary enters Idris. The shining glassy towers repel demons, unless they are corrupted by demon blood. Glass is a symbol of holiness and purity, but because of its clear nature, it shows darkness easily. When Cinderella's stepsisters drip blood on the glass slipper, they are revealed as impure. In just this way, Sebastian taints the glass towers and so reveals who he is.

CITY OF BLOOD

Magnus dreams of a "city all of blood, with towers made of bone, and blood ran in the streets like water" (*Lost Souls* 304). He then quotes the Bible "A land of darkness, as darkness itself; and of the shadow of death, without any order, and where the light is as darkness" (Job 10:22). Job, persecuted by Satan, begs God to give him peace for a short time before he must go to that land of darkness: death itself. Later, Clary has the same dream: "a city like Alicante, but the demon towers were made of human bones and the canals ran with blood" (*Lost Souls* 391). This is a possible future, the world invaded by demons and ruled by Sebastian.

CITIES OF LOST HOPES

The *City of Ashes* is so named as the Silent Brothers are slaughtered in their city and Jace and Clary learn they can never be together. Jocelyn spends the entire book unconscious, with Luke and Clary helpless to awaken her. Simon dies, becomes a vampire, and accepts that he'll never have Clary. The City of Bones of course is literally fashioned from Shadowhunter ashes, and in this book it goes from graveyard to slaughterhouse. In various famous expressions, passion, dreams, love, and fire all burn down to ashes when endangered. Most of the main characters, from Valentine to Simon, watch their desires dissolve into nothingness in the middle book. Ashes more literally references the ashes from Valentine's burned ship that swirl around them all at the book's conclusion – his plans, like Clary's and Simon's, have literally gone up in smoke.

The pairing of "dust and ashes" is even more common – a reminder that humans and all their ambitions are short-lived. Over the London institute gates is a Horace quote: We are dust and shadows (*Clockwork Angel* 90). Will notes that Shadowhunters especially have short lives followed by cremation.

The *City of Fallen Angels*, as Clare reveals, is "metaphorical." As she explains:

> The tagline for the book was "Who will be tempted by darkness?" and the book is about temptation and falling prey to darker impulses. Simon falls when he bites Maureen; Alec when he frees Camille; Clary when she raises the dead; and Jace, of course, most spectacularly of all. We all fall from grace, is the message. (Jewell)

Myths and Motifs in *The Mortal Instruments*

Lost Souls is just as disturbing: Sebastian, of course, is the ultimate lost soul, but Jace has been possessed and Clary risks her life to free him. All three commit treason against the Clave and its angels. Sebastian of course creates a new race of warriors who fit this definition, children of the demons and lost souls in truth. Jordan the werewolf tries to find love and forgiveness with Maia. And Simon addresses the overwhelming concern of his own damnation. The Mark of Cain too becomes important, as is the question of whether Jace and Sebastian "are more heaven's than hell's." This book more than any other forces the characters to put their souls on trial and beseech heaven's judgment on their actions.

The *City of Heavenly Fire* reflects the heavenly war that's coming – Shadowhunters against Sebastian's evil Shadowhunters. In the Bible, God sent divine fire down to kill those who had angered him, like Aaron's sons. The fire is one of purification and cleansing, but also heaven's wrath. Jace quotes the Bible: "For a fire is kindled in mine anger, and shall burn unto the lowest hell, and shall consume the earth with her increase, and set on fire the foundations of the mountains" (Deut. 32:22). Of course, this heavenly fire now burns inside him. With Sebastian's demon powers, they are the two champions of the war of light and darkness. Fire also suggests the passion of love. "Will love be their salvation or destruction?" is a tagline. In the end, all three trilogies show a trip from darkness through greater darkness into light and salvation, reflected in the titles.

Angels in Popular Culture

Clare adds: "I love writing about angels because the mythology is so rich and enjoyable. There are so many texts to read" ("Cassandra Clare's Interview with German Magazine, Daisuki"). In fact, angels have featured as main characters in many popular movies as well as books: *Wings of Desire, The Prophecy, Michael, Meet Joe Black, Dogma, The Preacher's Wife, It's a Wonderful Life*. The struggle between angels and fallen angels appears on the *X-Files, Xena, Charmed*, and other shows. *Many Waters* by Madeline L'Engle (a sequel to *A Wrinkle in Time*) shows the fallen angels consorting with human women and God sending Noah's flood to cleanse the earth of them.

The Archangel Uriel advises Harry Dresden in his series. The television show *Angel* and Diane Duane's *Young Wizards* series feature The Powers That Be: immortal spiritual forces that give advice on God's behalf. In many fantasy universes, helpers such as Gandalf or Mercedes Lackeys' horse-shaped Companions are specifically supposed to be angels, though the fluffy wings don't appear. Further, in L. Jagi Lamplighter's *Prospero Lost*, elves are fallen angels, and in Laura Anne Gilman's *Retriever* series angels are one of many nonhuman species. There are angelic superheroes from Angel on *X-Men* (a mutant who resembles an angel) to the actual angel Zauriel who joins the Justice League. And of course, who's more angelic than Superman, the modern flying man who travels the world saving the day?

Paranormal romance series such as Kristina Douglas's *The Fallen* and Gena Showalter's books or erotic fantasy like *Kushiel's Dart* feature fallen angels who seek humans to love. Sharon Shinn's *Archangel* series is about a planet where a colony ship transformed some people into angels, who can call upon God (as they think) to cure illness and bring rain with their beautiful voices. Every book is filled with the angels' quests for their human soulmates.

Fallen angels and their love affairs with mortals appear in teen novels like *Fallen Angel* by Heather Terrell and *The Space Between* by Brenna Yovanoff. The later follows a daughter of Lilith and Lucifer as she combs the earth for her half-brother and finds herself dazzled by another half-angel. *A Temptation of Angels* by Michelle Zink features a teenage girl in Victorian London, who is a Keeper, descendent of the angels and preserver of the world.

Other series use the images of angels to create aliens manipulating man for their own aims or to better mankind in Terence Blacker's *The Angel Factory*, *Battlestar Galactica*, and *Babylon 5*. The Ori on *Stargate* demand worship, but more resemble demons bristling with hellfire. *Doctor Who* offers the terrifying "weeping angels" aliens. Phillip Pullman's *His Dark Materials* shows angels who are closer to the institutionalized church with its inquisition than avatars of God. Actual angels who aren't as benevolent as they appear are also in Neil Gaiman's *Neverwhere* and Sarah Douglass' *The Crucible* series.

When asked about her favorite YA book of 2011, Clare replied, "One is *Daughter of Smoke and Bone* by Laini Taylor. It's set in Prague and has to do with angels and magic, and a really lovable main character. I really love that" (Brissey, "Mortal Instruments, Infernal Devices Author"). *Daughter of Smoke and Bone* is a groundbreaking angel series. Akiva, an angel broken by a never-ending war, comes to earth and falls in love with a human girl named Karou. Though she pretends to be an art student, she has another, secret life collecting teeth and bringing them to her master, a granter of wishes. As Akiva and Karou fall in love, they realize the war is continuing and they are not on the sides they had once believed. The book is filled with surprises from beginning to end.

Angel books often reflect angels' warlike natures, and bring the war of heaven down to earth. *Angelfall* by Susan Ee features a post-apocalyptic Bay Area, where the angels have descended to tear civilization apart. Teenage Penryn quests with the injured and wingless angel Reffe, whom she believes is her only link to her vanished seven-year-old sister. In the post-apocalyptic or otherwise evil angel stories, there are a few good angels remaining to save humanity. The war isn't always divided into angels and demons, but we are reminded that it is in fact a war in heaven. In Clare's series, Sebastian and Valentine are the antagonists – all angels are on the side of God, if not precisely humanity. However, Lilith's arrival in the second trilogy reminds readers the battle for heaven is continuing.

The Books of Raziel by Sabrina Benulis, beginning with *Archon*, introduce a young woman named Angela Mathers, who is obsessed with visions and dreams of angels. She's ostracized, for there's a prophecy that someone with red hair like hers will destroy the world. Angels and demons are combing the streets for the key to the Book of Raziel and the power to control the universe. *The Fallen* by Thomas E. Sniegoski follows Aaron Corbet, a boy who thought he was human until he discovers he is Nephilim – half angel, half human. Along with the angel Camael, Aaron embarks on his destiny – to be the Nephilim chosen to heal the rift between fallen angels and God. L.A. Weatherly's *Angelburn* features evil angels who feed on innocents, leaving them mentally damaged. However, the angels have found a single person capable of stopping them, a half-angel teenager named Willow. To do so, however, she must force herself to confront the angelic side of her own nature and discover what she can do. On the run for her life, Willow meets Alex, an A.K., or Angel Killer and they team up against the threat.

> Dean: I thought angels were supposed to be guardians. Fluffy wings, halos – You know, Michael Landon. Not dicks.
> Castiel: Read the Bible. Angels are warriors of God. I'm a soldier.
> ("Are You There, God?")

On *Supernatural*, the angel Castiel carries Dean out of Hell. Since Castiel is actually "roughly the size of your Chrysler Building," he and his brothers must occupy humans (with permission) to interact in the world – demons do the same. The Apocalypse is coming, and all the angels are choosing sides for the great conflict. Uriel, Michael, Raphael, and all the expected main players show up in the story, battling Lilith, Lucifer, and hordes of demons.

Vampires

John Heinrich Zopfius in his Dissertatio de Uampiris Seruiensibus, Halle, 1733, says: "Vampires issue forth from their graves in the night, attack people sleeping quietly in their beds, suck out all their blood from their bodies and destroy them. They beset men, women and children alike, sparing neither age nor sex. Those who are under the fatal malignity of their influence complain of suffocation and a total deficiency of spirits, after which they soon expire. Some who, when at the point of death, have been asked if they can tell what is causing their decease, reply that such and such persons, lately dead, have arisen from the tomb to torment and torture them." (Summers 1-2)

All stories are true, Jace reports. Vampires are one of the world's oldest and most widespread legends – almost every culture has a myth about the angry dead, risen from the grave to suck the blood of the living. The monsters are the Adze in West Africa, the Cihuateteo to the Aztecs. In China they are Jiāngshī, in the Philippines, the Sigbin. The Celtic Leanan Sidhe drains the life from her victims like a succubus while Celtic Glestigs were said to drink the blood and milk of cattle. The Vikings told tales of walking dead known as Draugr (Curran 23-30).

Vampires are considered the unblessed dead, and that is the reason holy symbols repel them. Drinking blood is particularly forbidden in the Bible. Blood is the essence of life, and while people who follow the Bible are permitted to eat meat, they are prohibited from taking the creature's lifeforce or spirit. In the original Hebrew, this word is often translated as soul.

> It is written: If any man whosoever of the house of Israel, and of the strangers that sojourn among them, eat blood I will set my face against his soul, and will cut him off from among his people: Because the life of the flesh is in the blood: and I have given it to you, that you may make atonement with it upon the altar for your souls, and the blood may be for an expiation for the soul…Since then the very essence of life, and even more, the spirit or the soul in some mysterious way lies in the blood we have a complete explanation why the vampire should seek to vitalize and rejuvenate his own dead body by draining the blood from the veins of his victims. (Summers 14-15)

Vampires essentially prey on the living and take their souls to sustain themselves.

> As all other demoniacal monsters the Vampire fears and shrinks from holy things. Holy Water burns him as some biting acid; he flies from the sign of the Cross, from the Crucifix, from Relics, and above all from the Host, the Body of God. All these, and other hallowed objects render him powerless. He is conquered by the fragrance of incense. Certain trees and herbs are hateful to him, the whitethorn (or buckthorn) as we have seen, and particularly garlic. (Summers 131)

The word vampyr may come from the Mediterranean vam-pir, blood-monster or from Russia, derived from the words for blood-drunkenness. Simon's thirst compares to this drunkenness, as it's a truly uncontrollable need. Further, when he drinks human blood, it is unforgettable.

Throughout Europe, the terrifying concept of risen corpses spread. Some tales were based on real life cases of catatonic people buried, only to "return to life," or corpses that looked healthy and flushed after death. Diseases and plagues striking the population were sometimes blamed on the walking dead who must be draining otherwise healthy people. A number of folk remedies spread for dealing with this problem, though destroying the body entirely was the most popular.

> In some Slavonic countries it is thought that a Vampire, if prowling out of his tomb at night may be shot and killed with a silver bullet that has been blessed by a priest. But care must be taken that his body is not laid in the rays of the moon, especially if the moon be at her full, for in this case he will revive with redoubled vigour and malevolence. (Summers 208-209)

The popularity of gothic novels led to vampires' appearance in fiction. Polidori's *The Vampyre* (1819), written at the same party as Mary Shelley's *Frankenstein*, features a dissipated aristocratic vampire modeled after Lord Byron. Lord Ruthven is charismatic but selfish, charming his victims and then draining or seducing them. He enjoys dragging a young lady from the highest pinnacle of virtue into utter degradation. After affairs with him, some women become listless and drained, while others are filled with a wild madness.

Varney the Vampire arrived in England in 1847. Its popularity led to its being serialized in one of the horror magazines known as "dreadfuls." In 1897, during a gothic revival, Irish writer Bram Stoker published *Dracula*. In readers' minds, the book linked the vampire firmly with Eastern Europe and Vlad the Impaler. From that moment through today, *Dracula* with its novel and subsequent films defined vampires – thin, tall, pale, and well-dressed, with a thick Eastern European accent.

The silent 1919 film *Nosferatu* with its grotesque Count Orlok (which was heavily sued for not obtaining permissions from the Stoker estate) added much to the horror of the tale. Its vampire is truly grotesque, monstrous, and terrifying. 1931's *Dracula,* staring Bela Lugosi, became the best-known portrayal of the cruel, aristocratic vampire who was nonetheless sexy and alluring. "After 1931, whenever millions of theatergoers would think of the Count, they would see Lugosi's face" (Bibeau 106). Many vampire films followed, starring Christopher Lee as the vampire in an entire series of movies, but Lugosi was ingrained on the American consciousness. Nonetheless, the Spanish language version of the 1931 Dracula, filmed on the same set with an alternating schedule and different cast, has a large cult following. One critic insists, "If you want to watch the undead stalking the lifeless, go for the Anglos. But if you want to watch chemistry, sex, drama, and full-bore crazy-guy-shouting, check out the Spanish *Dracula*" (Bibeau 103).

Stoker's Dracula uses the power of corruption, infecting his victims with the power of the devil until they can no longer so much as touch a cross. Dracula mesmerizes his victims and tempts them to let him in and conceal their loyalty to him as he slowly turns them. This novel doesn't contain the concept of victim and vampire drinking each others' blood, but other series such as *Buffy* and *True Blood* do. The concept of vampire and victim sharing blood adds a quality of deliberateness to the transformation – on some level, the victim must accept. Simon feels drawn to Raphael's hotel, and he finally journeys there, giving in to the compulsion and letting the vampires bite him.

Of course, today, paranormal fiction is incredibly popular, and with it the concept of the attractive vampire. Dracula and the early vampires were mesmerizing and hypnotic but also fundamentally evil. Anne Rice and Chelsea Quinn Yarbro were the first to pioneer the attractive vampire as both sex symbol and protagonist. Yarbro's St. Germain travels the world, hiding his vampire nature as he embarks on romantic and heroic adventures. Rice's Lestat is a beautiful French aristocrat and also a sadistic killer. His vampire is also modern, and even fronts a rock band, which he names for himself. In the 1994 film, Lestat is played by Tom Cruise, with Brad Pitt as his protégé Louis de Pointe du Lac. Many series followed: *Buffy the Vampire Slayer* and *Angel*, *Forever Knight*, *Moonlight*, *Twilight*, and today, *True Blood*, *Being Human*, and *The Vampire Diaries*. *Forever Knight* was the first show with a benevolent angst-filled vampire: Nick Knight, a cop, prowls the streets solving crimes. The show is melodramatic and serious, compared to the humor and tongue-in-cheek quality of the more popular *Buffy the Vampire Slayer*.

Clare notes:

> The idea that making a character a vampire is making them de facto evil, a "bloodsucker" (Simon's a vegetarian, and drinks animal blood out of bottles), a loathsome figure, is a very dated one. It is not how modern media generally portrays vampires. Edward Cullen, Lestat, Angel, Spike, the hot brothers from The Vampire Diaries, Mitchell from Being Human, Bill and Eric from True Blood, are not loathsome and horrible, they're badass beloved sex symbols. (And they're all, as far as I can tell, Christian.)

> When I started writing the TMI books my cousins begged me to have a Jewish vampire in the books, because vampires were cool…Simon is Jewish because I had literally never read a book with a Jewish vampire in it and I wanted there to be one. He's Jewish because I've had tons of kids (and adults – Michelle Hodkin, who wrote The Unbecoming of Mara Dyer****, did a signing with me in Long Island and the first thing she said to me was that she was so glad Simon was Jewish) come up and be thrilled that a Jewish guy got to be a hot kickass immortal vampire, that Jews are not shut out of what is (like it or not) a massive mainstream cultural trend.) ("Simon Lewis, Jewish Vampire")

Myths and Motifs in *The Mortal Instruments*

Camille Belcourt, the lovely silver-blonde, green-eyed vampire, is likely a reference to Carmilla (or perhaps she's supposed to be the original Carmilla). *Carmilla* is a Gothic novella written in 1872 (25 years before *Dracula* and six years before the events of *The Infernal Devices*) by Joseph Sheridan Le Fanu. This is the fictional casebook of Dr Hesselius, often known as the first occult doctor in literature.

The heroine, Laura, grows up in a solitary castle deep in the forests of Styria. After a nearby carriage accident, Laura mysteriously acquires a friend of her own age: Carmilla. To Laura's surprise, she realizes she once had a vision of Carmilla as a child and woke feeling she had been bitten. As the girls grow closer, Carmilla makes romantic advances toward Laura and the book turns surprisingly erotic. Carmilla's obsessive pleas ("You are mine, you shall be mine, and you and I are one for ever") appear in Camille Belcourt's possessiveness.

There is a mysterious resemblance between Carmilla and an ancient portrait. Further, Laura has nightmares of a feline hellbeast slipping into her room at night and biting her chest. Her health declines. At last, they meet a general whose niece once befriended a similar girl named Millarca and suffered the same series of attacks. He drove the cat-beast away, and his niece immediately dropped dead. Carmilla attacks, and she and the general recognize each other. He explains that her names Millarca and Carmilla are both anagrams for the original name of the vampire Countess Mircalla Karnstein. Baron Vordenburg, a vampire hunter, joins them and helps them find the countess's tomb. They destroy her body and Laura is saved – the vampire is laid to rest.

This is a standard pattern for the classical vampire tale – the wise doctor and fearless warrior struggling to save a young human victim from the vampire's corruption. Gothic literature tackled the supernatural, especially people's fears and horrors. The concept of the Slayer or Vampire Hunter, seen in Baron Vordenburg and *Dracula*'s Doctor Van Helsing continues through many works of fiction to the latest – Clare's Shadowhunters.

Slayers

Slayer fiction shares many tropes with vampire fiction: holy symbols and specialized weapons are key. The slayers face not only physical trauma but also temptation in the battle between heaven and hell.

Many say *Buffy the Vampire Slayer* defined the slayer genre. From her 1992 film to her 1997 television show, she evolved into a strong, capable teen who could dust vampires and demons with a single kick, all while mouthing off cleverly and making it to prom on time. Her team of friends and fellow warriors emphasized that it was all right to be a bookish computer geek, a librarian, or an unskilled teen with no superpowers at all – one could still save the world. And they did. A lot.

The spinoff *Angel* follows Buffy's former boyfriend, the only known vampire with a soul, as he attempts to make up for his past misdeeds by battling demons in Los Angeles. He too has a team, of which he is the head, and he officially runs a detective agency, while Buffy must hide her night job from her mother and her teachers. Buffy's story is a metaphor for growing up, often described as the "high school is hell" plot, with all of her problems brought to demonic life. Angel's problems are more adult, from job security to a teenage son.

Supernatural features famous demons from Azazel to Lilith, as the heroic demon fighting brothers Dean and Sam must occasionally make unholy bargains with them to preserve their loved ones. Though they ally with angels sometimes, the Winchester boys are classic demon hunters, seeking out evil through the world with their occult weapons.

The film *Van Helsing* was intended as a sequel to Anthony Hopkins' portrayal in the 1992 *Dracula*, but many elements were changed as the movie's release was pushed back. In the end, it was crowded with Frankenstein, Wolfman, and many other characters Universal had the rights to. Van Helsing becomes a youngish action hero with "Indiana Jones hat and has wicked ninja stars and a machine-gun-style crossbow" – a far cry from the novel's bookish professor (Bibeau 111). Other films crowd the genre: *Abraham Lincoln, Vampire Hunter*; *The Brothers Grimm*; *Underworld*; and so forth.

The *Anita Blake: Vampire Hunter* series by Laurell K. Hamilton is a hard-boiled detective series complete with female action hero. In Anita's world, vampires and werewolves exist alongside mundanes, and are even gaining rights. But, as with the Shadowhunters' series, when one steps out of line, she's there. Anita is unusually religious for a demon hunter, and also has a necromancy power that lets her raise zombies. Intriguingly, her great vampire nemesis of her first adventure is named Valentine. While Hamilton comments that she hadn't intended to write a sexy vampire story, Anita finds herself eventually having relationships with werewolves and vampires as she's drawn deeper into the occult world.

Sarah Rees Brennan's first work, *The Demon's Lexicon*, features classic demons, with possession, magician's circles, and all the rest, not to mention the Goblin Market famed in Rossetti's poetry. There are even marks, which once given, offer one person power over another. The brothers Nick and Alan Ryves spend their lives on the run from demons and often fighting them. Nick is a selfish hotshot untouched by emotion who's an amazing fighter. However, when a boy is marked by demons, Alan volunteers to take half the mark on himself. The only person Nick truly loves is under a death sentence, and the two boys set out on a quest to slay the demons summoners and wipe their marks clean before Alan perishes. As they travel, Nick discovers the startling secrets of his origin and the powers he's only begun to tap.

Novels about brave demon hunters have been coming out in hordes recently. *The Slayer Chronicles* introduces an entire world of slayers, with one special child born each generation. Joss McMillan, seeking revenge for his sister's death, may become the youngest slayer in history…if he survives. The *Demonata* series by Darren Shan features a family of werewolves trapped in a terrible demon's bargain – each generation, they turn into mindless monsters. However, his family members can defend him – one can play a series of chess games against the terrible Lord Loss for the power to save one person, while another family member descends into the demon realm to fight Lord Loss himself.

The Demon Trapper's Daughter by Jana Oliver introduces Riley Blackthorne. In a world where demons wander the streets, Riley is an apprentice demon trapper, delivering her quarry to the church. However, she finds herself embroiled in a mystery of demons fixated on her and corrupted holy water. At last, angels appear to her and offer to save the dying boy she loves…if she'll be their chosen one and stop the apocalypse. Rachel Hawkins wrote the *Hex Hall* series, which features portals, an Institute, and many other paranormal staples. In the books, Sophie Mercer is sent to Hex Hall, a reform school for wayward Prodigium, as witches, faeries, and shapeshifters are called. There she has the usual romantic and magical adventures while battling her fair share of demons. *Maggie Quinn: Girl vs Evil* by Rosemary Clement-Moore sees high schooler Maggie Quinn solving mysteries and ferreting out demons in her everyday world. Mercedes "Mercy" Thompson likewise battles the undead to save the day. Jane Yellowrock is an investigator and vampire hunter in Faith Hunter's books. *Every Other Day* by Jennifer Lynn Barnes features a sixteen-year-old named Kali, who transforms into an invincible demon hunter every other day…and not always the right day.

Pride and Prejudice with Zombies, and the similar books that followed all see incongruously genteel young ladies pulling out weapons and dispatching the monsters, all while trying to keep their demure etiquette in place. Though they're meant as parody, Tessa shares a little with these bizarre action heroines.

Vampire hunters have roots in the oldest legends, just as vampires do. The Dhampir, in Romany and Eastern European tradition, is the child of a vampire and human. He's born with incredible strength and a sense of when vampires are near. He travels from town to town seeking monsters to destroy, for as long as he lives. The dhampyr guardians in *Vampire Academy* are trained to protect the Moroi (good, mortal vampires) from the Strigoi, the classic evil undead. *The Night Huntress* books feature a young woman who hunts the vampire father who destroyed her mother's life. In *The Saga of the Noble Dead*. Magiere and Leesil are con-artists who pretend to be a Dhampyr and a vampire…until they discover the real thing. Vampire Hunter D is also a dhampir. He hunts in a post-nuclear world, year 12090, in a Japanese series, including two anime films.

American comic books offer several impressive slayers. In the *Underworld* series, Lucian is the first lycan and can change into werewolf form. He turns from protector of vampires to one who hunts them. Demali Richards is "the Neteru," a superheroine who can sense demons and then kill them with her mystical Madame Isis blade. Initially appearing in Marvel Comics during the 70's, Blade, a half vampire/half human hybrid, slays the vampires who made him with his trusty sword. In 1994, he debuted in his first color comic, *Blade: Vampire Hunter*. Blade is known as the "Daywalker."

Werewolves

Werewolves, like vampires, are humans infected with demon diseases in Clare's work. The traditional werewolf comes to us from western Europe, though there are older mentions in world folklore. A first-century Roman novel described wolf transformation, and berserkers in Norse sagas believed their rage transformed them into beasts.

In the French and Germanic traditions, a man could become a wolf by wearing a wolf's skin or a magic belt of wolfskin. Others were transformed by rubbing the body with special ointments or casting spells. Lycanthropy, as it was called, was more than folklore: it was seen as witchcraft, and thus, as a sin against God (Robbins 329).

In Fahrenholz in the year 1682 a number of people were accused of being able to transform themselves into wolves and were put on trial.

> In early days it was recognized that a werewolf might be a person who was afflicted with a horrible mania, and Marcellus Sidetes, who lived in the reigns of Hadrian and Antoninus Pius, circa A.D. 117-161, wrote…that Lycanthropy is a disease, a kind of insanity or mania when the patient was afflicted with hideous appetites, the ferocity, and other qualities of a wolf. He further tells us that men are attacked with this madness chiefly in the beginning of the year, and become most furious in February; retiring for the night to lone cemeteries and living precisely in the manner of ravening wolves. (Summers 166)

The concepts that a werewolf bite could transform a person into a werewolf, and that the change would occur on the following full moon are barely seen in folklore and instead originate in the popular 1941 movie, *Wolf Man*. This film also introduced the use of silver to repel the beasts and the

Myths and Motifs in *The Mortal Instruments*

half-wolf, half-man form seen in some popularized werewolves. *Wolf Man* was a commercial success, and many other werewolf films followed, including *I Was a Teenage Werewolf*, *American Werewolf in London*, and *The Howling*. These perpetuated the concepts introduced in *Wolf Man* and made concepts like the full moon and silver bullets a permanent part of the trope (Curran 123-125).

Witches and Warlocks

Witches and warlocks are half-human, half-demon, and thus sterile crossbreeds. Jace explains that they are the strongest of the Downworlders, since they're the direct offspring of demons (*Bones* 104).

In hundreds of fantasy novels, including *Lord of the Rings* and classics like *King Arthur*, the wizard is the all-powerful problem solver and mentor. His nearly inexplicable magic is used to save the day for the humble hero. This is subverted somewhat in Magnus Bane, as he insists for the hundredth time that he doesn't want to be dragged into the Shadowhunters' many problems. Magnus isn't an old, bearded asexual wizard – he's young and hot with spiked hair, glitter, and exotic outfits. He falls for Alec, involving himself further in Shadowhunter affairs to a depth that aloof wizards usually don't. Clare comments, "Everyone pictures wise, ancient, beardy wizards. I wanted to write a wizard who was young, a New York raver, a party boy" (Link and Black 173).

Fairies

Fairies, usually called the "good folk" to ward off their notice, "are said to be of a midle Nature betuixt Man and Angel, as were Dæmons thought to be of old" (Kirk 5). Fairies have various origins. Clare's book wonders whether they are a cross between angels and demons or "fallen angels, cast out of heaven for their pride" (*Bones* 104). According to some legends, the fairies were once a group of angels who refused to take sides in Lucifer's rebellion against God and his loyal angels. Afterwards, these angels were not thought evil enough to go to hell, nor saintly enough to stay above, so they were sent to a midway place – earth.

Fairies can be found in every country, in our oldest works of literature, for they are most often demigods – less powerful gods or former gods left in a newer culture's literature. Sometimes they are ancestral spirits, helpful house brownies, or other "good folk." They are the dryads and naiads of Greek myth, Germanic Nixies, the Bediadari of Malaysia; the Chilean volcano spirits known as Pillan; the Hindu, Buddhist, and Jain Yakshas; the Japanese Yōkai, which include kitsune, oni, and other supernatural beings.

Sidhe (pronounced 'shee'), the Irish and Scottish Gaelic name for fairies, literally means "people of the (fairy) hills." The original concept of fairyland, the realm "under the hill" was the land of the dead. This is why food and drink are prohibited – if one eats the food of the dead, one becomes like them. In the old tales, it is said that "Seers, or Men of the Second Sight, (Fæmales being seldome so qualified) have very terrifying Encounters with them" (Kirk 7-8). While most people cannot see through fairy glamours, a few have the sight and go through life aware of the Otherworld.

Folklore offers the concept of cold iron to guard against fairies:

> Metals, and Iron of the North, (hence the Loadstone causes a tendency to that Point,) by ane Antipathy thereto, these odious far-scenting Creatures shrug and fright at all that comes thence relating to so abhorred a Place, whence their Torment is eather begun, or feared to come hereafter. (Kirk 14)

As with other supernatural creature, running water and religious tokens are said to offer mortals safety. Fairies must speak the truth and will keep their oaths, but they are known for being tricky with the exact wording.

Along with folktales, ballads such as "Tam Lin" and "Thomas the Rhymer" contribute much to our concept of fairyland. From "Tam Lin" we get the teind, a sacrifice of a human or fairy to hell that inspires many modern fantasy novels. Both describe the fairies' unearthly beauty, especially that of the enticing queen. Most legends, including these, address the concept of the fairies stealing mortals for their own amusement.

Thomas the Rhymer also known as "True Thomas" was one of the early works that emphasized fairyland as a third path between heaven and hell. As the queen tells Thomas while abducting him:

> "O see ye not that narrow road,
> So thick beset with thorns and briers?
> That is the path of righteousness,
> Tho after it but few enquires.
> "And see not ye that braid braid road,
> That lies across that lily leven?
> That is the path to wickedness,
> Tho some call it the road to heaven.
> "And see not ye that bonny road,
> That winds about the fernie brae?
> That is the road to fair Elfland,
> Where thou and I this night maun gae.
> "But, Thomas, ye maun hold your tongue,
> Whatever ye may hear or see,
> For, if you speak word in Elflyn land,
> Ye'll neer get back to your ain countrie."
> (Child Ballad 37)

Myths and Motifs in *The Mortal Instruments*

Shakespeare's *A Midsummer Night's Dream* is equally influential, offering the vision of the Fairy Court with its king and queen. When they quarrel, all their tiny subjects fall into disarray. Further, Robin Goodfellow, or Puck appears. His words indicate how fairies spend their time: harassing mortals with cruel pranks.

> I am that merry wanderer of the night.
> I jest to Oberon and make him smile
> When I a fat and bean-fed horse beguile,
> Neighing in likeness of a filly foal:
> And sometime lurk I in a gossip's bowl,
> In very likeness of a roasted crab,
> And when she drinks, against her lips I bob
> And on her wither'd dewlap pour the ale.
> The wisest aunt, telling the saddest tale,
> Sometime for three-foot stool mistaketh me;
> Then slip I from her bum, down topples she,
> And 'tailor' cries, and falls into a cough;
> And then the whole quire hold their hips and laugh,
> And waxen in their mirth and neeze and swear
> A merrier hour was never wasted there.
> (*A Midsummer Night's Dream*, II.i.43-47)

A Midsummer Night's Dream offers many instances of glamour and trickery. A magic flower makes all the wrong people fall in love, including the fairy queen herself. When Bottom, the human entrapped by the fairies, is released, he decides it was all a beautiful dream. King Oberon and Queen Titania display qualities like that of Clare's fairy queen – especially the manipulation, selfishness, and desire to see mortals squirm. From ancient ballads to the urban fantasy of the past few decades, the concept of fairies as beautiful, morally dubious characters has only grown. Clare's fairies are malicious, as they are in the oldest of traditions, long before Disney's Tinkerbell.

Holly Black's trilogy (*Tithe, Valient, Ironside*) shares several themes and motifs with Clare's: a girl grows up thinking she's human, but as a teenager, she meets a mysterious, irresistible figure and discovers her heritage lies in his world, as does her future. She chooses him, though she adventures with a geeky, male best friend who knows all kinds of science fiction trivia. (Holly Black's character is called Corny, a name that he despairs over as "King of the Dorks.") Though he's actually human and her connection to normality and childhood, he too becomes ensnared in the magical world. In the end, the heroine wins with a clever trick and claims the man she loves as well as her own power.

Both young women, struggling with identity, must face the children they could've been. Clary befriends Isabelle, who grew up in Shadowhunter culture and is an adept warrior, but she also connects with Sebastian, the demon child her father got to raise. Likewise, Kaye travels into the Seelie Court to retrieve the real Kaye – the human girl that was stolen so she, a fairy changeling, could take her place. Like Jace and Simon, Kaye reveals her true identity to her mother and is rejected, but her foster-mother soon relents.

Most of all, fairies aren't nice and sweet, but terribly cruel. The good and evil fairy queens of Black's series both torture Roiben to watch him squirm, and the good one tries to force him to kill his own sister. Clare's queen likewise makes Jace and Clary kiss for her entertainment. Worse, both queens betray the protagonist couple, twisting their bargains.

Clare's fairy queen is in fact supposed to be the one from Black's series (Link and Black 179). In those books, fairies are summoned with a bloody leaf dropped in the water – Jace's summoning in *City of Ashes* may be that very token.

Clare also mentions growing up with the beloved urban fantasy work *War of the Oaks* by Emma Bull. Eddi McCandry discovers fairies in the streets of Minneapolis and gets drawn into their conflict. The story features red caps, phoukas, brownies, and British fairies of all types as Eddi struggles between the Seelie and Unseelie courts, the latter of which is ruled by the Queen of Air and Darkness. In the end, she battles the queen in a rock band playoff that determined the fate of both courts and enables her to rescue her true love. The war of the Seelie and Unseelie courts features in many series, and *The Dark Artifices* may eventually reveal the Unseelie court with its own queen.

Steampunk

Cassandra Clare writes:

> I actually got the idea for *The Infernal Devices* before I got the idea for *The Mortal Instruments*. It started with a strong mental image: the image of a Victorian-era girl and a boy standing on a bridge in London while creepy-looking mechanical monsters came after them....While I was writing the *Mortal Instruments*, the story of the Devices remained in the back of my head, nagging at me, and I would occasionally make notes about the plot and characters so I wouldn't forget about them. As I built the world of the MI series, I realized I wanted Devices to take place in the same world, and that the mythology of one could be easily folded into the story of the other. ("The Infernal Devices")

From the image of clockwork automatons, the story evolved into Steampunk.

Myths and Motifs in *The Mortal Instruments*

Steampunk has been a growing trend in the past decade. It's Victorian science fiction, usually with clockwork and airships used to accomplish the science fiction part, rather than computers or rockets. Automatons are popular. It's historical fiction, but with retro science fiction and often the paranormal thrown in. Some authors create secret societies of monster-fighters and inventors, while others set their stories in alternate universes altogether. Clare explains:

> Steampunk is very hard to define. There are a number of definitions to be found here, including this one from Tinker Girl at Brass Goggles, that I like: "Steampunk is a genre of fiction set somewhere in the 1800's during the Victorian Era. The fictional part comes in that technology has gone a bit skewed - though the exact methods vary, generally steam-powered devices that would have been impossible or unfeasible at the time are found to exist. Examples include steam-robots, flying castles, under-water bases, moon rockets, time machines etc." ("The Infernal Devices")

Jules Verne and HG Wells' books are considered representative: They define this trope, as do the movies adapted from their stories. Related is secret history, historical fiction in which there's an event or secret world unknown to the public. Clare's series is this – history is taking place as usual, but vampires, werewolves, and other Downworlders are kept secret from the mundanes, as are the clockwork monsters.

Of course, Clare's work blends romantic poetry and gothic references with clockwork monsters and angelic magic. This mixture of classics and science fiction is typical for Steampunk, which includes Sherlock Holmes, Captain Nemo, and Alice in Wonderland as much as it does historical figures. In fact, Clare plays with this concept in her story "I Never," published in the anthology *Geektastic*. When a teen who's been playing Cathy Earnshaw on her friend's cross-genre online RPG doesn't feel like she fits in with geek culture, her new friend replies, "There's nothing about being someone from a book, even a classic book, that makes you less geeky than someone from a movie. Or a TV show. Or whatever" (95). The game mixes characters from *Sherlock Holmes, The Matrix, Watership Down, Smallville, Dracula*, and every other fictional story imaginable, a bit like Clare's world of vampires, warlocks, and Steampunk, in which "all stories are true."

The Steampunk and Secret History genres have the benefit of welcoming multicultural heroes not usually seen in books of this era. Not only is Jem mixed-race, but the Council includes a Middle Eastern man, Asian woman, and East Indian woman, representing parts of the British Empire. While these characters might not have been received in the highest levels of British

Government, the Clave can be more progressive as it makes its own rules. Likewise, feminism is a common theme, as spunky girls tired of propriety become inventors, soldiers, and superheroes within their secret societies.

Many series take place in London with its balls and emphasis on propriety: London *is* Victorian culture to many readers. It's the world of Dracula, Queen Victoria, royalty and scandal, contrasted with the rough-and-ready America of Twain or Alcott.

Gail Carriger's beloved *Parasol Protectorate* takes place in a London with vampires and werewolves, like Clare's series. The heroine, Alexia, is "soulless," an abnormality perfectly set up to destroy those with too much soul – paranormal creatures. Armed with magnificent, invention-filled parasols, she does just that while falling in love and having delightful adventures across England. Like Clare's series, there's an emphasis on maintaining political alliances and truces between the species as powerful vampires and werewolf packs jostle for power, and hope for Queen Victoria's good graces. And Carriger's Alexia Tarabotti is an action heroine as tough as any, all while wearing a bustle.

As the authors of *The Ministry of Peculiar Occurrences* explain it:

> Steampunk, at least the way we see it, gets its "punk" not in its dystopian view of the world or even in its gritty edge. The "punk" in "Steampunk" comes from going against convention that, through creativity and declaration of one's individuality be it through style, gadgets, or attitude, sets one apart. In our own work, the "punk" is embodied in Eliza D. Braun, an agent from New Zealand. Coming from the farthest reaches of the Empire where women have the right to vote, where the "natives" co-exist with the "colonials," and where everyone speaks their mind frankly and honestly, she goes against the standard norms at the home office in London, England. She is paired up with Wellington Thornhill Books, Esquire, a man of the manor born now serving at the Queen's pleasure. She is everything he is not, and vice versa; and it is their chemistry and unorthodox approach to peculiar occurrences that make them unique within a society based on conformity. All this, and they're having a smashing good time while doing it. Well, at least, Eliza is. ("What is Steampunk?")

Behemoth by Scott Westerfeld is more blatantly alternate-world. It's World War One, but the Germans have giant mechanical walkers, and the Brits, airships constructed of living creatures in complex symbiotic ecosystems. The First World War has become one of ideology – the species-crossing Darwinists versus the technologically-minded Axis powers. Against this backdrop, a young airship officer who's a girl in disguise struggles to find a way to be with her prince charming – the young heir to Austria and son of the murdered archduke. Like many Steampunk series, this trilogy features a girl unusually tough for her time struggling to find her role in the world. The technology is colorful and inventive, but the romance and plight of the characters against the backdrop of war forms the story.

The Girl with the Steel Corset is a delightful superhero story much like *The League of Extraordinary Gentlemen* (itself completely Steampunk as well). The heroine is the daughter of Doctor Jekyll and has inherited his particular ability. Add to this a girl inventor, violent automatons, and superhuman abilities from the substance H.G. Wells discovered in the center of the earth, and they're off on many adventures.

Girl Genius, a web and print comic by Phil and Kaja Foglio, has become one of the classics of Steampunk. There are also novelizations of the comic's first two major arcs, called *Agatha H. and the Airship City* and *Agatha H. and the Clockwork Princess* respectively (a popular title in Steampunk, clearly). Agatha spends much of the first story running around in her underwear (nineteenth century full-length underwear at least). An inventor and student at the local Transylvania Polygnostic University, she can create amazing devices and defend herself with martial arts. When she's kidnapped by the tyrannical Baron Wulfenbach and his amiable son Gilgamesh, she's taken aboard their airship. There, she learns she's a Spark – a magical inventor whose devices can come to life. She's also the daughter of famous folk heroes, with a mission to oppose Wulfenbach's despotic reign…even as the heroes of good are determined to get her killed and Gil is busy proposing marriage. "People keep giving me rings – but I think a small death ray might be more practical," she comments.

Inventors are common in the Steampunk world – from real-life Edison, Tesla, and their friends to a spectrum of fictional crazy inventors. Superhero-type stories are common, as they use the inventions and sometimes more paranormal powers to fight evil, much as Shadowhunters do. Clare adds:

> I love the aesthetic of steampunk and tried to work it in in small ways, most notably in the existence of the mechanical human-seeming automatons that figure significantly into the plot, and in Henry's endless inventing of all sorts of mechanical devices that really didn't exist in the Victorian Era – but hey, there weren't really vampires and werewolves in London, either. ("The Infernal Devices")

Steampunk is satirized with Henry's inventions, especially his lethal bonnet. Likewise, Magnus wonders if he's wearing two pairs of goggles as a fashion statement, referencing the goggles most Steampunk costumes include.

Infernal Devices

"THE INFERNAL DEVICES ARE WITHOUT PITY. THE INFERNAL DEVICES ARE WITHOUT REGRET. THE INFERNAL DEVICES ARE WITHOUT NUMBER. THE INFERNAL DEVICES WILL NEVER STOP COMING" (*Clockwork Princess* 48). Benedict Lightwood writes these words in blood on the wall of his study while "slowly going mad." They also appear in Mortmain's stronghold. These are the prophecy of doom that Tessa and the Shadowhunters must work to avert, or the infernal devices, the automatons, will destroy the entire world of the Nephilim.

The title for the series comes from a Steampunk trope: Jules Verne's *An Antarctic Mystery* originated the phrase: "Captain…is it not the case that all these men perished, some in the attack on the schooner, the others by the infernal device of the natives of Tsalal?" Clare notes, "'Infernal Device' is a Victorian-era term that means a sort of deadly device or bomb. The term is something of a steampunk idiom, most notably appearing as the title of K.W. Jeter's classic book *Infernal Devices*" ("The Infernal Devices"). Jeter's *The Infernal Devices* is one of the earliest and most defining works of the genre. It offers mad scientists, space travel, time travel, clockwork robots, and more. When asked how much she was influenced by Jeter's book, Clare responded:

> A. I didn't read it until I'd already started *Clockwork Angel*, and then in part for the same reason I read Michael Connelly's *City of Bones* when I found out it existed – I wanted to make sure it was sufficiently unlike my book of the same title that no one would get confused. And boy is it. Jeter's book is subtitled "A Mad Victorian Fantasy" and it really is – it's this totally parodic, black-humoured romp through a weird alterna-Victorian setting where everything is exaggerated or bizarre and there are half-human, half-fish Lovecraftian monsters – I mean, I really do recommend reading it, it's hilarious. I think it influenced me in the sense that along with Tim Powers and James Blaylock, Jeter really invented the steampunk genre – the aesthetics of it, the essence, are due to writers like him. ("*Clockwork Angel*: An exclusive Q&A")

In fact, Jeter was the one to invent the word "Steampunk":

> The term "Steampunk" originated in the late 1980s with a cheeky letter to *Locus Magazine* from science fiction author K. W. Jeter. Jeter was trying to find an accurate description of works by himself (*Morlock Night*), Tim Powers (*The Anubis Gates*), and James Blaylock (*Homunculus*). While Jeter coined the word, it was William Gibson and Bruce Sterling that brought the genre attention with the book *The Difference Engine* (1992).

MYTHS AND MOTIFS IN *THE MORTAL INSTRUMENTS*

...

Over the years, steampunk has evolved into more than just a sub-genre of Science Fiction and Fantasy. Steampunk now extends into fashion, engineering, music, and for some, a lifestyle. With the Victorian British Empire or American Wild West as the backdrop, steampunk projects are a challenge of making something elegant out of random bits and bobs. Picture *MacGyver* or *The A-Team* in the 1800's. Consider Dick Van Dyke's Caractacus Potts and his creations in *Chitty Chitty Bang Bang*, or the ingenious contraptions from Artimus Gordon's laboratory in the television show *The Wild, Wild West*. What others see as junk or scrap parts, steampunk artists transform it into something new and expressive, be it an original creation or a modification of a modern convenience. ("What is Steampunk?")

CHAPTER 4
LITERARY ALLUSIONS

The Mortal Instruments and the Classics

This quote begins *City of Bones* and provides the source for the series title:

> I have not slept.
> Between the acting of a dreadful thing
> And the first motion, all the interim is
> Like a phantasma or a hideous dream;
> The genius and the mortal instruments
> Are then in council, and the state of man,
> Like to a little kingdom, suffers then
> The nature of an insurrection. (*Julius Caesar* II.i.64-71)

Between planning and doing a dreadful thing, the time in between is like a terrible dream, as Brutus protests. The "genius and the mortal instruments," the unconscious and the body, are trapped in discussion. As they conspire together, they overtake the conscious mind.

The "genius" is the mind or spirit. In the Roman world, each person had a guardian spirit of a sort, which influenced his actions and his fate. In the context of Shadowhunters, this might be their angel blood or the angels they summon to strengthen their blades.

Mortal Instruments likely refer to human agents – Othello for instance calls his hands and eyes his "speculative and active instruments." (I.ii.271). However, some critics consider Brutus's "mortal instruments" to mean human passions. Whether the Shadowhunters represent God's human agents, or the human passions thrown into heaven's battle against the demons, this is a series about their efforts to hold back the darkness of Valentine's rebellion, even while battling their own feelings and romances and saving one another. As Simon notes, "If Heaven didn't want it that way, we ought never have been given the ability to love" (*Lost Souls* 425).

Myths and Motifs in *The Mortal Instruments*

Julius Caesar is the story of idealists like Brutus plotting Caesar's death – an immoral, treacherous act – in order to save the republic and create a better world. Several critics interpret the quote as the conspirators' inner conflict between their guardian spirits or higher consciences and the passions that inspire them to fight for the honorable side. Not only do Valentine and Sebastian (not to mention Hodge and the Circle) rebel against the establishment, but Jace, Clary, and the Lightwoods all break Clave law while battling for what they know to be right, whether it's rescuing Simon or stopping Valentine. *Julius Caesar* is a tale of Brutus and his fellow conspirators balancing the law and their personal loyalty to Caesar with what they know is good for the republic. The teen Shadowhunters likewise must choose between the Clave and the right thing to do. Alec tells Jace they must trust the Clave "because otherwise everything turns into chaos" (*Glass* 90). However, as it turns out, the Inquisitors lie and serve their own agendas, while the Council is bogged down in meetings and fails to act. The time has come for Clary and Luke, like Brutus, to change the system.

Dante's Divine Comedy

> I did think of Mortal Instruments as a trilogy when I first constructed it because I was a huge fan of trilogies as a kid. There's a theme that runs through it that's [inspired by] Milton and *The Divine Comedy*. There are little epigraphs at the beginning of each section: the first is the hero's descent, the second is about hell and the underworld, and the third as an ascent out of the underworld. I think of it as Clary's heroic journey. ("Cassandra Clare: Bringing the Shadows to Light")

As Clare describes, Dante's *Divine Comedy* includes three sections: Inferno, Purgatorio, and Paradiso. These follow Dante's journey through Hell, Purgatory, and Heaven as he finds spiritual enlightenment. Clary's own journey can be seen as a metaphor for this: She crosses into the dark, demon-filled magical world, and then spends the middle of the story in a kind of Purgatory, unable to be with Jace. In the third book, she reaches the "heaven" of Idris.

In Dante's first stage, he stumbles fearfully through a dark wood and his way is blocked by magical beasts: a leopard, a lion, and a she-wolf. He is trying to reach the towering mountain in the distance, which symbolizes spiritual salvation, but the way is difficult to achieve. He explores the circles of hell, each of which punishes sinners in a unique way. Similarly, Clary's quest is blocked by antagonists, most of whom are demons. She is only guided out of the darkness by Jace and the Lightwoods. On her path through the otherworld of monsters and terrors, she encounters many sinners suffering torments, from Hodge to Madame Dorothea.

City of Bones is divided into sections: part one is called "Dark Descent" after a quote from *Paradise Lost*. Certainly Clary's entrance into the Pandemonium Club (Pandemonium is the fallen angels' city in *Paradise Lost*) represents a descent into an urban hell, filled with teens in goth attire. Part Two: "Easy is the Descent" is a quote from the *Aeneid*, by Virgil, Dante's guide in *The Divine Comedy*. In fact, Virgil's *Aeneid* was one of the models for Dante's *Inferno*. Despite the title, this portion of the story guides Clary to a higher spiritual plane, as she discovers the truth about her memories from the Silent Brothers and Magnus Bane, the wise ones of the story. Treacherous Dorothea and Hodge are revealed as their true selves as well. Part Three: The Descent Beckons is a stage of testing, in which Jace and Clary discover the truth about Valentine and must choose between good and evil. Epilogue: The Ascent Beckons comes at book's end as Clary searches for a way to reclaim her mother and Jace. She has discovered the secrets of her past, but not until the third book will she achieve salvation for all the Shadowhunters.

Dante is guided on his quest by Virgil, just as Clary is by Magnus Bane. Virgil, who represents all ancient knowledge, guides Dante to the edge of Purgatory, and then, since he's not allowed to go further, the saintly Beatrice guides Virgil the rest of the way. In just this way, Magnus Bane helps the teen Shadowhunters and guides Clary to Idris, though as a Downworlder, he's forbidden to enter. As Clary and Jace evolve, each becomes the angelic guide for the other, leading toward salvation.

An angel bearing a flaming sword guards the gates of Purgatory. With his sword, the angel marks seven P's on Dante's forehead – each will vanish as Dante passes a level of Purgatory. This too seems a tie to the Shadowhunters and their runes.

At the time of Dante's writing, the Pope and the Holy Roman Emperor were battling for political power – Valentine's rebellion against the Clave mirrors this struggle. The Holy Roman Emperor's power in Italy and the rest of Europe was supported by the medieval aristocracy, bound to the old ways rather like the aristocratic Shadowhunters. The emerging middle class favored the Pope and a new form of government. Clary and her friends, the young generation, manage to revolutionize the Clave and provide Council seats for the Downworlders.

Other themes include the fallen angels' misery as they are cut off from paradise. Hodge, a fallen angel himself, speaks sadly of Idris, and betrays his loved ones only so he can return there. The cries of the fallen angels are similar:

> "Here sighs and cries and shrieks of lamentation
> echoed throughout the starless air of Hell;
> at first these sounds resounding made me weep:

> tongues confused, a language strained in anguish
> with cadences of anger, shrill outcries
> and raucous groans that joined with sounds of hands,
> raising a whirling storm that turns itself
> forever through that air of endless black,
> like grains of sand swirling when a whirlwind blows.
>
> And I, in the midst of all this circling horror,
> began, "Teacher, what are these sounds I hear?
> What souls are these so overwhelmed by grief?"
>
> And he to me: "This wretched state of being
> is the fate of those sad souls who lived a life
> but lived it with no blame and with no praise.
> They are mixed with that repulsive choir of angels
> neither faithful nor unfaithful to their God,
> who undecided stood but for themselves.
>
> Heaven, to keep its beauty, cast them out,
> but even Hell itself would not receive them,
> for fear the damned might glory over them."
>
> And I. "Master, what torments do they suffer
> that force them to lament so bitterly?"
> He answered: "I will tell you in few words:
>
> these wretches have no hope of truly dying,
> and this blind life they lead is so abject
> it makes them envy every other fate.
>
> The world will not record their having been there;
> Heaven's mercy and its justice turn from them.
> Let's not discuss them; look and pass them by…"
> (3.30-51)

IN HOC SIGNO VINCES AND THE CIRCLE

The Circle's motto is *in hoc signo vinces*, "by this sign we will conquer." Constantine said these words on a march, when he saw a cross of light above the sun, and with it the Greek words for "In this, conquer." The following night, he dreamed Jesus told him to use the sign against his enemies, and Constantine used the sign as his standard. The original "cross of light" is described as "a long spear, overlaid with gold" with a transverse bar. "On the top of the whole was fixed a wreath of gold and precious stones, and within this the symbol of the Saviour's name, two letters indicating the name of Christ by means of the initial letters, the letter X intersection P at the centre" (Hassett).

This motto has been used to represent singleminded devotion and power across the world, used by the Knights Templar, military battalions, churches, schools, and more. More chillingly, George Lincoln Rockwell, the founder of the American Nazi Party, wrote a political manifesto called *In Hoc Signo Vinces*. This may be a deliberate link, as the Circle is known for its intolerance and devotion to racial purity.

Valentine is a fundamentalist, believing in blood purity and absolutism like the Nazis and other reviled figures. (Magnus Bane appears to reference this when he warns Jace not to disavow responsibility for what his people have done.) His motto is Deus Volt, "Because God wills it," the motto of the crusaders who killed thousands in religious wars, all for the glory of God. Lucifer certainly believes in God. However, his sin is pride, as he is certain he is better than mankind. Valentine too believes he's better than ordinary humans, who should give their children to help the Shadowhunters.

Ave Atque Vale

The final three words of this touching poem by Gaius Valerius Catullus inspire the Shadowhunters' words upon a death:

> Through many countries and over many seas
> I have come, Brother, to these melancholy rites,
> to show this final honour to the dead,
> and speak (to what purpose?) to your silent ashes,
> since now fate takes you, even you, from me.
> Oh, Brother, ripped away from me so cruelly,
> now at least take these last offerings, blessed
> by the tradition of our parents, gifts to the dead.
> Accept, by custom, what a brother's tears drown,
> and, for eternity, Brother, 'Hail and Farewell'.

The ancient Roman poet acknowledges that nothing can comfort his grief – he doesn't even have the solace of belief in an afterlife. It seems very much in the spirit of Parabatai, bidding farewell to a spiritual brother as well as a brother in arms. At the same time, Jem and Will come to realize that every goodbye contains a greeting as well in the words "hail and farewell," and is a mixed blessing of happiness and sorrow. Tennyson, a romantic poet popular in Will and Tessa's day, references this poem in his own: As such, he recalls a simpler time of olive groves and Roman ideals, much as the Shadowhunters do with their knowledge of the classics.

> Frater Ave Atque Vale
> Row us out from Desenzano, to your Sirmione row!
> So they row'd, and there we landed-"O venusta Sirmio"

Myths and Motifs in *The Mortal Instruments*

> There to me through all the groves of olive in the summer glow,
> There beneath the Roman ruin where the purple flowers grow,
> Came that 'Ave atque Vale' of the Poet's hopeless woe,
> Tenderest of Roman poets nineteen-hundred years ago,
> 'Frater Ave atque Vale' - as we wandered to and fro
> Gazing at the Lydian laughter of the Garda Lake below
> Sweet Catullus's all-but-island, olive-silvery Sirmio!
> (Tennyson 293)

Doctor Faustus

In *Doctor Faustus*, Faustus chants the same summoning ritual used in *Lost Souls* to summon Azazel. *Doctor Faustus* is the story of an expert in many subjects who grows prideful and decides to experiment in forbidden magic. He summons the demon Mephistophilis and they agree that in return for his soul, Faustus will gain twenty-four years of absolute power. A good angel and a bad angel appear to him and each advise him. However, Faustus signs the contract in blood and gains amazing powers, until his time ends and he's dragged down to hell.

Though Faustus acts like a warlock, he parallels Sebastian—despite Clary's influence in *Lost Souls*, Sebastian decides to be the villain of his tale. He bargains with Lilith and gains a demonic army as a result. However, it's certain that his demonic alliances will someday crumble and he, like his father, will be sent straight to hell. Both stories emphasize that taking power from evil forces always comes at a price.

Will, Tessa, and the Library

Cassandra Clare wrote *Clockwork Angel* while reading many books from the time period and before. She notes:

> For six months I read only books written during, or written about, the Victorian period. I did a lot of reading of first-hand sources: journals kept at the time period, the travel accounts of tourists visiting England from America (since Tessa is American, in London for the first time) and newspapers of the period. (Interview with Cassandra Clare)

It's evident as Will and Tessa spar through literary references and each chapter is begun with a quote. These include Tennyson, Byron, Horace, Swinburne, Henley, Kipling, Wilde, Browning, Rossetti, Keats, and Shakespeare, all popular writers of Tessa's time. Most of the romantic poets are listed here. Not only are they appropriate for the era, but romantic writers in particular were fascinated with myth and the fantastical. Will and Tessa share a number of books they've read, including *Dante's Inferno*, *Tale of Two Cities*, *Ivanhoe*,

Alice in Wonderland, The Moonstone, Armadale, The Woman in White, and *Lady Audley's Secret*. Tessa dreams of herself and Will as the ever-parted Tristan and Isolde, and compares him to classical heroes.

But fundamentally, each considers him- or herself a fictional character. Will sees himself as the rogue in *A Tale of Two Cities*. Tessa sees herself as penniless, plucky Jane Eyre. Each offers the other a different vision – Will tells Tessa she can be a warrior like Boadicea. She tells him his hero was noble deep inside. Tessa also compares Will to Achilles and Jason, but Will points out that they died badly. Both are obsessed with books: Seeing Poet's Corner in Westminster Abbey is "like being among friends" for Tessa (*Clockwork Prince* 9). Will falls in love with Tessa while reading her heartfelt letters to her brother. In *Clockwork Prince*, he tells her that their shared love of books is what has turned to real love between them. Reading her letters enabled him to dream and feel with her. "I dreamed what you dreamed, wanted what you wanted – and then I realized that truly I just wanted you. The girl behind the scrawled letters." (468). He's also known for his pithy quotes.

> Tessa craned her head back to look at Will. "You know that feeling," she said, "when you are reading a book, and you know that it is going to be a tragedy; you can feel the cold and darkness coming, see the net drawing tight around the characters who live and breathe on the pages. But you are tied to the story as if being dragged behind a carriage and you cannot let go or turn the course aside." His blue eyes were dark with understanding – of course Will would understand – and she hurried on. "I feel now as if the same is happening, only not to characters on a page but to my own beloved friends and companions." (*Clockwork Princess* 68)

As Clare notes, "Tessa filters everything through her knowledge of books – the way she expects people to behave versus the way they actually do behave, etc." ("*Clockwork Angel*: An exclusive Q&A"). At the moment of crisis in their romance, Tessa tells Will that she no longer sees him as this hero or that, but as a real person. When Will proposes, he tells her he wants to share the storybook of their lives forever.

THE BRONTES

On her blog, Clare mentions that Charlotte Branwell is named for Bronte siblings Charlotte and Branwell, adding, "Anne, Emily and Charlotte went on to write famous novels. Branwell gambled himself into bankruptcy and finally drank himself to death. He is in part the model for Nate" ("Clockwork Princess Trailer Questions").

Jane Eyre by Charlotte Bronte is a mixed Cinderella and Beauty and the

Myths and Motifs in *The Mortal Instruments*

Beast story in which mistreated orphan Jane goes to work for the mysterious Mr. Rochester. However, Mr. Rochester cannot wed Jane or anyone else, for he is tied to his mysterious gothic mansions full of secrets, cursed by the burden of the past. Tessa and Will have a similar relationship as he combines savagery and charm in a bewildering alternation, always dwelling on the curse that prohibits him from finding love.

More intriguingly, Jane and Tessa begin their stories the same way – both are orphans thrust into the care of cruel women – either the Dark Sisters or Jane's cold Aunt Reed. Both are punished and tortured, reminded that they are the unfavored children. However, both find surprising opportunities in the gothic mansion or church where the traditional rules don't apply. Jane, governess to Mr. Rochester's illegitimate child, finds her employer falling in love with her. Tessa discovers the Shadowhunters, who value her shapeshifting powers and encourage her to be an emancipated woman. When Will calls out for Tessa in the Welsh countryside and she hears him, she recalls Rochester's hoarse whisper calling to Jane Eyre in her dreams. As she wanders, she stumbles across a rundown cottage and again imagines herself as Jane on her adventures. Both heroines find independence without depending on the men in their lives, and find ways to rescue their men and find a happy ending. Plain, brown-haired Jane seems to be a strong model for Tessa to follow.

A Tale of Two Cities

Tale of Two Cities and *Great Expectations* are my favorite Dickens books, and *Clockwork Princess* was always meant to be a loose retelling of *Tale of Two Cities*. ("Clockwork Princess Questions & Answers – Spoilery")

"It was the best of times, it was the worst of times." This quote begins *A Tale of Two Cities*, describing the French Revolution in Paris and London. This novel, written at the height of Charles Dickens' career, remains a classic to this day.

Charles Darnay and Sydney Carton both love Lucie Manette. Darnay is a former French aristocrat, a very good man though often naïve and foolish. Carton, a disreputable English barrister, has lived his life drinking and lazing about. He feels his life is worthless and appears to care for nothing, much like Will. However, like Will, he views the heroine of the story as the talisman that inspires him to be a better man. He professes his love, but she chooses to wed Darnay. Carton promises Lucie:

> For you, and for any dear to you, I would do anything. I would embrace any sacrifice for you and for those dear to you. And when you see your own bright beauty springing up anew at your feet, think now and then that there is a man who would give his life, to keep a life you love beside you. (158)

At the book's end, Charles Darnay is found guilty of treason and will be sent to the guillotine. To save Lucie's true love, Carton takes Darnay's place and dies. His famed last thought is, "It is a far, far better thing that I do, than I have ever done; it is a far, far better rest that I go to than I have ever known" (386).

Clare specifically sees Will as Sydney Carton (*Cassandra Clare's Clockwork Princess Bus Tour*). It's not surprising Will sees himself as the self-hating character, especially after his truly good best friend wins Tessa's heart. He quotes Carton's love speech to Tessa:

> All through it, I have known myself to be quite undeserving. And yet I have had the weakness, and have still the weakness, to wish you to know with what a sudden mastery you kindled me, heap of ashes that I am, into fire – a fire, however, inseparable in its nature from myself, quickening nothing, lighting nothing, doing no service, idly burning away. (157)

Like Carton, Will appears to care for nothing before he falls in love. After, however, he's determined to break the curse and find a way to protect Tessa. In the second book, he flings himself over her and takes the injuries she would have gotten. He also sacrifices his own happiness so Tessa and Jem can be together. In the third book, he tells Tessa he gladly would have sacrificed himself to save Jem for her.

He bares his soul and tells Tessa his true feelings after she's already engaged, much as Carton does with Lucie. "How you must despise me," Will says, echoing Carton's words (*Clockwork Princess* 196). For both, this is a major turning point, in which they set aside their dissipated behavior and become men of greater honor and nobility. Both sacrifice themselves to preserve the happiness of the couple. However, Jem does not get the girl (until the epilogue, at least) – he is the one to make the sacrifice so Tess can live happily ever after with the bad boy who is more noble than he first appeared.

Dickens' story is also subverted through the main characters' independence and goodness: Magnus assures Will he's not Sydney and his love has become more than destruction. Tessa tells Will she doesn't want to be Lucie who did nothing to save Sydney. When Tessa manipulates Mortmain, she thinks of Lucie appealing to Sydney Carton, but Mortmain tells her he has no better nature to appeal to. In the end, Tessa admits that she and Will are not characters, but real people, with real hopes and dreams.

Themes from Dickens

"If you could say, with truth, to your own solitary heart, to-night, 'I have secured to myself the love and attachment, the gratitude or respect, of no human creature; I have won myself a tender place in no regard; I have done nothing good or serviceable to be remembered by!' your seventy-eight years would be seventy-eight heavy curses; would they not?" (*A Tale of Two Cities* 320)

This quote mirrors Tessa's comment in her letter to Nate that if no one loves a person, that person ceases to exist. Will keeps that letter and quotes it to Magnus as he struggles to break the curse. Love and the importance of being loved are a major theme in the trilogy.

> The children had ancient faces and grave voices; and upon them, and upon the grown faces, and ploughed into every furrow of age and coming up afresh, was the sign, Hunger. It was prevalent everywhere. Hunger was pushed out of the tall houses, in the wretched clothing that hung upon poles and lines; Hunger was patched into them with straw and rag and wood and paper; Hunger was repeated in every fragment of the small modicum of firewood that the man sawed off; Hunger stared down from the smokeless chimneys, and started up from the filthy street that had no offal, among its refuse, of anything to eat. (*A Tale of Two Cities* 34)

Dickens frequently wrote about the plight of the poor, and this book is no exception. Likewise, Jem and Tessa drive to Whitechapel, and on the way they see the ill and dying poor, the starving refuse of the city, shut away and forgotten.

> A wonderful fact to reflect upon, that every human creature is constituted to be that profound secret and mystery to every other. A solemn consideration, when I enter a great city by night, that every one of those darkly clustered houses encloses its own secret; that every room in every one of them encloses its own secret; that every beating heart in the hundreds of thousands of breasts there, is, in some of its imaginings, a secret to the heart nearest it! Something of the awfulness, even of Death itself, is referable to this. (*A Tale of Two Cities* 15)

Human beings constitute perpetual mysteries to one another and always remain somewhat locked away, never fully reachable from the outside. In fact, prisons are another motif, as Lucie's father and Darnay are literally locked up while Carton struggles to break through his own worthless personality. Tessa begins the novel locked up, and Jessamine ends the second book in a similar state. The others are constrained by their bodies and curses: Charlotte's womanhood in a man's world, Jem's addiction, Will's curse. Secrets are at the base of the conflicts in *The Infernal Devices*: Jem and Will each hide the great secrets that influence every moment of their lives, while Tessa quests for her origins and the Magister hides his identity and history. Like Will's hidden passion for Tessa, Carlton's love for Lucie remains equally a secret to the world until his final sacrifice.

Sacrifice is another important theme. Sydney Carton's death at the end secures a new, peaceful life for Lucie, Charles Darnay, and even Carton himself. By sacrificing himself, Carton gives his life meaning. As he dies, the narrative suggests that he will be resurrected, just as France's old regime is dying to create a newer, better world. Jem believes in a similar type of resurrection and rebirth, and he tells Tessa that he is dying faster and risking his life so that he can be a Shadowhunter and save others.

The motif of doubles in *A Tale of Two Cities* is likewise significant. First is the opening quote: "It was the best of times, it was the worst of times." The story is split between London and Paris, just as *The Infernal Devices* divides between the mysterious Downworld and the everyday world of London. Clare notes:

> I believe that all cities have a shadow self. [In Mortal Instruments,] I tried to use a lot of locations in Manhattan that were abandoned and no longer have a purpose. I lived in London for several years when I was growing up, and it's the city I know second-best to Manhattan. There are so many wonderful locations in London where there used to be something amazing in a spot that no longer exists, but some echo of it remains. ("Cassandra Clare: Bringing the Shadows to Light")

Tessa is encouraged to see through the illusions to the world underneath. Further, her world, like that in *A Tale of Two Cities*, is shrouded in shadows and mysteries.

On a more individual level, most characters in both have doubles or shadows: Lucie is loving and nurturing, contrasted against the bloodthirsty Madame Defarge. Tessa is equally kind and capable, contrasted with the cruel Dark Sisters or selfish Jessamine. Good, successful Darnay is a poignant reminder to Carton of what he could have been, just as Jem is a shining example for disreputable Will.

Further, *The Mortal Instruments*' world is a mirror of *The Infernal Devices*, which takes place a century before, yet involves the same Shadowhunter families and conflicts. Events from one story influence the next as these two series parallel each other – the Herondales, Lightwoods, and Fairchilds fight against the laws of the hidebound Clave and the dark menace overtaking their world.

The Gothic Tradition

Will teases Tessa for her addiction to Gothic novels, which were enjoying a resurgence at the time, though they were considered "sensational literature" or "trash" rather than highbrow art. The original goths were a Germanic people who eventually split into the Eastern Goths or Ostrogoths and the Western Goths, or Visigoths. They attacked the Roman Empire many times, beginning around 267 C.E., until the Visigoths finally sacked Rome in 410 C.E. Centuries later, the European high culture was still heavily modeled on the Roman influence, from architecture to art. "Gothic" was the term for the counterculture – all wild and barbarous, Germanic rather than classical Roman. The term "gothic" was an insult at first, like saying someone was raised by wolves. However, it soon caught on. As the Romantic poets of the 1820's or so began writing about goblins and ghosts, the word gothic came into play (Bibeau 138-139).

Romantic literature and gothic were both interested in myth and legend such as King Arthur, and both employed emotion and larger than life grandeur to tell their stories. Romanticism was an imitation of medieval literature, while the gothic focused on the repellent, grotesque, and supernatural. Gothic combined the presence of God with older icons – ancestral spirits, monsters, and demons. Angels likewise often appear in gothic art as images of protection. The hero who's laboring under a terrible curse, the ancient undying foe vowing revenge, the heroine like Jessamine who is seduced and falls from grace – all are staples of the genre.

The young gentleman dying of a wasting disease that makes him cough blood (traditionally consumption) is also a staple of the 1800's, as is his lingering, terribly sad death. In fact, as Clare revealed, Jem was inspired by Keats, the poet dying of tuberculosis and coughing up blood while forbidden to wed the girl he loved. The image of the beautiful dying boy "seemed very romantic to me," Clare noted (*Cassandra Clare's Clockwork Princess Bus Tour*).

The first major Gothic novel was Horace Walpole's incredibly popular *The Castle of Otranto* published in 1764 – it's not surprising Tessa and Will both enjoyed it. *Vathek* by William Beckford (1786), *Mysteries of Udolpho* by Ann Radcliffe (1797), and Mary Shelley's *Frankenstein* (1818) all followed. Will of course offers Tessa a copy of *Vathek* with a silly poem in the front since he knows she enjoys this type of novel.

As a reaction to the strict world of Victorian manners and rationality, gothic novels saw a revival around the 1870's in which the Clockwork series takes place. The mourning culture, inspired partly by Prince Albert's early death, helped to fuel this interest. The vampire novel *Carmilla* was published six years before the events of *Clockwork Angel*, though *Dracula* came a few decades later. In Tessa and Will's days, *Faust* (1846), *Wagner the Wehrwolf* (1847) and *Varney the Vampire* (1847) gained a new popularity. Many romantic poets mentioned in the trilogy, such as Coleridge and Keats, used traces of the gothic. Dickens's novels too display a trace of gothic, especially in

Great Expectations, as Miss Havisham paces her rotting mansion.

Gothic literature involves various tropes: ruined, haunted castles and dark dungeons. Labyrinths, winding stairs, shadows and darkness, magic and the supernatural all are common. Of course, many of these elements are present in the *Infernal Devices* trilogy, particularly in the Institute's ancient cathedral, complete with dusty storerooms, winding staircases, and so forth. The Dark sisters' home with its terrifying basement of corpses, the vampire gathering with its room of death and secret peepholes: all are classic gothic. This is also subverted in a few places – the ancient crypt of the Institute is now Henry's modern workshop, and Jem jokes that Will has likely lured him and Tessa into the Institute's storeroom to murder them. The Silent Brother who terrifies Tessa is benign, and the vampires and warlock are helpful.

The Infernal Devices is in fact a modern gothic trilogy – about a hero and heroine bound by their love of gothic fiction. Starting chapters with epigraphs was popular in the time the novel takes place – Tessa's beloved *The Hidden Hand* does so, with many of the same authors. In Gothic, the heroine is desperately curious – something Tessa describes as her "besetting sin" (*Clockwork Angel* 102) and often needs rescue. The villains and heroes are tormented through ancestral curses and driven by passion. This describes Will of course, and also to some degree Nate Grey, the Lightwood boys, and Aloysius Starkweather, the ancient keeper of the York Institute. Unrequited or forbidden love is a theme as well.

> Gothic heroes and heroines are on their own, stumbling alone, sometimes in foreign countries, through appalling complexities of decision and action, obliged to find their own solutions or go under; estrangement from family ties is their normal condition....Protagonists are frequently orphans, or they are foundlings or adopted, their family origins mysterious. (Tracy)

Tessa sees herself as Jane Eyre early in the book – an early feminist and solver of a great mystery in a gloomy gothic world. Charlotte Brontë's *Jane Eyre* (1847) and Emily's *Wuthering Heights* are both a type of feminist gothic with decaying mansions, mysteries, and ghostly hauntings. Both books explore women's entrapment within the world of the home, forced to obey the patriarchy, however wrong and cruel it may be. Tessa begins her story tied to the bed and doomed to wed the Magister, and she struggles to find the path she desires. When they finally begin their romance, Tessa sees Will as Emily Bronte's "Heathcliff on the moors," an image of rebellion as well as romance (417). Cecily, whom Will sees as mad and energetic like Bronte's Cathy, likewise shows up at the Institute protesting that she has nowhere to go. Both Tessa and Cecily find themselves penniless, expected to live with their male relatives and politely starve, with no other outlet for their energy and ambitions. For both girls, the Institute offers a modern egalitarian world, in which women can fight, support themselves, and choose their own lovers.

When Mrs. Black spirits her away to Mortmain in *Clockwork Princess*, Tessa decides not to act like a foolish heroine, but her situation mirrors one in many ways, from her confused "Where are you taking me?" to the hero riding hellbent to her rescue. In Mortmain's mountain, Tessa becomes a traditional gothic heroine in truth – the villain has kidnapped her and taken her to his stronghold of monsters. There he imprisons her, and plans to wed her by force. Only when Tessa uses her angel pendant and saves everyone, including her heroes, does she escape the novel pattern. There are other subversions of the genre: When Will informs Tessa that the brave rescuer is always right, another gothic staple, Tessa informs him two books later that he's made a foolish mistake and trapped them both with his thoughtlessness. Will continues to remind Tessa of the gothic, taking her to famous moors and castles for the rest of his life. They are the gothic heroes, but by the end, they're taking control of their own story.

The Hidden Hand

Tessa protests to Will that *The Hidden Hand* with its far-fetched situations and daring-do is not her *favorite* novel, merely one of her favorites. When E. D. E. N. Southworth's *The Hidden Hand* was serialized in the *New York Ledger* in 1859, Southworth was America's most-read female novelist. She serialized her forty or so novels in *The New York Ledger*, one appearing as soon as the previous had concluded, so for roughly thirty years, one of her novels was in the paper and being devoured across America.

Little Women contains a short satire of Southworth's work, as Jo begins a career by writing stories in imitation of the extremely popular Mrs. S. L. A. N. G. Northbury (a rather obvious reference). In chapter 27, "Literary Lessons," Jo glances at a youth's newspaper and, upon seeing the illustration, wonders "what an unfortuitous concatenation of circumstances needed the melodramatic illustration of an Indian in full war costume, tumbling over a precipice with a wolf at his throat, while two infuriated young gentlemen, with unnaturally small feet and big eyes, were stabbing each other close by, and a disheveled female was flying away in the background, with her mouth wide open." The story turns out to be one of "that class of light literature in which the passions have a holiday, and when the author's invention fails, a grand catastrophe clears the stage of one-half *the dramatis personae*, leaving the other half to exult over their downfall" (215).

Tessa sees herself as Capitola Black, or Cap Black, heroine of *The Hidden Hand*. This heroine wears boy's clothes, and like Jo, is an unapologetic tomboy, and stays that way.

> She is also the progenitor of the many female action heroines, especially female detectives, who populate fiction today. These are the women characters whose energy, curiosity, sass, street savvy, and above all compelling sense of justice lead to adventures where they uncover secrets, right wrongs, and defend true morality over social custom. The basic message of these popular novels now, like the message of *The Hidden Hand* then, is that the essence of true womanhood lies within and can never be compromised by merely unconventional behavior. (Introduction, *The Hidden Hand*)

In rural Virginia, Capitola ranges the countryside on horseback seeking adventures. She fights duels, rescues maidens, and rejects a spiritless life of sewing and indoor work. Though she grew up a street waif and knows little more than that, she is secretly the heiress to a great fortune, stolen by her villainous neighbors. Tessa has a link to Capitola besides her bravery – Tessa too grew up ignorant of her heritage but is the heiress to a great magic and mysterious heritage, all orchestrated by the Magister. Both heroines learn to outwit the patriarchy, using cleverness and persuasion rather than outright violence.

> Southworth shows, women need to develop more strategic wit than men; since they cannot expect ultimately to triumph over hostile men by brute strength, they need to carry the day by cleverness. To the extent that women become accomplished strategists like Capitola, sexual boundaries are again destabilized; if men are stronger than women, they assuredly are not smarter. (Introduction, *The Hidden Hand*)

On the street, Capitola disguises herself as a boy to seek employment:

> While all the ragged boys I knew could get little jobs to earn bread, I, because I was a girl, was not allowed to carry a gentleman's parcel, or black his boots, or shovel the snow off a shopkeeper's pavement, or put in coal, or do anything that I could do just as well as *they*. And so, because I was a girl, there seemed to be nothing but starvation or beggary before me. (Southworth 40)

Throughout the novel, she continues to dismiss women's traditional decorum as ludicrous and counter-productive. "Cap, my little man," she tells herself at a particularly suspenseful moment in the plot, "Be a woman! don't you stick at trifles!" (Southworth 344). Tessa too mourns how little choices are open to her before she meets the Shadowhunters. This was a common problem for women of the time, unable to take most jobs or find ways of supporting themselves if they lost their male relations. As Tessa trains, she marvels at how easy it is to move in men's clothing and how much freedom self-defense can bring her. At one point, Capitola imitates the sobbing Clara Day, her far more feminine friend, just as Tessa must disguise herself as the feminine Jessamine and charm Nate. After, both reveal themselves as the far more emancipated heroines of the story, not its listless victims.

> By making Capitola attractive to readers and to all the other characters in the book, male characters included, Southworth indicates that attraction grounded in admiration and esteem is far more satisfying to both sexes than attraction based on pity. The message for women is to be more like Capitola; for men, it is to appreciate Capitola-like women. (Introduction, *The Hidden Hand*)

London Poems

Poems about the city of London itself are frequent in the book. William Blake, for instance, wrote about the misery of the lower class in London's industrial revolution, describing the hopelessness and tragic early deaths in his *Songs of Experience*. In Blake's "London" (1798), the urban wanderer roams the empty streets near the Thames, where he meets in every face "[m]arks of weakness, marks of woe" and hears in every voice "[t]he mind-forg'd manacles" (213-214).

Will quotes the following line out of Blake's longest poem – "Jerusalem The Emanation of the Giant Albion": "I behold London; a Human awful wonder of God!" (*Clockwork Angel* 461). This line casts London as divine, though industrial and manmade, a counter to the demonic clockwork men of the series. As he says the line, he contradicts it and reflects that London may be the entrance to Hell. Intriguingly, this poem blends the concepts of Industrial Britain and the Bible with its angels and saints fighting God's war.

> London became perceived as exemplary of the sublime for the Romantics for many reasons: it was growing geographically without seeming control; it was the hub of the country's imperial commerce and trade with the external world; it had become the mixing board of extreme luxury and poverty; as well as the seeming victim and beneficiary of a spiraling population being sucked in to the vortex of the city from elsewhere. (Barfield and Spaar)

> Bring me my bow of burning gold;
> Bring me my arrows of desire:
> Bring me my spear: O clouds unfold!
> Bring me my chariot of fire!

These four lines from "Jerusalem" introduce chapter 21 of *Clockwork Princess* as the heroes head into battle. In the original poem, these lines follow:

> I will not cease from mental fight,
> Nor shall my sword sleep in my hand:
> Till we have built Jerusalem,
> In England's green & pleasant land.
> (488-489)

The poem retells a story that young Jesus traveled to England and visited Glastonbury. In the poem, Jesus speaks of the Second Coming and a better world, creating heaven in England, in place of the "dark Satanic Mills" of technology. Tessa, Charlotte, Will and the others are fighting for a world free from Mortmain's machines of death, which cover the green Welsh hills with blood. As the heroes take arms, they are determined to bring about God's kingdom, which Tessa does with her angel.

Dickens tended to see "the sublime city as inhuman negation, terror and deathliness," while Blake's poem is filled with awe, offering contrasting visions as Tessa, Will, and Jem journey from the slums of Whitechapel to a golden age of peace for the Shadowhunters (Barfield and Spaar).

The chapter in which Jem and Tessa visit Blackfriars Bridge is introduced by a snippet from the following poem:

> The River's Tale
> Prehistoric
> By Rudyard Kipling
>
> Twenty bridges from Tower to Kew –
> (Twenty bridges or twenty-two) –
> Wanted to know what the River knew,
> For they were young, and the Thames was old
> And this is the tale that River told: –
>
> "I walk my beat before London Town,
> Five hours up and seven down.
> Up I go till I end my run
> At Tide-end-town, which is Teddington.
> Down I come with the mud in my hands
>
> And plaster it over the Maplin Sands.
> But I'd have you know that these waters of mine
> Were once a branch of the River Rhine,
> When hundreds of miles to the East I went
> And England was joined to the Continent.
>
> "I remember the bat-winged lizard-birds,

Myths and Motifs in *The Mortal Instruments*

The Age of Ice and the mammoth herds,
And the giant tigers that stalked them down
Through Regent's Park into Camden Town.
And I remember like yesterday
The earliest Cockney who came my way,
When he pushed through the forest that lined the Strand,
With paint on his face and a club in his hand.
He was death to feather and fin and fur.
He trapped my beavers at Westminster.
He netted my salmon, he hunted my deer,
He killed my heron off Lambeth Pier.
He fought his neighbour with axes and swords,
Flint or bronze, at my upper fords,
While down at Greenwich, for slaves and tin,
The tall Phoenician ships stole in,
And North Sea war-boats, painted and gay,
Flashed like dragon-flies, Erith way;
And Norseman and Negro and Gaul and Greek
Drank with the Britons in Barking Creek,
And life was gay, and the world was new,
And I was a mile across at Kew!
But the Roman came with a heavy hand,
And bridged and roaded and ruled the land,
And the Roman left and the Danes blew in –
And that's where your history-books begin!"
(713-714)

Rudyard Kipling, of course, is best known today for *Just So Stories* and *The Jungle Book*. "The River's Tale" was written by Kipling to serve as the introduction to a history of England for schoolchildren by C.R.L.Fletcher. The poem emphasizes the eternal nature of the river, following from the beginning of prehistoric times through London today. As such, it links Tessa's time with our own as it continues to flow through the present. It's not surprising that Jem, who believes time is a wheel and he can be reborn someday, loves the river. As they meet there each year for over a century, the river emphasizes their steady timelessness, involved in the world yet apart from it.

Tessa likewise quotes Spencer's "Prothalamion," which sets the Thames in a pastoral world of frolicking nymphs, brave knights, and glorious beauty. The magic in the poem reminds readers that Jem and Tessa are also in a tale of magic and romance, with nymphs and fairies materializing in the river. Here is the first stanza:

Prothalamion
E. Spenser

Calm was the day, and through the trembling air
Sweet-breathing Zephyrus did softly play—
A gentle spirit, that lightly did delay
Hot Titan's beams, which then did glister fair;
When I, (whom sullen care,
Through discontent of my long fruitless stay
In princes' court, and expectation vain
Of idle hopes, which still do fly away
Like empty shadows, did afflict my brain,)
Walk'd forth to ease my pain
Along the shore of silver-streaming Thames,
Whose rutty bank, the which his river hems,
Was painted all with variable flowers,
And all the meads adorn'd with dainty gems
Fit to deck maidens' bowers,
And crown their paramours
Against the bridal day, which is not long:
Sweet Thames! run softly, till I end my song.
(Palgrave, LIII).

"Oranges and Lemons" is a schoolyard rhyme and game that references the churchbells around London. An opium addict sings this in *Clockwork Prince*. Any number of books and television shoes quote it to increase the story's London feel, from *The Avengers* television show to *Doctor Who*.

Oranges and lemons,
Say the bells of St. Clement's.

You owe me five farthings,
Say the bells of St. Martin's.
When will you pay me?
Say the bells of Old Bailey.

When I grow rich,
Say the bells of Shoreditch.

When will that be?
Say the bells of Stepney.

I do not know,
Says the great bell of Bow.

Myths and Motifs in *The Mortal Instruments*

Here comes a candle to light you to bed,
And here comes a chopper to chop off your head!

On the Tombs in Westminster Abbey

Will quotes the first four lines of this poem to scare Tessa and Jem.

On the Tombs in Westminster Abbey
F. Beaumont

Mortality, behold and fear
What a change of flesh is here!
Think how many royal bones
Sleep within these heaps of stones;
Here they lie, had realms and lands,
Who now want strength to stir their hands,
Where from their pulpits seal'd with dust
They preach, "In greatness is no trust."
Here's an acre sown indeed
With the richest royallest seed
That the earth did e'er suck in
Since the first man died for sin:
Here the bones of birth have cried,
"Though gods they were, as men they died!"
Here are sands, ignoble things,
Dropt from the ruin'd sides of kings:
Here's a world of pomp and state
Buried in dust, once dead by fate.
(Palgrave LXVII).

All of these poems combine to increase the sense of place: Just as sitcoms today reference the same books and shows that everyone's enjoying, these London poems indicate a shared culture, a shared knowledge of the popular literature and rhymes of the time. When Tessa and Will quote them, they're not only sharing their love of books, they're sharing their worldview.

"Come into the Garden, Maud"

Jessamine is a romantic heroine, devoted in fact to being a romantic heroine who is wooed and cossetted. However, she is inherently selfish and even turns traitor to the Clave. Her name is intriguing. Jessamine is a flower that, while it resembles honeysuckle, is actually poisonous. Her last name, Lovelace, sounds like "Loveless," appropriate for a character who uses people rather than caring for them.

Nate describes Jessamine as Tennyson's lovely Maud, "In gloss of satin and glimmer of pearls." (*Clockwork Prince* 253) Will adds the line "Queen rose of the rosebud garden of girls," on seeing a disguised Tessa (260). The Tennyson poem "Come into the garden, Maud" shows jessamine blossoms stirring to the tune as dancers swirl at a ball. The poem also idealizes a weak, beautiful female who is beginning to "faint in the light of the sun she loves/To faint in his light, and to die." In fact, Nate isn't surprised when Tessa (disguised as Jessamine) pretends to feel faint – that's what he expects of helpless females even one as strong and capable as Jessamine. Likewise, he lets the Shadowhunters catch Jessamine and take her off to be tortured, showing how little he cares for her. She is an object, like the girl of the poem, meant to be admired rather than respected. Jessamine loves the poem, Tessa doesn't.

> COME INTO THE GARDEN, MAUD
> Alfred Lord Tennyson
>
> Come into the garden, Maud,
> For the black bat, night, has flown,
> Come into the garden, Maud,
> I am here at the gate alone;
> And the woodbine spices are wafted abroad,
> And the musk of the rose is blown.
>
> For a breeze of morning moves,
> And the planet of Love is on high,
> Beginning to faint in the light that she loves
> On a bed of daffodil sky,
> To faint in the light of the sun she loves,
> To faint in his light, and to die.
> All night have the roses heard
> The flute, violin, bassoon;
> All night has the casement jessamine stirr'd
> To the dancers dancing in tune;
> Till silence fell with the waking bird,
> And a hush with the setting moon.
> ...
>
> Queen rose of the rosebud garden of girls,
> Come hither, the dances are done,
> In gloss of satin and glimmer of pearls,
> Queen lily and rose in one;
> Shine out, little head, sunning over with curls,
> To the flowers, and be their sun.
>
> There has fallen a splendid tear

Myths and Motifs in *The Mortal Instruments*

From the passion-flower at the gate.
She is coming, my dove, my dear;
She is coming, my life, my fate;
The red rose cries, "She is near, she is near;"
And the white rose weeps, "She is late;"
The larkspur listens, "I hear, I hear;"
And the lily whispers, "I wait."

She is coming, my own, my sweet;
Were it ever so airy a tread,
My heart would hear her and beat,
Were it earth in an earthy bed;
My dust would hear her and beat,
Had I lain for a century dead;
Would start and tremble under her feet,
And blossom in purple and red.
(250-252)

"Boadicea"

Far in the East Boadicea, standing loftily charioted,
Mad and maddening all that heard her in her fierce volubility,
Girt by half the tribes of Britain, near the colony Camulodune,
Yell'd and shriek'd between her daughters o'er a wild confederacy.
…
Hear Icenian, Catieuchlanian, hear Coritanian, Trinobant!
Me the wife of rich Prasutagus, me the lover of liberty,
Me they seized and me they tortured, me they lash'd and humiliated,
Me the sport of ribald Veterans, mine of ruffian violators!
See they sit, they hide their faces, miserable in ignominy!
Wherefore in me burns an anger, not by blood to be satiated.
Lo the palaces and the temple, lo the colony Camulodune!
There they ruled, and thence they wasted all the flourishing territory,
Thither at their will they haled the yellow-ringleted Britoness –
Bloodily, bloodily fall the battle-axe, unexhausted, inexorable.
Shout Icenian, Catieuchlanian, shout Coritanian, Trinobant,
Till the victim hear within and yearn to hurry precipitously
Like the leaf in a roaring whirlwind, like the smoke in a hurricane whirl'd.
Lo the colony, there they rioted in the city of Cunobeline!
There they drank in cups of emerald, there at tables of ebony lay,
Rolling on their purple couches in their tender effeminacy.
There they dwelt and there they rioted; there – there – they dwell no more.

> Burst the gates, and burn the palaces, break the works of the statuary,
> Take the hoary Roman head and shatter it, hold it abominable,
> Cut the Roman boy to pieces in his lust and voluptuousness,
> Lash the maiden into swooning, me they lash'd and humiliated,
> Chop the breasts from off the mother, dash the brains of the little one out,
> Up my Britons, on my chariot, on my chargers, trample them under us.'
>
> So the Queen Boadicea, standing loftily charioted,
> Brandishing in her hand a dart and rolling glances lioness-like,
> Yell'd and shriek'd between her daughters in her fierce volubility.
> Till her people all around the royal chariot agitated (57)

Tennyson's poem recalls one of Britain's great heroes. Queen Boadicea, after being tortured and humiliated by her Roman overlords, led her people in a great rebellion. Through today, she is the symbolic warrior woman of early Britain, fiery spirit of her people. Will describes her to show Tessa that women have a warrior spirit as well as men.

However, there are also subtler links between the stories. The book *Clockwork Angel* begins with Tessa being tortured by the Dark Sisters at the order of the Magister. He, like the Romans, is the establishment. After Will arrives, Tessa rebels against the Dark Sisters and attacks them. Alone in the dark with the Magister, she finally fakes her own suicide to trick him. Boadicea literally committed suicide according to many sources so she wouldn't be captured by the enemy. Through the trilogy she remains a feminist icon of strength and power, contrasted with fainting Victorian heroines.

CHAPTER 5

A DEEPER LOOK AT THE SHADOWHUNTERS AND THEIR BOOK

Timeline

The Mortal Instruments series takes place in 2007, the year *City of Bones* was released. It's August in *City of Bones*, September in the next two books, the end of October in *City of Fallen Angels*, November in *City of Lost Souls*. If *Heavenly Fire* takes place in December, that would be appropriate to bring about a new rebirth out of the darkness, much as *Clockwork Princess* does.

In 2008, after the events of *City of Heavenly Fire*, Jem and Tessa speak in the epilogue to *Clockwork Princess*. Tessa mentions *City of Glass* took place a few months before, and they reflect on how much their world has changed. *The Dark Artifices* takes place five years later, with the characters dealing with the changes to their world. Clary and her friends are adults, and the next generation of teenagers is finding their path.

The Infernal Devices series takes place more than a century before, in 1878 between April and December. Clare left gaps in the family tree of *Clockwork Princess* as she's considering writing a series set in the early 1900's about the generation after Will and Tessa's (*Cassandra Clare's Clockwork Princess Bus Tour*).

Names

Clary

As Jace points out on their second meeting, Clary appears to be named for the herb Clary Sage (41). Since this herb improves one's magical sight, allowing one to see fairies and the supernatural, it's a logical choice for our heroine. She not only has the sight herself, but the runes that come to her in visions are her special power. She can also see, thanks to her outsider upbringing, that the Shadowhunters and Downworlders must make peace if they are to survive. She takes the podium at the end of book three to guide people into both kinds of seeing.

Sight and looking are often emphasized around Clary. Simon asks Clary to "really look" at him as he pushes her to see how his feelings are evolving (*Bones* 341).

> "You can come either willingly or unwillingly."
> Clary couldn't believe her ears. "Are you threatening to kidnap me?"
> "If you want to look at it that way," Jace said, "yes." (*Bones* 44)

This sequence, almost directly after the clary sage reference, emphasizes that there are two ways of looking at everything – Jace is pushy and rude but not malevolent. Vampires, warlocks, and werewolves likewise are trying to protect themselves. Clary's eyes have been shut to much around her, from her mother's scars to her next door neighbor's powers (and possession!). Only by seeing who people truly are will Clary be able to succeed on her quest. "Seeing through glamour is easy. It's people that are hard" Clary tells Simon (*Bones* 341).

The author's penname may come from this root, and many fans think Clary is named at least partly for the author's chosen name. On her site, however, the author responds, "[Clary's] not named after me. She is named after my friend Valerie Frayre, and my friend Clary." (FAQ)

The name Clarissa means bright or clear, just as Clary does. Deeper meanings of the name suggest the person will be a light of inspiration for others, much like a shining star. People with this name are traditionally leaders, with their creative ideas, new perspectives, and courageous determination.

Clary doesn't like having Jace call her Fray, since it reminds her of Simon. However, perhaps on some level, she knows it's not her real name. In later books she's called Clarissa Morgenstern, suggesting it's her true identity. Meanwhile, Jocelyn changes this last name, growing from Jocelyn Fairchild the innocent princess to Jocelyn Fray who battles in the midst of a great war against Valentine (fray is another word for battle). A last name of Morgenstern for each of them suggests a world of being tied to Lucifer and battling true evil in their lives. However, at the same time, Morgenstern means morning star, an image, like the last name Skywalker or Lightwood, of light and angelic powers. The fourth book, *City of Fallen Angels*, reminds readers that the saintly bringers of light have the farthest to fall.

Jace

Jace's name is notable because it's a construct. As he reveals at the end of book one, he has been Jonathan Christopher the entire time, hidden in plain sight. Clary, questing for knowledge of the past and her lost brother, is blindsided. Yet, as the Cain-and-Abel retelling *East of Eden* points out, "Names are a great mystery. I've never known whether the name is molded by the child or the child changed to fit the name. But you can be sure of this – whenever a human has a nickname it is a proof that the name given him was wrong." Calling himself Jace suggests not only that he's rejecting the name Jonathan Morgenstern, demonic son of Valentine, but that Jonathan is not the name he should have been given. His constant insistence that everyone call him Jace emphasizes that he's forming his own identity and becoming who he chooses, not who Valentine intended. At the end of *City of Glass*, Clary supports this belief, encouraging him to take the last name of his loving adoptive parents, not his birth father or childhood father. By doing so, he becomes Jace *Light*wood, a force of light in the world. This is a strong match for Clary Morgenstern, the morning star.

J.C., his initials, most often stand for Jesus Christ. In fact, Jace does die to save his people and is resurrected in book three. In *Lost Souls*, Clary sees him as a picture of a saint, kneeling and gazing upward, his face flooded with holy light. He appears to have a halo at times (*Bones* 138). All the descriptions of him use the word gold, from his eyes to his hair.

The other Jonathan Morgenstern is Jace's shadow, all he easily could have been but chose not to be. The same age, with the same upbringing and intended destiny, only their angel and demon blood separates them. Jonathan clearly references Jonathan Shadowhunter, creator of the Nephilim. Jonathan Morgenstern attempts to follow his example and create a new race. In the Bible, Jonathan is best known for his platonic love for David, who was an adopted brother to him. To the king, Jonathan is the good one and David the hated traitor, but the reality is more complex. David is the people's hero, and Jonathan, merely the king's sheltered son. There is also a Jonathan in the story of Hanukah (discussed below), who continues his father's rebellion against the corrupt authority. As he perpetuates his father Valentine's legacy, Jonathan Morgenstern's struggle in the series is with Jace, angel to his demon.

Sebastian

> Antonio: Will you stay no longer? nor will you not that I go with you?
> Sebastian: By your patience, no. My stars shine darkly over me; the malignancy of my fate might, perhaps, distemper yours; therefore I shall crave of you your leave that I may bear my evils alone. It were a bad recompense for your love to lay any of them on you.
> (Shakespeare, *Twelfth Night* II:i:1-7)

Sebastian's name may derive from Shakespeare's *Twelfth Night*, from this quote, which introduces Part Two of *City of Glass*. The play is about doubles and twins – the twins Sebastian and Viola are separated in a storm, and Viola disguises herself as her brother. Viola becomes the page to Duke Orsino but mourns that she can't tell him of her love, since she's disguised as a boy. The comedy goes on as people confuse them and fall in love with the wrong people, until it all works out in the end. *City of Glass* involves Sebastian's quest to find Clary, the lost sister he craves. Clary loves Jace, but he is forbidden to her. Meanwhile, Jace and Sebastian, both Jonathan Morgenstern, are confused with each other, until the chaos is finally sorted out at the story's end. The name, coupled with the *Twelfth Night* quote, may be a clue for the more literary fans that Sebastian is a double and twin – not what he seems.

The quote itself is interesting because Sebastian's "stars shine darkly" and he has a malignant fate – because of the circumstances of his birth, he will have an unlucky life, filled with an evil destiny, misery, and pain. While Shakespeare's Sebastian is speaking from despair, and actually falls into wealth and happiness in the play, the words certainly apply to Jonathan Morgenstern, cursed with demon blood so that everything he touches is corrupted. When Clary meets Sebastian, she thinks of her childhood fantasy, of a handsome prince cursed so everyone he loved would die (*Glass* 115). Clare of course gets to flesh out this concept in *The Infernal Devices*. However, Clary's small prophecy comes true – Sebastian's family of Jace, Clary, and Jocelyn suffer greatly for their association with him. The Lightwoods and Penhallows are likewise tortured, as are Luke and Amatis.

Sebastian's Verlac family crest is "a water serpent rising out of a lake" (*Glass* 157). Of course, this is a subtle clue that he is the serpent in the Eden of Alicante, arrived to destroy the place with treachery. Clare comments that Ver-lac is a French compound name, much like Light-wood or Heron-dale in English:

> Sebastian's last name, Verlac, is also compound. Ver means worm or serpent (like a wyrm type thing) and lac means lake. The thing I liked about it was that ver sounds a lot like verre, which means glass. Verrelac however is not a name. But if you just sound it out, it does sound a bit like Glass Lake. Which seemed fitting. (Clare, "Random Question")

In medieval art, the Archangel Michael is often depicted battling a serpent or dragon, which was a metaphor for the devil. Sebastian is the serpent of the lake rather than the serpent in the garden. With his crest and name, to say nothing of the creepy feeling he gives Clary, Jonathan Morgenstern is setting out to be the devil of the story.

Sebastian "wants to be Jonathan Shadowhunter reincarnated but on the side of the demons, not the angels" (*Lost Souls* 405). His bracelet reads "If I cannot move heaven, I will raise Hell." He's quoting Juno in the *Aeneid*: Juno (in her typical role as jealous stepmother) hates the hero Aeneas and hurls storms and battles against him. At last, she seeks aid in the underworld, crying, "If I cannot move heaven, I will raise Hell." If the powers of good and decency won't obey her, she will use the forces of evil to persecute a hero of the light, all through pettiness and cruelty.

Simon

Saint Simon is best known for his martyrdom, which is shared by the series character. Simon is turned into a vampire against his will, and then he surrenders himself to Raphael and the other vampires, knowing he is offering his life for peace. He only survives because he volunteers to take the mark of Cain, another sacrifice, for whoever wears it is cast out of society. Further, he willingly gives up Clary because she doesn't love him romantically.

In *City of Lost Souls*, the Angel Raziel makes a more direct reference when he compares him to Simon Maccabee (Simon the Hammer). The story of Hanukah (described in the First Book of Maccabees) tells of the sons of Mattathias, who started a rebellion against their Syrian conquerors. Maccabee means hammer, and it may have been adopted as an acronym for their leader, Mattathias *or Matityahu Kohen ben Yochanan*. It's also said that Maccabee is an acronym for the Torah verse that was the battle-cry of the Maccabees, "*Mi chamocha ba'elim –,*" "Who is like You among the heavenly powers, Lord!" Raziel calls Simon "Simon Maccabee" and gives him the sword with the words "Who is like God?" inscribed on it.

In the Bible story, first Judah and then Jonathan led the army, but Simon took a prominent part with his counsel and leadership. After Jonathan's capture, Simon was elected leader. Eventually, under his leadership, the state of Judea was freed. Simon removed idols from the country and rededicated the temple, a celebration of sacred menorah lighting that led to the modern Hanukah. "Thus the yoke of the heathen was taken away from Israel in the hundred and seventieth year" of the Seleucid era. The elders of the land resolved that Simon should be the high priest "forever, until there should arise a faithful prophet" (I Macc. 4.35-41), likely the messiah who would end war forever.

When Jace is captured by Valentine, then later captured by Sebastian, Simon becomes more than a counselor for the Shadowhunter teens and becomes a force of sacrifice and goodness. He is the one to summon Raziel and offer his life, just as he offers his life to Raphael. Both times, he succeeds and brings a new weapon to the side of light.

Lucian Graymark/Luke Garroway

"Luke Garroway I picked because it sounded a bit like loup-garou, which is French for werewolf," Clare explains (FAQ). Lucian, his original name, is another name of light, making him another warrior for goodness and fallen angel, like the Morgensterns. However, Greymark, while suggesting a wolf's grey pelt, also suggests that his motivations are more shadowed. He is a Downworlder in a battle of Shadowhunters against the Clave, and the "Grey" reminds readers that he is one of those shadows, infected with the blood of demons though he struggles towards the light.

Tessa Grey

The last name Grey is a vague, shadowy name, suggesting a mysterious curtain over Tessa's origins. In fact, this proves to be true. "Tessa's one of my favorite names and there's a reason she has the last name Grey and Clary has a name like that," Clare commented intriguingly (*Cassandra Clare's Clockwork Princess Bus Tour*)

Teresa, Tessa's real name, is the name of several saints, including Mother Teresa. Oddly, the villainess of *A Tale of Two Cities* is named Thérèse. However, she is generally known as Madame Defarge, and similarities are minimal.

For literature majors like Clare, the name Tessa strongly conjures associations with *Tess of the d'Urbervilles*, published in 1891. This is a tragic novel about a rather helpless heroine, who is seduced, lied to, betrayed, and so forth. Tessa Grey resolves to be none of these things. At the same time, her relationship with the apparently cruel Will and her engagement to the saintly Jem echoes Tess's love for Angel Clare and her seduction by the cad Alec. Hardy's masterpiece has a theme of mankind suffering when separated from nature, a theme that also appears in Mortmain's clockwork monsters and Will's dislike of the crowded, polluted London. Another important theme is the sexual double standard that destroys Hardy's Tess – she loses her virginity, and Angel, who once had an affair, and committed the "same sin," as Tess poignantly reminds him – cannot forgive her. Hardy supports Tess, subtitling the book "a pure woman faithfully presented," and reminding readers how unfair her censure is. As such, the book is an early work of feminism. Tessa Grey struggles with Victorian morality and the sexual double-standard, and Sophie's life is nearly destroyed because of it. Both girls struggle to maintain their social acceptability, even as they come to embrace the freedom of the Shadowhunters' life.

Zachariah

Zachariah was the father of John the Baptist, struck dumb because of his lack of faith. Jem must undergo a time of blindness and muteness as one of the Silent Brothers before he is redeemed through the mercy of heaven.

Zachariah was also an Old Testament prophet who recalled the nation's history and warned of the future. Someone who has lived a hundred years, since the first signing of the Accords, seems a logical prophet to advise about the Shadowhunters' future. The Book of Zachariah is a sort of apocalypse story, describing the glories that await Israel in "the latter day," the final conflict and triumph of God's kingdom. His vision of the future may be important in *City of Heavenly Fire*, a book that apparently changes the Shadowhunter way of life forever.

Other Names

Max and Isabelle are named for my grandparents. Alec's name was originally Alex, but Alec is a more interesting version of Alexander, I think. Simon and Maia are named after friends of mine, while Maryse, Robert, Jocelyn and others are simply names I picked out of baby name books and the like. (FAQ)

Raphael is based on a friend's younger brother (whose name is Gabriel, and I was tickled that it was an angel's name, so I changed it to Raphael, another angel's name.) Simon is sort of a combination of my boyfriend and my best friend. Magnus is based on a friend of mine – a guy who used to wear a ton of glitter and outrageous outfits, but there was this real keen intelligence under all the glitter and partying, which is what interests me about Magnus... I'll say that Magnus is the most fun to write, and Simon is the most like me. ("Interview: Cassandra Clare")

Archetypes and Tarot

Tarot is a world of archetypes – the queen, the fool, the lovers. And apparently it's a world of Shadowhunters as well. Cassandra Jean Piedra has drawn a set of Mortal-Instruments-inspired tarot cards, with characters assigned to their roles by Clare. These cards, available on Clare's Tumblr page (http://cassandraclare.tumblr.com/tagged/shadowhunter-tarot) or Cassandra Jean's website (http://cassandrajeanart.blogspot.com), reveal something of the characters and their archetypes and roles.

The Blackthorns (coming in her 2015 series) are called the Changeling, the Believer, the Genius, the Artist, and so forth, in keeping with their archetypes. Clary's card is "The Creator," and she perches on a lioness with a hunting falcon or eagle nearby, surrounded by her runes. Jace is the Angel, strength, with gold wings and a lion. Simon the Daylighter replaces the sun card. Sebastian of course is Death.

The Lovers, shown with Clary and Jace on one side and Alec and Magnus on the other, carries a message to follow one's heart, even through difficulty, good advice for both sets of characters. Simon's sun indicates freedom – casting off old loves and finding new ones, reaching a higher level of spirituality. All this and more happens to Simon on his journey. Clary's World card signifies feeling the weight of the world and is a card of completion – Clary indeed has a power no one else does and uses it to redeem the world. This card indicates clear flashes of important spiritual insights and a rise to great heights. Jace is the Strength card, suggesting the importance of mind over matter and the need to focus on goals. In the love quarter, Strength indicates a strong relationship filled with support, with skill in the workplace…even if it's demon fighting! It is a spiritual card as well.

Tessa, veiled, takes the Star card, Jem with his beloved violin takes the place of Temperance, and Will as the unlucky Hanged Man. The star means inspiration, just as Tessa is a spiritual light for Jem and Will. The card is a powerful one, which means its bearer can accomplish anything. The Hanged Man indicates a crossroads - one with only two options. Will can commit to Tessa or let her go, an issue he struggles with through all three books, though this is complicated by his curse and loyalty to Jem. Temperance is a card about balance and different kinds of relationships, from family to friends. Mild Jem is certainly balanced in all things, as a compensation for the drug that's killing him and the sacrifice he makes by fighting. This card suggests trying different paths to find one's life solution, something a dying Jem will need to try.

Ordinary tarot has four suits, cups, wands, swords, and pentacles, which evolved into the suits on playing cards. In Clare's deck the stele suit replaces wands, which are also known as staffs, spears, or rods. This traditionally is a suit of passion, ambition, spirituality, and creative endeavors: Anything a person might put their energy and soul into. Alec is the knight of steles, his family king, queen, and princess. Since the stele is like a royal scepter, this makes sense. The stele or staff is a masculine symbol, suggesting subtly that all four Lightwoods are masculine oriented – Maryse and Isabelle are women trying to compete in a man's world with their fighting skills and leadership, for example. The Inquisitor's steles are lined up like prison bars, and Amatis and Stephen argue as three steles are tossed up like a handful of shattered pieces. Will's steles seem to trap him.

The "seraph blades" or swords are another masculine symbol, representing the mind and voice. It is a suit of sharp ideas and sharp tongues, a love of facts and calculations. On the darker side, it can indicate anxieties. On one, Tessa kneels blindfolded before two blades, trapped between Jem and Will. Not only is she caught in a love triangle, but she is blind to her past, which holds the secrets of her future. It is her mind that is blindfolded, much like Clary's was. Jessamine is blindfolded as well, with swords like prison bars to show what her knowledge and treacherous tongue have gotten her. Nathaniel Grey is likewise surrounded by swords, as well as the Ouroboros box of forbidden knowledge.

Myths and Motifs in *The Mortal Instruments*

Jonathan Shadowhunter, Jocelyn and Valentine, and Hodge, all warriors of the intellect and participators in the masculine world of politics and ambition, are the royalty of this suit.

Benedict Lightwood, splashed with blood, is the king of rings. His sons are knight and page. A pentacle is a stone, disk or coin (sometimes set in a ring) so this is likely the corresponding suit. (In Harry Potter, Slytherin's ring corresponds to the pentacle, while the Elder Wand, Hufflepuff Cup, and Sword of Gryffindor cover the others). The family rings of course indicate family honor and loyalty. A ring may indicate dominion over some element, like Solomon's ring. As such, Jace's ring suggests that he's an heir to the Morgenstern legacy, as is Clary, to whom he passes it. Pentacles suggest practicality, the warm strength of earth. This is the suit of health, money, luck and work, the suit of the physical. It relates to our body, our home, our valuables. Pentacles is the slow-growth, long-term suit, the suit about creating something real, about social responsibility and interaction. In the *Infernal Devices* trilogy, all three Lightwoods must make these decisions.

The feminine Cup which once gave Shadowhunters the power of runes is left. The runes suit features Tess and Will in the library together, Magnus and Alec kissing for the fearless rune, and so forth. Cups represent emotions of the heart, the search for beauty, vision, and divine love mixed with the flow of gentle water, so this is no surprise. As we observe Tessa and Will sharing their incredible passion for books or recall Clary bursting open the ship with the strength of her desperation, we understand more about this suit.

As Clare plays with these archetypes, she reveals her visions for the characters: Tessa and Simon bring light to others, Jace is Clary's strength, while Clary herself is the entire world.

Easter Eggs

> "In *City of Fallen Angels*, Jace is in prison in the Silent City. He's in one of the jail cells, and he sees the initials JG scratched on the wall. So, umm, spoiler! That's Jessamine. …The more detailing and the more layering you do, the more real the world seems. This thing that was done 150 years ago is still there on the wall of the Silent City. And now you know how it got there. It just makes you feel like the Silent City has a history. (Bressia, "Cassandra Clare talks 'Clockwork Prince'")

In fact, similar spoilers and shared references, commonly known as Easter Eggs, appear throughout her series. This is hardly surprising when the *Infernal Devices* introduces the ancestors of the more modern series, complete with long-lived characters like Magnus and Camille. Many of these clever references are listed below. In an interview, Clare added:

I would say that I'm really looking forward to this adventure of alternating the series publications – first we'll have Clockwork Angel, then City of Fallen Angels, then Clockwork Prince, then City of Lost Souls, etc. It allows me to salt tiny details through the narrative that reward close reading. There are literally characters who show up in the end of Angel who reappear at the beginning of Fallen Angels; Jace notices some graffiti in Fallen Angels that ties into something in Lost Souls. I think it's going to be really fun! ("Clockwork Angel: An exclusive Q&A")

Characters

- Magnus Bane as magical problem solver: "I am not at your beck and call," Magnus said. "I helped with de Quincey because Camille requested it of me, and Will once, because he offered me a favor in return. I am a warlock. And I do not serve Shadowhunters for free." (*Clockwork Princess*). Magnus also says it will never be his responsibility to manage wayward Shadowhunters. This echoes his disgruntlement in New York.
- Camille as untrustworthy ally
- Brother Enoch
- Ragnor Fell
- In *Fallen Angels*, Magnus and Camille meet again. They discuss their former relationship, London, and Will Herondale (and how he resembles Alec). Looking at her, Magnus has a flashback to his old friends. In a short story published in the paperback release of *Clockwork Angel*, Magnus's first meeting with Jace and Alec triggers a similar flashback.
- Tessa appears at the *City of Glass* party. Magnus is talking to her, dressed Victorian style. Clare adds that Tessa wears white because she is indeed in mourning (*Cassandra Clare's Clockwork Princess Bus Tour*). In *Clockwork Princess*, it's revealed what they were discussing.
- Church the cat appears in both. Church was a Persian cat Mrs. Dark planned to sacrifice to aid her necromancy. By experimenting on him, she gave him eternal life. He appears to sense demonic powers and act wary of them. Clare notes that in addition "he's a bit evil" (*Cassandra Clare's Clockwork Princess Bus Tour*).
- Brother Zachariah looks at Jace and says he could have recognized him as a Herondale. He's very protective of Jace and adds, "Old ties exist between the Herondales and the

Brothers. We owe him help" (*Fallen Angels* 270). He adds he has a "particular interest" in Jace's well-being (*Lost Souls* 276). It seems quite clear that Zachariah is Jem, even before *Clockwork Princess* clarifies matters.

- Brother Zachariah also references his past more specifically when he comments, "I was once a Shadowhunter like you. I lived like you do. And like you, there were those I loved enough to put their welfare before anything else – any oath, any debt" (*Lost Souls* 278)
- Clary asks, "Were you ever in love? Before the brotherhood? Was there ever anyone you would have died for?" There was a long silence. Then: "*Two people*," said Brother Zachariah. (*Lost Souls* 517). The fact that he's willing to speak of this and still sounds so close to the Shadowhunters and their problems foreshadows the epilogue of *Clockwork Princess*.
- There's a mention in *Clockwork Princess* that Meliorn is going to America. Later Magnus and Church set off as well.
- Henry offers Magnus his first skin glitter.
- Azazel compliments Magnus for destroying Marbas, which happened in *Infernal Devices*.
- Cecily tells Gabriel he can make the Lightwood name shine again. By the time of the other series, it does.
- Tessa asks Jem's uncle if he plans to have children and suggests he leave them the Carstairs sword – this will be the ancestors of Emma Carstairs in the Los Angeles series.
- Tessa meets Ithuriel, and then Tessa's angel leaves the Herondale mark on Will's shoulder, later seen on Jace's shoulder.

Character Echoes

- Jace hates ducks, as does Will. Perhaps this is some kind of racial memory?
- Will and Jace both pick fights with werewolf packs when they're upset.
- Simon and Will both deal with biting vampires and the side effects thereof.
- Tessa is trapped in a Malachai Configuration, much like Jace is.
- In *Infernal Devices*, Magnus breaks up with Camille, described in the City books, and also shows glimpses of his relationship with Alec several times. He thinks to himself that he must do something about "this annoying softhearted impulse to assist the desperate...That, and his weakness for blue eyes" (*Clockwork*

Prince 139). He mentions black hair and blue eyes are his favorite combination. Magnus also pretends to fall for Will to make Camille jealous. As he explains, Will has far more passion than most people, especially a long-lived vampire. The same passion draws him to Alec later, and all of these moments foreshadow their relationship.
- Gabriel insists his father's a worm in a conversation similar to the "Simon's a rat" one in *City of Bones*. He is misunderstood just as his descendent Isabelle is.
- "I know about parabatai," said Magnus, an angry, dark undercurrent to his voice. "I've known parabatai so close they were almost the same person; do you know what happens, when one of them dies, to the one that's left–?" (*City of Lost Souls* 152)
- Rude Inquisitors appear in both series.
- In the modern series, Camille mentions the Lightwoods never give up.

Names

- Shadowhunter families like Lightwood, Herondale, and Wayland. Jem mentions in the epilogue that the battles in both books have involved epics of Fairchilds, Herondales, and Lightwoods.
- Alec's middle name is Gideon, after Gideon Lightwood. Isabelle's middle name is Sophia, after Sophie Collins. Gabriel and Cecily's child was Alexander Lightwood, ancestor to Alec Lightwood.
- Henry's middle name is Jocelyn, indicating a repeated family name (he's married to a Fairchild). They are Jocelyn and Clary's ancestors.
- The family tree in *Clockwork Princess* reveals that Will and Tessa named their children James and Lucie, the latter most likely after the heroine of *A Tale of Two Cities*. She wed Tatiana Lightwood's child and James wed into the Carstairs family. Thus Jem is not only related to Emma Carstairs, their descendent, but also to his namesake James Herondale and his descendent Jace. (Jace and Emma are related but about four generations back. Of course, it seems likely all Shadowhunters are distantly related to some extent.)
- A Scott still leads the Praetor Lupus.
- Magnus waved a hand. "All Lightwoods look the same to me." This will be ironically untrue later.
- Brother Zachariah comments, "Jonathan' is a fine old Shadowhunter name, the first of names. The Herondales have

always kept names in the family" (*Lost Souls* 517). Jace's birth father was named Stephen William Herondale, clearly Will's namesake.

Issues of the Time

- The Accords are a source of contention in both series. In the earlier one, mention is made of Downworlders having Council seats – it's dismissed as ridiculous, but Clary and Luke make it happen a century later.
- The Pandemonium Club is a popular hangout.
- Magnus mentions Praetor Lupus and its founder had reasons to investigate demon drugs. This refers to the events of *Clockwork Prince*.
- The epilogue of *Clockwork Princess* reveals that great changes have happened, altering the Silent Brothers' options, among other things. These events will certainly be seen in *City of Heavenly Fire*.

Items

- The Dark Sisters have a globe like Clary's, with Idris in the center of Europe.
- The *Book of the White* is hidden in Tessa's room in one series and the Wayland manor in the other.
- Isabelle's ruby necklace is worn by Camille in *Infernal Devices*. In *Clockwork Princess*, it passes from Camille to Magnus to Will to Cecily, Isabelle's ancestress.
- The Soul-Sword and a trial by the sword are discussed in *City of Ashes*, and used in *Clockwork Prince* and *City of Lost Souls*.
- "Henry invented the Portal and the Sensor and fire messages, and all the things they use today," Clare noted. She added that the characters of *Infernal Devices* would be amazed that Henry became the most famous of them all (*Cassandra Clare's Clockwork Princess Bus Tour*).
- A copy of *Tale of Two Cities* signed "With hope at last, William Herondale" appears in *Clockwork Princess* and also in Sebastian's safehouse in *Lost Souls*.
- The clockwork angel (and a book on demon pox!) are in the Institute in *Lost Souls*.
- Magnus keeps some of Woolsey Scott's things around, including the silver snuffbox Woolsey gives him in *Clockwork Princess*.
- Charlotte fights with an electrum whip, like Isabelle's.

- Amatis gives Jace a Herondale family tree in a silver box. This may be the one written in *Clockwork Princess*. Though the silver box has herons on it, it evokes a memory of Jem's Kwan Yin box that he gives to Will Herondale.
- The Carstairs sword will undoubtedly appear in *Dark Artifices*.

Jace and Will, Tessa and Clary

Tessa and Clary are both outsiders, both young ladies who have lost their families through violent attacks and now seek their loved ones and protection, along with the place they truly belong. As such, links are obvious between the two series. Clare comments:

> I was trying to do a bit of paralleling, with the way Clary falls in with the Shadowhunters. Tessa's experience is different because she's a Downworlder. They sign the Accords so the Shadowhunters can live with Downworlders in an uneasy truce. In the Mortal Instruments series, the Accords were signed many years in the past. I wanted to set a book right after the Accords were signed, where the tensions are still really high between the Shadowhunters and Downworlders. Tessa showing up and being a Downworlder and yet being their only hope of defeating the Pandemonium Club creates a tension that wasn't there for Clary, because Clary was also a Shadowhunter. ("Cassandra Clare: Bringing the Shadows to Light.")

Tessa, like Clary, thinks she's a normal human, but when rescued by her future love is taken to the Institute and learns about the shadow world. She has powers never before seen. Clary's are due to her angel and Shadowhunter blood while Tessa's powers are a mixture of demon and Shadowhunter. Both have been engineered by evil forces: Valentine and the Magister respectively. Clary is a book lover like Tess. Neither ever does what she's told. Both girls end up having an evil or otherwise traitorous brother. Both feel romantic pressure from the villain, the Magister and Sebastian. Both have two boys with radically different personalities competing for them, plus a foil of a glamorous girl who knows how to dress and makes the heroine feel sloppy.

Jace and Will have even stronger parallels, as they have similar attitudes and personalities. Both are born Shadowhunters, talented and fearless, with a particularly snarky attitude. Both quote literature a lot, in multiple languages. Each takes his foster brother for his parabatai. Further, both Will and Jace are from the lush, quiet countryside, Jace from a manor house in Idris and Will from Wales. Clare describes, the "landscape being a match for Will's personality: beautiful but also remote, one of those places that's not easy to access, but worth the effort in the end." She adds:

MYTHS AND MOTIFS IN *THE MORTAL INSTRUMENTS*

A lot of people are reading Will as Jace. That isn't surprising, as they are 1) obviously blood related and 2) share a similar sense of humor and a way of using humor as a deflector against real feelings. I think of Will as almost a commentary on Jace's character, but that will be more clear in book two, when you learn there are ways in which they absolutely aren't alike at all. ("Author Interview: Cassandra Clare," *The Mortal's Library*)

It's true that different family traumas are motivating their standoffish behavior. But in fact, both have learned as children that loving is a weakness. When the heroine shows up, both must fight their instincts to be with her. In book four, Jace turns into a kind of Will, both so fearful that they'll hurt the ones they love that they reject them and act cold. Only in unguarded moments do they reveal their true feelings. Jace never has a friend or even meets another child until he's ten. Before that, he has an indulged life of servants and gifts, with his father as his only companion. They travel the world together. However, his father also teaches "that to love is to destroy and that to be loved is to be the one destroyed" (*Bones* 206). Clary is appalled, but Jace believes his father made him strong.

"It's like you never feel anything at all," Clary complains (*Bones* 318).

Tessa is likewise frustrated with Will's hot-and-cold behavior towards her. It is finally revealed in the second book that Will believes he must alienate others to protect them. Though this contrasts with defensive Jace, who protects himself, both Shadowhunters push people away with sarcastic quips:

> "How rude. Many who have gazed upon me have compared the experience to gazing at the radiance of the sun." Will tells Jem (*Clockwork Angel* 343)

> "You're the first Shadowhunter I've ever met."

> "That's too bad," said Jace. "Since all the ones you meet from now on will be a terrible letdown. (*Fallen Angels* 144)

Their parallels run even deeper, as Will was created from Jace's character: "Jace was originally named Will, but Jace is a name I always liked, and it needed to be something that could be short for Jonathan (and now the name Will shows up in *Clockwork Angel* instead)" (FAQ). It's also interesting that Jace becomes the adopted brother of the Lightwood children, his distant cousins. His ancestor Will also gave Cecily the ruby pendent Isabelle now wears. The ancient love between their families and the Carstairs may show up in *Dark Artifices*. Likewise, Jem and Tessa may check in on his cousins many-times-removed and her last descendant, Jace.

Nods and Homages to Other Series

Through Simon and to a lesser extent the others, references abound to *Spiderman, Dungeons and Dragons*, comics, movies, and more. Clary loves *Forbidden Planet* in New York. Simon plays in a garage band. Magnus hoards comic books. And their constant references to all they've watched and seen embed this story in the larger universe of fantasy while keeping it something modern teens can understand. Basically, this is a fantasy series for fantasy fans.

The references also remind readers that their heroes are, in fact, fictional. All stories are true, including this fantasy epic. For instance, two unnamed characters in the café have a debate on which wizard would win in a fight, Dumbledore or Magnus. This calls attention to the fact that Magnus, while a powerful wizard like Dumbledore, is just as fictional. Clary and Simon decide that Anne Rice's Lestat already covered the vampire rock star bit, and he has no need to repeat it. Other more particular shout-outs abound:

- Val and Luis from Holly Black's *Valiant* are seen at one point. The Fairy Queen is supposed to be the same one as in Black's series.
- A badge on Clary's bag says "Still Not King," a reference to Clare's famous *The Lord of the Rings* fanfic *The Very Secret Diaries*. A "Still Not King" pin is also seen in Ruth's bag in *Valiant*.
- Manga is popular among the characters: Max is frequently seen reading *Naruto,* and Clary asks him if Simon wants to spend the evening with her watching *Trigun*. Clary also thinks about how a church looks like one of her favorite anime scenes involving a vampire priest.
- Magnus listens to Elka Choke's "Alack, for I Can Get No Play."
- Simon is described in the fourth book as wearing Jeph Jacques's "Clearly I Have Made Some Bad Decisions" shirt, and Cassandra Clare also mentions his series "Magical Love Gentlemen."

Themes and Motifs

I don't think of these as two separate series so much as a single overarching story of the Shadowhunter families of the Waylands, Herondales, Fairchilds, and Lightwoods. These books are all thematically linked by issues of family, blood and choice. Are you destined to be what you are from birth, or do you get to choose? What makes someone your family – is it love, or blood ties? Can what your blood relatives did in the past still reverberate in your own life? Can you escape your destiny? In a sense, the story of the *Infernal Devices* makes the story of the *Mortal Instruments* possible. ("*Clockwork Angel*: An exclusive Q&A")

Myths and Motifs in *The Mortal Instruments*

Clare notes how many shared themes the two series carry. (*The Dark Artifices* will doubtlessly share these as well.) Some of her themes like tolerance are woven subtly into the tales, while others prove to be major plot points. Kid power and feminism abound, as is common in YA fantasy. But at the same time, Clare finds a way to make hard-hitting points about the world in which we live.

Love is the Greatest Source of Strength

"L'amor che move il sole e l'altre stelle (My will and my desire were turned by love, the love that moves the sun and the other stars)" Dante Alighieri, *The Divine Comedy*. Jace defines this as saying that love is the most powerful force, and later adds that the greatest kind of love is faith. He quotes this at the beginning of *City of Fallen Angels* to remind Clary what they mean to each other (76).

At the climax of the third book, both he and Clary resist Valentine and keep fighting through the strength of their love for each other. Yet Jace forgets this crucial lesson and distances himself from her because of his demonic dreams. Though he loves her, he doesn't trust that her presence will strengthen him. He doubts he deserves to be happy, so he sets them on a destructive spiral through most of *Fallen Angels*. The pair must struggle to remember this lesson and find their way across all obstacles in *City of Lost Souls*.

Jem's love for Will and Tessa apparently keeps him alive for years beyond his projected lifespan, and Tessa's love grounds him for over a century, keeping him more human than the other Silent Brothers. Likewise, Will reads to Tessa from Dickens's *David Copperfield*: "I hope that real love and truth are stronger in the end than any evil or misfortune in the world" (*Clockwork Princess* 513).

At the same time, love is a weakness – Lilith and Mortmain both use love as weapons to force Simon and Tessa to follow their commands, Fortunately, both heroes mange to find strength in the threats to their loved ones and defeat the evil forever.

Love Triangles

Twilight and *The Hunger Games* are very different from each other; however, the love triangles are startlingly similar.

> When one compares only the love triangles, a cascade of similarities present themselves. The heroines, both considering themselves gawky and unlovable, have two boys competing for them. One is wealthy, pale, high-class, and set apart. He's a pacifist and model of restraint. The other is "the boy next door," darker-skinned, happiest in the outdoors or working with his hands. This one is more hot-tempered, even violent

as he trains in combat. Family pressure guides her toward this one, a childhood and family friend. After some struggle, the heroine chooses the first. Why do both heroines choose the same way? What does this reveal about today's young women and their fantasies? (Frankel, *Katniss* 53-54)

All right, Jace isn't a pacifist and Simon isn't a savage (though he does have outdoorsy talent with a bow and performs in a rock band). However, Clary's two men otherwise fit this trope perfectly. All three heroines have a prince charming, set apart and used to the perks of magic or wealth. He's isolated, a bit brooding and controlled. He also has artistic skills: Peeta is a painter, Edward a musician like Jace. These skills and magical or high-class background encourage the heroine to grow toward a higher spiritual plane – he gives her unique opportunities and offers a catalyst to a new way of thinking. In turn, the heroine is his first love, the one who changes his entire outlook. This pattern appears in other recent stories, including *The Selection, Divergent, Delirium, Tiger's Curse, True Blood, The Vampire Diaries,* and *Snow White and the Huntsman.*

A racial metaphor appears when Katniss picks pale indoor-raised Peeta over olive-skinned Gale and Bella chooses the dead-white Edward over Native American Jacob. This may reflect "an image of the paleness of aristocracy, privilege, and civilization deeply rooted in America's European ancestry as desirable. For the wealthy, pale prince to choose the less privileged commoner echoes Cinderella, an enticing fairytale for women that cuts deep into our childhood fantasies" (Frankel, *Katniss* 60). Indeed, when Clary dreams of dancing with both of them at a ball: Simon is dressed in black, with "dark hair" and "lightly browned skin" while Jace is in white "and his hair and eyes looked more gold than ever" (*Bones* 161). The coloring theme repeats here, with Jace highlighted in gold like royalty.

Tessa, Jem, and Will have a much more unusual love triangle: Tessa loves both of them equally but in different ways. The two men would do anything rather than hurt each other, unlike most romantic rivals who view each other as competitors. Most unusually of all, Tessa finds a way to be with them both. Clare explains:

> I really wanted to write a love triangle that was a perfect triangle. Most love triangles are really sort of a love "V." Point A and point B and a girl or boy who's beloved by those two people. But I wanted to do something that was a real triangle where every point has a relationship. So, you know, Will and Jem's blood brother relationship was as important as their love for Tessa and her love for them. So no part of this triangle could be broken without heartbreak. And that is what I think makes

Myths and Motifs in *The Mortal Instruments*

it difficult to read because you can't conceive of how you could get out of this situation without smashing one point of that triangle. And smashing any point is going to bring pain to everybody else. (Brissey "Cassandra Clare Talks Clockwork Prince")

Tessa ends up with the active, ill-mannered Will instead of the aloof, controlled Jem. Jem, a musician with exotic silver hair and eyes, is the pale artistic prince. This choice seems more in keeping with nineteenth-century gothic fantasies than the twenty-first century ideal. Indeed, only in recent times has the heroine always chosen the prince: Jane Eyre prefers dark, savage Rochester over her polite cousin. Cathy, a savage herself, is famous for loving gypsy-born Heathcliff over the aristocratic Linton.

> In the days of Victorian repression and before, women confined to their homes dreamed of the smoldering gothic hero, dark and melancholy, who would tear them from their dull, safe princes. He might be the mysterious sheik, the evil vampire, the dark foreigner. Today, however, teens see too much brutality. The savage, all around us in our lives and on the news, has lost his savor. Girls are retreating to the safer Cinderella fantasy of their childhood. Fairytale adaptations are overwhelmingly popular right now, with a resurgence in young adult novelizations, movies, and television shows. (Frankel, *Katniss* 60)

Clare encountered confusion and criticism from some fans who were annoyed that Tessa finds a way to get both lovers without having to choose. She responded by pointing out that life isn't this neat and tidy: most people love more than one person in their entire lives, especially after one dies or leaves forever.

> The *Clockwork* series has a love triangle, but it is also *about* love triangles, and like I've said before, is about what I wanted to say about love and about life. We are taught by many romance narratives that one can feel only one great love in a lifetime. Even if, as in the example here, the person you married, and loved, has been dead eighty years, the idea has been entrenched in us by media that loving someone else next, as much, diminishes or undermines that love. It is the purpose of the Disney "happily ever after" coda – we don't *want* to know what happens after the couple gets together: we assume an unclear sort of happiness awaits, but don't want to know if they fight, or one of them dies first, or any of the things that happen in actual life. Their love story ends when the curtain comes down, and therefore they are preserved in happiness forever, like flies in amber – and none of the messiness of real life, of loss and death, of cycles of happiness and sorrow, of the inevitability of aging, ever touch them at all.

I think this is an actually damaging way to think about love. Love, even romantic love, is not something you only feel once and forever, and to have loved one person does not make love that you feel later less. Love isn't a zero sum game: we're not issued a bucket of love at birth and the more of it we give out, the less we have (in fact, the opposite is true.) Very few people remain with their first loves forever; very few people *love only one person romantically ever in their lives*. Yet we are told that is the ideal we should strive for. That if love is followed by loss life is destroyed, and an attempt to move on cheapens the love we had before. It's a narrative I've seen ruin people's lives, literally, and so it's one I both reject, but wanted to explore. ("Clockwork Princess: Spoiler Questions and Answers")

There are other less central love triangles in the Shadowhunters' books as well. Luke and Simon share several plot points after Hodge warns Clary that she's treating Simon as her mother treated Luke. Hodge notes: "When your mother was young, she had a best friend, just as you have Simon. They were as close as siblings…As they grew older, it became clear to everyone around them that he was in love with her, but she never saw it. She always called him 'friend.'" (*Bones* 334). Both men lose their loves to a flashier, more attractive teen. After, both act recklessly and thus are turned into Downworlders. Both are even skilled with the bow. And both must settle for a platonic friendship with their loves, though Luke gets more after decades of waiting. However, while Valentine betrays Luke and tries to kill him, Jace gives his blood to save Simon. The new generation is healing the mistakes of the old.

Simon and two girlfriends becomes another love triangle in the second trilogy, or perhaps a love quadrangle with Jordan thrown in. Simon's dating two girls causes pain to all of them, while the ignored Maureen loses her life. Love triangles are messy and awful – they lead to emotional pain, or more physical pain in Maia's case. However, people like to feel desired and fought over. And with today's fairytale resurgence, love triangles are taking a new hold on teen fiction.

Neutrality

Another quote from Dante's *Inferno* doesn't appear in the series but seems relevant: "The hottest places in hell are reserved for those who, in times of great moral crisis, maintain their neutrality." In a world of good Shadowhunters and evil demons, there are neutral figures from fairies and vampires to Magnus Bane. Clary's anger at their limited help is justified, as they all must share the world. Magnus helps throughout both series – though he insists he isn't interested in mortal problems, he intervenes to help Tessa and Will, just as he helps Clary, Jace, and the Lightwoods, even going into battle on repeated occasions. Characters like Raphael and Camille, who run whenever there's danger, are far more contemptible.

Words and Actions

As Tessa's Aunt Harriet comments, men reveal themselves by their actions not their words. This is prophetic for Will, who claims to go out drinking and wenching every night but is in fact lying. Sebastian begins to convince Clary to sympathize with him, but she sees his violence as he kills for pleasure. Luke, by contrast, rejects Clary and says he's not her father, but after a lifetime of caring for her, she knows he actually is, or should be. She orders her mother to go after him and marry him.

Prejudice

Clary sees in a vision that Valentine's intolerance is actually born of jealousy. She enables Downworlders and Shadowhunters to share abilities and trust each other like brothers, ending the feud. Sebastian claims that Valentine's idiotic prejudice ruled him and Sebastian is now wiser. However, he and Jace speak mockingly of mundanes who don't realize the sacrifice Shadowhunters make for them, and Jace says the Shadowhunters deserve to rule over them. Clary calls Luke a "slimy downworlder" (*Bones* 385) upon discovering he's a werewolf, but she quickly regrets it, especially when another werewolf dies defending them.

Later Clary compares Valentine's pureblood policies to "one of those creepy white power guys" (*Bones* 405). He's like Voldemort, leading a secret society within the magic world willing to wipe out mundanes for blood purity and power. When Valentine tells the Angel Raziel he's fighting heaven's battle, Raziel retorts that heaven doesn't desire humans to kill other people with souls – clearly, religious wars and fundamentalist thinking are something Clare is fighting against.

Minorities appear often in the series—Aline and Helen are lesbians, Maia is mixed-race as are Magnus and Jem, Cristina Rosales in *Dark Artifices* is Mexican. "The head of the vampires is Hispanic and Christian: the vampires we see in the Hotel Dumort are white and black and Hispanic and Asian." ("Simon Lewis, Jewish Vampire"). The Clave meetings feature Shadowhunters from across the world. Most of these are heroic characters, but all of them are real people rather than stereotypes.

Simon, of course, is Jewish, and he's a sincere believer, judging by the number of time he tries to mention God. Clare comments:

> I wanted the scene where Simon recoils from the Stars of David

in his cell in City of Glass to mean as much for a Jewish reader as the scene in Dracula might to a Christian reader – that as deep an emotional and spiritual importance is attached to the Magen David by Jews as is attached to the crucifix by Christians. I was happy when one of my beta-readers, Steve Berman told me that the scene where Simon thinks he is going to die in City of Ashes so he tries to recite the Shema ** (Shema Yisrael Adonai eloheinu Adonai ehad) – but chokes on the words – made him cry.

…

And lastly, Simon is Jewish because of all the characters, he is the most like me, and *I* am Jewish…The general assumption is that I am Christian because the general default assumption, from my Western readers, is that everyone is. I'm glad Simon is not. ("Simon Lewis, Jewish Vampire")

It's easy for a writer to make all the characters white. By tackling this "default assumption," Clare creates a more varied, realistic world her many readers can identify with.

Clare also faces the judgments other people make, both in many angry comments fans have emailed to her (often suggesting books with gay characters should have "warning labels") and the hurtful comments people experience in real life. When Alec comes out as gay and Simon comes out as a vampire, both struggle with truly intolerant parents. For Alec in particular, Clare describes the thousand pinpricks of judgmental comments, including his father's wondering what "turned him gay." Clare's sympathies are on Alec's side, even as she shows the pain these thoughtless remarks offer. By depicting Magnus and Alec as loving, even while struggling through the same trust issues other couples face, Clare pictures their relationship sympathetically, and charms fans' sympathies in turn.

"Family is More than Blood"

Jace learns to accept that his fathers, either Valentine or his birth father, don't matter. His true identity is Jace Lightwood because that's who he's chosen to become. Many times Luke is mentioned as fathering Clary and Simon, endlessly giving them rides and taking them to his farm. They have a second home in his house all their lives.

In contrast to these are Sebastian's chilling demands for affection when he confronts Jocelyn or touches Clary in a creepy, incestuous fashion. Like Sebastian, Valentine presides over Jace and Clary at a disturbing parody of a family dinner. Clary is disturbed when Valentine and then Sebastian wants to drag her and Jace home to play happy families.

Myths and Motifs in *The Mortal Instruments*

"One can build one's own family," Jem says (*Clockwork Angel* 472). He, Will, Jessamine, Henry and Charlotte are all orphans, but they become a close-knit family of siblings. When Tessa arrives they welcome her as well. Tessa discovers that Nate, the brother she loved and protected all her life, has betrayed her. He actively hates her and wants to give her to the evil Magister. But Charlotte welcomes her to the Institute and makes it clear she's one of them. Even obnoxious Jessamine buys her dresses and urges her to borrow more. Will too comes to realize that "without Charlotte, without Henry, without Jem or Tessa or Sophie or even the bloody Lightwoods, he did not want to be a Shadowhunter. They were his family" (*Clockwork Princess* 473). He and Cecily can visit their parents, but to return home they must go to the Institute.

Kid Power

Maryse makes mistakes, from summoning the Inquisitor to not believing Jace is innocent in the matter of Valentine. When Jace is thrown in prison, Alec, Isabelle, and Clary rush to the rescue. Jace and Clary are the ones to stop Valentine, Isabelle slices off Sebastian's hand. In the third book, the adults spend most of their time in pointless, frustrating meetings while the teens literally save the world. The second trilogy sees Maryse torn between Jace and the Clave once more, while Clary and her friends save the day.

Luke is the only trustworthy adult. Even his early rejection of Clary is for her own protection. His werewolf status makes him an outsider, like Hagrid or Haymitch in other series. However, most of the adults are parents like Clary's and Simon's mothers, who must not be told the truth, or the hidebound, corrupt Clave. The Lightwood children grow up trusting the Clave and its Inquisitor, but both are proven to be hate-filled adults desperate to cling to power and seek revenge, not justice. In both timelines, it is led by a self-serving traitor. Tessa, Will, Charlotte, and their friends likewise save the day while the Clave squabbles and meets endlessly. The new generation is a bright light of hope destroying the corruption of their parents.

Feminism

Clare explains that messages of feminism are "very important," adding the following statement:

> I think we are now in a place where readers expect that girls will not hang back waiting for boys to save them, but will be fighting right alongside them. We are no longer surprised at the idea of a strong, tough woman warrior. One of the most common requests I get from readers is, "We want to see Clary fight more! We want to see her kill

more demons!" ("Cassandra Clare's Interview with German Magazine, Daisuki")

Jace notes that women have always been Iron Sisters and weapons teachers. He adds:

> There have always been women in the Clave – mastering the runes, creating weaponry, teaching the Killing Arts – only a few were warriors, ones with exceptional abilities. They had to fight to be trained. Maryse was a part of the first generation to be trained as a matter of course. (*Bones* 141)

Thus Charlotte fights but Jessamine doesn't.

Cecily fights with cleverness, goading the giant worm to bite itself. She thinks of herself as a heroine riding into the Shadowhunters' lair to rescue her brother. She doesn't want to "make an advantageous marriage and give the world children" (*Clockwork Princess* 377) – she wants to be a powerful Shadowhunter and warrior. Though Will fears for her, he supports her, giving her the ruby necklace and saying, "It will help keep you safe, which is how I want you, and help you be a warrior, which is what you want." (*Clockwork Princess* 252). Similarly, Tessa learns to fight, and Jem and Will respect her skills even while teaching her to improve them. Jem only tells her to stay out of a fight because she's in a giant ballgown – as he points out, even Will couldn't fight in such a thing. Tessa, of course, fights, runs, and cleverly escapes her captors, until she summons the angel's power to save everyone. Tessa explains, "We are cleverer and more determined and more patient than men. Men may be stronger but it is women who endure." (*Clockwork Princess* 118).

Benedict Lightwood is only repeating the beliefs of his time when he claims Charlotte cannot run the Institute, as women think only "with the emotions of the heart" (*Clockwork Prince* 21). However, when it's revealed that he has affairs with demons and ignores Clave law, his character is revealed as suspect. Consul Wayland similarly calls Charlotte "flighty, emotional, passionate, and disobedient," none of which is true (*Clockwork Princess* 74). Worse, he himself is corrupt. Consul Wayland only appoints Charlotte so he can rule through her – when she challenges his authority he blocks her from doing her duty. He craves power and control over the Shadowhunter world, even power he has no right to.

More importantly, Charlotte does a capable job in all aspects of her role, even though she must use her husband as a figurehead, a common tool of the time. Charlotte eventually becomes the first female consul, in a time when Victoria ruled but few women had political power. The entire Council (minus the scheming Consul) is behind her, even while she defies the law. She's wise, fair, clever, and compassionate – the perfect leader.

Myths and Motifs in *The Mortal Instruments*

"I think as women we've always been very used to growing up reading and identifying with male protagonists, especially in fantasy. There's a saying in publishing that girls will read about boys, but boys will only read about boys and it's important to give women strong heroines," Clare explains (Nathan). All of her series feature strong, powerful heroines on the Chosen One's path as well as female fighters. Tessa and Clary learn to fight but are not known for their combat skills. However, their magic allows them to save the day uniquely, in ways they choose for themselves.

> Nineties girl power has offered modern fans some flexibility. Their heroine can disguise herself as a boy to ride off to battle and behead warlords. She can marry or remain independent. She can be any race, color, age, nationality, or orientation, and be celebrated for who she is, as she is. She can wear Xena's cleavage-enhancing armor. She can be a superhero saving innocents as Elektra does, or Fray, on the dark streets of our future. Or she can be Buffy, the warrior girl in pink miniskirts and lip gloss, who will be the epic warrior as *she* determines and rewrite her own legend of the Chosen One. This is the new feminism, one that encourages each woman to make her choice and become the self she desires—whether in a white prom dress, a leather jacket, or both. (Frankel, *Buffy* 204)

Shades of Grey

Hodge describes "the moral absolutism of the young, which allows for no concessions" (*Bones* 374). Clary begins the story convinced there's only good and evil. But moments after Hodge's speech, she discovers her childhood protector Luke Graymark is as gray as his name – he's a Downworlder who lied and rejected Clary, but he's a good person who's been protecting her all this time. He tells her she is Valentine's daughter, and Jace discovers he's Valentine's son. The complicated world of loving evil people who have love to offer in return appears in Valentine and his son Jonathan. Jace thinks of himself as pure Shadowhunter, pure code. But when he discovers Valentine was his beloved father and it would be wrong to love Clary, he's conflicted. Hodge himself is a strong example of this. Clary discovers Hodge betrayed his entire family...but also called a healer for Alec. He truly loves his charges, but he also betrays them to have a life for himself with Valentine. Inquisitor Herondale is Jace's enemy, seeking revenge for her son's death; however, she does the right thing in the end.

Moral ambiguity comes up a great deal in the series. Clare explains:

> What interests me about the Shadowhunters is that they're warriors with a basically good purpose, whose good purpose has become

> distorted over time with laziness, arrogance and greed (living off the blood money of slaughtered Downworlders, for instance.) One of the main themes of the series is moral ambiguity (the Shadowhunters are not so good, the Downworlders are not so bad, except some of them are bad, but some of them aren't, and the Seelie Queen is bad, but maybe she isn't, and even the Angel is actually kind of vicious and terrifying) – but I think in order to have moral ambiguity, you need moral certainty as well. There is at least one moral certainty in the series: demons are evil. ("Cassandra Clare's Interview with German Magazine, Daisuki")

Even Mortmain is a figure of pity, as the more vicious of the Shadowhunters slaughtered his parents and set him on the path toward revenge. Further, he does good in creating Tessa, protecting her, and teaching her to use her powers. Tessa understands him and pities him somewhat, even while battling him to save her friends.

"We Always Have Choices"

When Jace faces his father and can't bear to kill him, when the Lightwoods are told to obey the Inquisitor, when Clary is tied up and helpless, all must realize that they have choices. Doing what they're told will doom the world, while acting for what they know is right can save it.

> Jem seemed to look through her then, as if he were seeing something beyond her, beyond the corridor, beyond the Institute itself. "Whatever you are physically," he said, "male or female, strong or weak, ill or healthy – all those things matter less than what your heart contains. If you have the soul of a warrior, you are a warrior. All those other things, they are the glass that contains the lamp, but you are the light inside." He smiled them, seeming to have come back to himself, slightly embarrassed. "That's what I believe." (*Clockwork Angel* 283)

Of course, depriving people of their choices, as Clary does Jace in *Lost Souls*, is a great betrayal. Jem points out that if Tessa asked him to betray his friends, as Nate did Jessamine, he'd know she didn't really love him. Likewise Simon explains to Clary that while he loves her and would give his life for her, he wouldn't kill innocents or burn down the world. He worries what "evil Jace" will ask Clary to do and whether she'll do it. Sebastian too demands heedless love and trust, demanding Clary's loyalty even as he murders and creates a race of evil Shadowhunters. As it's pointed out repeatedly, Sebastian can't really love.

Myths and Motifs in *The Mortal Instruments*

Forgiveness

"Do you think it's possible to do something so bad, even if you didn't mean to do it, that you can never come back from it? That no one can forgive you?" Simon asks (*Fallen Angels* 417). In fact, Jace, Simon, and Jordan all do unforgiveable things, but their friends and loved ones do in fact forgive them. In the Silent City, Jem says he'd excuse Tessa for committing any sin against him. He's equally generous with Will, admitting he'd forgive him for thoughtless cruelty without an apology. Similarly, Will knows that his Shadowhunter family would pity and love him if he told him the truth about his behavior. Luke echoes this at the end of *Fallen Angels* when he points out that truly loving someone means forgiving them anything.

Faith

As Charlotte says, "Faith has brought us this far; it will bring us a little farther. The Angel watches over us, and we shall win out" (*Clockwork Princess* 426). Jem shows faith in Will even when he's cruel and when finally he reveals he loves Jem's beloved. Charlotte and her friends show faith in Gideon then Gabriel, and both men finally respond with loyalty, offering her their faith in return. Even when Tessa and Will are imprisoned together in Mortmain's lair, she tells him that together they still have hope to overpower or trick Mortmain.

The Lightwood children have extraordinary faith in Jace, which never wavers, even when they discover his origins. Everyone in Clary's life: her mother, Luke, Simon, and Jace, all believe she can be something extraordinary. When the Shadowhunters willingly take on her runes, they find the key to save them all.

Of course, love means having faith in the other person. Jace and Jocelyn both come to realize that they can't protect Clary from all danger, or even stop her being a Shadowhunter. Alec tries to make Magnus's choices for him, and Magnus is infuriated. Tessa, Will, and Jem all feel great guilt for the others' fates, but must all come to understand that each chose the best path.

Lies

"Lies and secrets, Tessa, they are like a cancer in the soul. They eat away what is good and leave only destruction behind," her aunt's spirit warns her (*Clockwork Prince* 395). Jem tells Tessa his secret, though they don't know each other well, and Magnus pledges Alec that he'll tell him anything. Will is destroyed by the demon Marbas's lie, which takes everyone he loves from him. Likewise, the lie that Clary and Jace are related is their greatest source of misery. Traitors are everywhere, in both series, as Shadowhunters turn fundamentalist and self-centered. The worst liar is Jocelyn, who controls everything Clary sees and remembers. Everything Tessa and Clary know about themselves is a lie, and both quest to discover their stolen powers and heritages. Every lie becomes an obstacle and every truth brings the characters greater freedom.

Upcoming Projects

The Bane Chronicles

Ten Magnus Bane short stories are scheduled for 2013 leading up to the movie release date. The new series, called *The Bane Chronicles*, is being written by Clare and two other YA authors: Sarah Rees Brennan and Maureen Johnson. Brennan notes:

> I think Magnus is always fun for readers to have in a scene, because when other people are floundering in uncertainty, there's Magnus to say 'I know what's up.' …But the thing is, the text never encourages you to dismiss him: he's funny, but he's not a clown, he has the answers, but he's not an exposition machine. He's a magical mentor figure, but he's not at all in the Gandalf mode. He's one half of this gay romance that's charmed thousands of readers, but he's not defined by his relationship. He's so vivid, and he's so much his own person, that he's unforgettable." (qtd. in Markey)

Fans describe loving Magnus Bane for his looks, wardrobe, and funny wit, but mostly his ability to be himself and also give his heart to another person (Markey).

"The Bane Chronicles" is being published online and released through Amazon in an attempt to take advantage of today's new media. A publication date has not been set for the print collection, though it will likely come out in 2014, after the movie. The stories are on Amazon for order or preorder, while synopses of the stories with release dates are available at Cassandraclare.com.

The Film

Unique Features partners Bob Shaye and Michael Lynne will team with Constantin Film to produce *The Mortal Instruments: City of Bones*. The partners have set Jessica Postigo (*Operation Checkmate*) to write the script. "Cassandra Clare has created a truly unique, imaginative and universally appealing world seen through the eyes of a 16-year-old girl," said Robert Kulzer, who will produce for Constantin. Martin Moszkowiez (*Resident Evil*) will be executive producer (Fleming).

The props and set will be the closest to how Clare envisioned them in the book, as the designers have asked her for lots of tips (*Cassandra Clare's Clockwork Princess Bus Tour*).

Myths and Motifs in *The Mortal Instruments*

> "It was very reassuring to come on set and see everything covered in runes and replicated down to the last detail," Clare says. "The movie was definitely made by people who love the books and wanted to do right by them." (Brissey, "First Look")

Hollywood is certainly looking for "The Next Twilight," and *Mortal Instruments* may fit. Lots of YA series have been optioned recently: The films *Divergent* and *Daughter of Smoke & Bone* are coming soon, along with the rest of *The Hunger Games* series.

> Some industry insiders see Clare's Mortal Instruments series as the most likely to inherit the *Twilight* mantle. "I think that's the really big one. It's got the biggest fan base online from our experience," says Breanne Heldman, senior editor at MTV's NextMovie. *City of Bones*, the first in a planned six-book series, shares some of the ingredients that helped *Twilight* become a hit, like an Everygirl heroine, Clary – to be played by Lily Collins – who learns about the supernatural from a most appealing boy. "Jace, the male character – he's very Edward," says Heldman, "but with more attitude." (Vilkomerson and Lee)

Lily Collins and Jamie Campbell Bower star as the loving teens, with Jonathan Rhys Meyers from *The Tudors* as the evil Valentine. Clare describes being a fan of Robert Sheehan (Simon Lewis) from the British TV series *Misfits*, though she only met Lily and Jamie during auditions. Clare adds:

> I still find it amazing that they first time they met was in their audition for Clary and Jace! The first time I really got to talk to them was at dinner, and we were talking about the chemistry test Jamie did with Lily. Lily was our Clary and we were looking for Jace and I said, "You guys were amazing, anybody could see that Jamie just seemed to be Jace." (Nathan)

Describing them, she notes:

> They're very close and I begin to see them now in my head when I'm writing. I wrote Clary as very petite and delicate with freckles, because it's a lot of fun to do a reversal because she turns out to be strong, which is very like Lily. There's a sense of sweetness about her, but she can also transform into being really tough and strong and an ass-kicker, which is a lot of fun too. And Jamie IS Jace – he's exactly the same! Very sarcastic and funny and very beautiful.

The Shadowhunter's Codex

> Ms. Clare has eked out time to compile "The Shadowhunter's Codex" with the help of husband Joshua Lewis….The Codex, referenced in both

"The Mortal Instruments" and "The Internal Devices" is the official guidebook to the world of Shadowhunters. Through Clary's copy, readers will become privy to the warriors' history, demon taxonomy, rune catalog and training manual, among many other tidbits. Clary's drawings and notes are also included! (Wilkinson, "Cassandra Clare's 'Shadowhunter's Codex'")

This long-awaited guide to the Shadowhunters' world, complete with drawings of runes, lists of demons, and much more, is coming October 2013. The Shadowhunter's Codex is referenced often in the series, as the book Clary and Tessa use to learn about their new world. Tessa is even pictured holding the book on the cover of *Clockwork Princess* (*Cassandra Clare's Clockwork Princess Bus Tour*). Clary is described filling her copy with notes and sketches, and many quotes from the book are included in the series. Clare's website and Tumblr page offer even more. Fans will delight in holding Clary's copy and entering the world of the Shadowhunters for themselves.

The City of Heavenly Fire

City of Heavenly Fire, coming March 2014, will conclude Clary and Jace's epic. A few things are certain: Much of the conflict has been set up in *City of Lost Souls* as Sebastian creates a race of dark Shadowhunters. More and more demons have been pouring into the world, and Clary and her friends must try to find a way to block them. "A great war with the demons is coming, and the Clave is woefully unprepared," Sebastian warns (*Lost Souls* 345).

A year later, Jem tells Tessa that the recent conflicts have changed the nature of Shadowhunters forever, and the summary for *The Dark Artifices* hints at a similar recreation of the world as the Shadowhunters all "stand on the edge of oblivion." Some heroes will die or be grievously wounded, for this kind of revolution always has casualties. Most of our seventeen-year-old heroes will earn their adulthood through trial, battle, and heroism. And the book will be huge. Clare comments:

> I have already come to terms with the fact that City of Heavenly Fire is going to be gigantic. My future involves a lot of typing. There is no getting around it. I was in my editor's office today and she was like, "Clockwork Princess was long…so long…" and I pointed out that Heavenly Fire was going to be EVEN LONGER so she put her head down on her desk. I revived her with a cupcake. ("Clockwork Princess Questions & Answers – Spoilery")

She says to expect "a hard-fought battle and a lot of epic romance" (Minzesheimer). Indeed, romantic conflicts are also left to be wrapped up: Isabelle and Simon, Magnus and Alec, Jocelyn and Luke, Jordan and Maia, and of course Clary and Jace. Any number of these couples might marry at series end or at least declare a more permanent relationship. "I think it should seriously be called City of Delayed Weddings," Clare noted, though she refused to spoil whether Luke and Jocelyn (or any other characters) would tie the knot in the book. She added that readers are "unlikely" to see *Infernal Devices* characters besides Brother Zachariah, but that they will likely appear in the *Dark Artifices* books (*Cassandra Clare's Clockwork Princess Bus Tour*).

The Dark Artifices

Shadowhunter Emma Carstairs was orphaned in the epic battle of *The Mortal Instruments*. Now, she's determined to be the best of Shadowhunters. However, as she trains in the Los Angeles Institute, she finds herself falling for her best friend and parabatai Julian, the one person forbidden to her by Shadowhunter law. As this series returns to the intrigues of demons and fairies, it also reveals the truth behind the parabatai bond.

"The series follows Emma Carstairs, the fiercest warrior and most skilled young Shadowhunter since Jace Wayland, and Emma's sworn partner in arms, Julian Blackthorn," Margaret K. McElderry Books announced. "Despite Emma's complicated feelings for Julian, the two must band together to investigate a demonic plot that stretches from the warlock-run nightclubs of the Sunset Strip to the enchanted sea that pounds the beaches of Santa Monica." (Italie). The series is scheduled for 2015. Clare eagerly anticipates setting the book in her hometown, with beach and water magic. She notes:

> "The Dark Artifices" takes place in 2012. Five years after the events of "The Mortal Instruments." That would make the characters of "TMI" – Clary, Jace, Simon – 22, 23 years old (well, the ones who survive, anyway!). (Wilkinson, "'Mortal Instruments' Author")

"The Dark Artifices" series title comes from "The Annals of Imperial Rome" by Tacitus: "It would have been less ignominious to die by the dark artifices of Tiberius." When the Roman Valerius Asiaticus was falsely accused by the treacherous lady Messalina, he was only allowed the favor of choosing the manner of his death. He said, "It would have been less ignominious to die by the dark artifices of Tiberius or the fury of Caligula [his enemies], than thus to fall by the base devices of a woman" (Tacitus 214). A woman's treachery may come to play in the series.

As Clare reports: "I just liked the phrase. And all the kids in the [Blackthorn] family have Greek or Roman names – Helen, Julian, Marcus, Olivia and even Tiberius. (Poor Tiberius.)" She adds that the Blackthorns' father is a classicist, obsessed with Greek and Roman works. (Wilkinson, "'Mortal Instruments' Author"). "I know readers will come to love Emma, Mark, Cristina and Julian just as they have loved Jace, Clary, Will, Tessa and Jem," she said. "Readers have often asked what will happen in the Shadowhunter world after the events of the 'Mortal Instruments' and this series will give them a chance to find out" (Italie).

On Tumblr, she describes the enormous family, complete with Cassandra Jean's Shadowhunter Tarot cards that reveal aspects of their personalities. The eldest sister, Aline Penhallow's girlfriend Helen, shows up in *City of Lost Souls* as does her brother Julian. Clare notes:

> Mark and Helen have a different mother than the rest of their siblings. They have, as mentioned by Alec in City of Lost Souls, "some faerie blood." Above, Mark has the Tarot Card of the Chariot, which is for reasons I will not expound on here. ("Blackthorns and co")

The Chariot, reimagined as "The Changeling," surrounded by black dogs, represents an external battle or conflict. It also indicates a union of opposites like earth and water, requiring control to give them a single direction. The charioteer fights alone, armored against the forces that threaten him.

Next comes Julian or Jules, an artist and the caregiver of the family. He's more of a formal painter than Clary is. His best friend is Emma Carstairs, the born warrior who follows in Jace's footsteps. She carries a very special sword and is on a mission to find out what happened to her parents. Julian and Emma are parabatai and incredibly close. "Her best girl friend is Cristina, who came to the LA institute from Mexico City. I gave her the card of the High Priestess and surrounded her with roses because that's the meaning of her last name – Rosebush," Clare adds. Her tarot card is titled The Believer, on which she appears with heart, roses, and medallion.

> Cristina Rosales' name is taken from the first name and the last name of two different girls who attended a signing I did in Mexico City years ago. Almost everyone who came up to me asked if I would write a Mexican Shadowhunter girl so I said I would, if they would help me – I wanted to know what Mexican girls wanted out of a character who shared their heritage. *worldwidenotes* gave me the explicit note that Cristina should be "strong in her faith" so I decided to explore some of the intricacies of Shadowhunter faith through her. I haven't written a character who is strong in their faith before, and it's been interesting. I like Cristina a lot – she is shyer than Emma, but very strong and unwavering in her loyalty and morals. She wears a medallion above that says *Blessed be the Angel my strength which teaches my hands to war and my fingers to fight* (which is me, as usual, mauling passages from the Bible.) ("Blackthorns and co")

Myths and Motifs in *The Mortal Instruments*

Then we see the fifteen-year-old twins, Livia and Tiberius. Ty cares more for mysteries than fighting and wants to be a detective like Sherlock Holmes. "Livvy is the 'protector' because she protects Ty from everything, since he's hopeless at fighting and she's a skilled fencer and swordfighter. She also interprets the world for him when he finds other people's behavior confusing." Drusilla and Octavian, or Tavvy, are the youngest. Their shared card calls them The Dreamer and The Innocent. Dru is just old enough to have developed an important crush and Tavvy is too young for runes, but both have roles to play in the story.

The titles will be *Lady Midnight*, *Prince of Shadows*, and *The Queen of Air and Darkness*. The source of the latter, as Clare mentions on her blog, is a poem by A.E. Housman. The phrase is a reference to "the prince of the power of the air" in Ephesians 2.2, which is a force of evil (Housman, *Letters* 377). It's also used to describe the Unseelie Queen in Emma Bull's popular urban fantasy.

> Her strong enchantments failing,
> Her towers of fear in wreck,
> Her limbecks dried of poisons
> And the knife at her neck,
>
> The Queen of air and darkness
>   Begins to shrill and cry,
> 'O young man, O my slayer
>   To-morrow you shall die.'
> O Queen of air and darkness
>   I think 'tis truth you say,
> And I shall die to-morrow;
>   But you shall die to-day.
> (Housman, "Last Poems," 100)

The Iron Trial

The Iron Trial is the first book in an epic fantasy series that I'm cowriting with Holly Black. *The Iron Trial* will be released in September 2014 by Scholastic Books. Four books will follow, one for year of Call's life from twelve to seventeen, as he comes of age in a world where child apprentices train to be warriors and dark magicians seek to defeat even death. (FAQ)

"It's also fantasy, and also in our world, but the magic system is very different: it's elemental magic with five elements, and a magical history based in part on the robber baron era of American history," Clare comments ("Hello Ms. Clare").

The five elements would be earth, fire, air, water and spirit traditionally. Holly Black is known for her urban fantasy, from *The Spiderwick Chronicles* to *Tithe, Valiant,* and *Ironside*. Her recent *Curse Workers* series adds con artists to urban fantasy to create something startling, unique, and delightful. This new fantasy collaboration will certainly be quirky, funny, and unusual, as well as charming and creative. Some are calling the series "The Next Harry Potter," and Constantin Films has already snapped up the movie rights.

THE FUTURE OF SHADOWHUNTERS

Clare reports that the generation of readers who grew up on Harry Potter, "the first big teen sensation, feel connected by what they read. They want to share their experiences, usually online …. I think you find a big overlap between kids who are into fantasy and sci-fi and kids who build their own online communities" (Minzesheimer). As one of those fantasy fans with a busy online presence (as she started by writing a *Lord of the Rings* fanfiction series that's still a sensation today), she revolutionizes authorial web presence.

Cassandra Clare has extraordinary online activity, with daily Tumblr posts and active profiles on Facebook and Twitter as well as her own website. Online, she admires fan art and answers questions about the series. Interviews appear on book blogs across the world. There's even a Shadowhunters app for Apple and Android. This is turn has led to publisher support with innovative ideas.

> As the clock ticks down to the March 19 release of *Clockwork Princess*, the third and final book in Cassandra Clare's bestselling The Infernal Devices series, Simon & Schuster Children's Publishing has some innovative marketing plans in place for the novel's launch. One highlight of the campaign was the February 26 online chapter reveal, which YA readers controlled as they collectively tweeted the hashtag #ClockworkPrincess, unlocking the opening chapter word-by-word and enabling fans all over the world to read it simultaneously in real time. And there were lots of them: more than 560,000 tweets were sent in 27 hours, and the hashtag became a top trending topic on Twitter all over the world, including in the U.S., Spain, Italy, Guatemala, Singapore, and the U.K. (Lodge)

"We are always trying to bring something new to the table while promoting Cassie's books," says Anne Zafian, vice president and deputy publisher of

S&S Children's Publishing. "Since she has such good online outreach and social networking skills, it was great that, with the Twitter campaign, the first chapter could be revealed worldwide at one time" (Lodge). On March 19, 2013, coinciding with the release of *Clockwork Princess*, Clare embarked on a weeklong tour in a bus decorated with her book covers and movie promo, in a "cross-country billboard for both the book series and the upcoming movie," as she put it. She added, "Plus, it makes me feel like I'm in a rock band!" (Lodge).

While she delights in her fan responses, she also makes an effort to guide them toward tolerance and do good in her community: Fans that make a donation to the Trevor Project, the leading national organization providing crisis intervention and suicide prevention services to homosexual youth, will receive an exclusive snippet from "The Bane Chronicles." One of those fans will also win a *City of Bones* book signed by the cast and an autographed picture of Godfrey Gao (Magnus Bane) (Markey). She's also hosting a drawing: all those who donate to Project for Awesome will have a chance to be kissed or killed in *City of Heavenly Fire*, and will receive a short story as well.

Of course, publicizing is a full-time occupation, but that isn't all Clare is up to – she has many more writing projects planned:

> "Fortunately, I have much to work on and look forward to," she says. "There are the Bane Chronicles, a series of e-novellas that I'm co-writing with Maureen Johnson and Sarah Rees Brennan, releasing starting this April; The Shadowhunter's Codex [October 2013]; City of Heavenly Fire, the conclusion to The Mortal Instruments [March 2014]; and a brand-new series, The Dark Artifices [2015], which is going to bring me a whole new generation of Shadowhunters to write about." (Lodge)

Across the world, she delights fans with her online postings and her increasingly thick books. One thing is certainly true: On and off the web, this author is making a statement for tolerance, feminism, and the quest for one's own personal power.

Myths and Motifs in *The Mortal Instruments*

BIBLIOGRAPHY

Primary Sources

Alcott, Louisa May. *Little Women*. USA: Little, Brown, and Co., 1922.

Alighieri, Dante. *The Divine Comedy*. Trans. Mark Musa. Indiana: Indiana University Press, 1995.

"Are You There, God? It's Me, Dean Winchester." *Supernatural: The Complete Fourth Season*. Dir. Philip Sgriccia. Warner Brothers, 2008. DVD.

Blake, William. "Preface: Milton" The Poems of William Blake. Ed. W.H. Stevenson. New York: Longman Group, 1972. 488-489

The Book of Enoch. Trans. R.H. Charles. London: Society for Promoting Christian Knowledge, 1917. The Sacred Texts Archive. http://www.sacred-texts.com/bib/boe/index.htm.

Catullus, Gaius Valerius. "Ave atque Vale." *Poem Hunter*. 2003. http://www.poemhunter.com/poem/ave-atque-vale.

Child, Francis James. "Thomas the Rhymer." *The English and Scottish Popular Ballads*. Boston, New York, Houghton, Mifflin and Company, 1886-98. The Sacred Texts Archive. http://www.sacred-texts.com/neu/eng/child/ch037.htm.

Clare, Cassandra. "Author Interview: Cassandra Clare," *The Mortal's Library*, 29 Aug 2010. http://themortalslibrary.blogspot.com/2010/08/author-interview-cassandra-clare.html?spref=tw.

–. "The Blackthorns and Co." March 6 2013. Blog Post. http://cassandraclare.tumblr.com/post/44598318611/the-blackthorns-and-co.

–. "Brother Zachariah" June 2012. Blog Post. http://cassandraclare.tumblr.com/post/23301325236/brother-zachariah.

– . "Cassandra Clare: Bringing the Shadows to Light." *Mystical Lit Lounge*. 20 May 2010. http://pandemoniumclub.livejournal.com/tag/official%20clare%20news:%20interview.

– . *Cassandra Clare's Clockwork Princess Bus Tour*. Menlo Atherton High School Performing Arts Center, Menlo Park, CA. 23 Mar 2013. Personal Appearance.

– . "Cassandra Clare's Interview with German Magazine, Daisuki" *Daisuki*. 12 Jan 2010. http://pandemoniumclub.livejournal.com/tag/official%20clare%20news:%20interview.

–. *City of Ashes*. New York: Simon & Schuster, 2008.

–. *City of Bones*. New York: Simon & Schuster, 2007.

–. *City of Fallen Angels*. New York: Simon & Schuster, 20011.

–. *City of Glass*. New York: Simon & Schuster, 2009.

–. *City of Lost Souls*. New York: Simon & Schuster, 2012.

–. *Clockwork Angel*. USA: Margaret K. McElderry Books, 2010.

–. *Clockwork Prince*. USA: Margaret K. McElderry Books, 2011.
–. *Clockwork Princess*. USA: Margaret K. McElderry Books, 2013.
–. "City of Glass: A Dark Transformation." *Extras, Outtakes/Deleted Scenes & Short Stories from The Mortal Instruments books! Goodreads*. 3 July 2012. http://www.goodreads.com/topic/show/945398-extras-outtakes-deleted-scenes-short-stories-from-the-mortal-instrume.
–. "Clockwork Princess: Spoiler Questions and Answers." 25 Mar 2013. Blog Post. http://cassandraclare.tumblr.com/post/46238458552/clockwork-princess-spoiler-questions-and-answers.
–. "Clockwork Princess Questions & Answers – Spoilery." 8 Mar 2013. Blog Post. http://cassandraclare.tumblr.com/post/44845464969/clockwork-princess-questions-answers-spoilery
–. "Clockwork Princess Trailer Questions." Feb 2013. Blog Post. http://cassandraclare.tumblr.com/post/43688151249/clockwork-princess-trailer-questions
–. "FAQ." *Cassandra Clare: New York Times Bestselling Author*. http://www.cassandraclare.com/frequently-asked-questions/about-the-books.
–. "Hello Ms. Clare." 8 Mar 2013. Blog Post. http://cassandraclare.tumblr.com/post/44506026913/hello-ms-clare-im-enjoying-your-shadowhunter.
–. "I Never." *Geektastic: Stories from the Nerd Herd*. Ed. Holly Black and Cecil Castellucci. New York: Little, Brown, and Co., 2009. 81-110.
–. "The Infernal Devices: Frequently Asked Questions" Shadowhunters.com. http://www.shadowhunters.com/theinfernaldevices/faq.php.
–. "Interview: Cassandra Clare." *The Reader's Quill*. 6 Nov 2008. http://www.readersquill.com/2008/11/interview-cassandra-clare.html.
–. "Introduction." Clare, *Shadowhunters and Downworlders* ix-xiii.
–. "Random Question." April 2012. Blog Post. http://cassandraclare.tumblr.com/post/27358116912/random-question-was-the-real-sebastian-verlac-a.
–. "Simon Lewis, Jewish Vampire." June 2012. Blog Post. http://cassandraclare.tumblr.com/post/31293907714/simon-lewis-jewish-vampire.
"*Clockwork Angel*: An exclusive Q&A with Cassandra Clare." *Novel Novice*. 18 Aug 2010. http://novelnovice.com/2010/08/18/clockwork-angel-an-exclusive-qa-with-cassandra-clare
Dionysius the Areopagite. *The Celestial Hierarchy*. *The Esoteric Archives*. http://www.esoteric.msu.edu/VolumeII/CelestialHierarchy.html.
Dickens, Charles. *A Tale of Two Cities*. USA: Signet Classics, 2007.
Housman, A. E. "Last Poems." *The Collected Poems of A.E. Housman*. New York: Henry Holt and Co., 1965.
–. *The Letters of A. E. Housman*. Oxford: Oxford University Press, 2007.
"Of the Art Goetia." *The Lesser Key of Solomon*. Ed. Joseph H. Peterson. USA: Weiser Books, 2001. http://www.esotericarchives.com/solomon/goetia.htm.

Myths and Motifs in *The Mortal Instruments*

Kipling, Rudyard. *Complete Verse*. New York: Anchor Books, 1989.

de Manhar, Nurho. *The Sefer Ha-Zohar or The Book of Light*. Ed. H.W. Percival. New York: Theosophical Publishing Company, 1914. The Sacred Texts Archive. http://www.sacred-texts.com/jud/zdm/zdm000.htm.

Milton, John. *Paradise Lost*. New York: The Modern Library, 2007.

Palgrave, Francis T., Ed. *The Golden Treasury*. 1875. http://www.bartleby.com/106/67.html.

Sepher Rezial Hemelach: The Book of the Angel Raziel. Ed. Steve Savedow. USA: Weiser Books, 2000.

Shakespeare, William. *The Riverside Shakespeare*, 2nd ed. Boston: Houghton Mifflin, 1997.

Shelley, Mary Wollstonecraft. *Frankenstein: or the Modern Prometheus*. New York: The Cornhill Publishing Co., 1922.

Southworth, E. D. E. N. *The Hidden Hand; or, Capitola the Madcap*. 1859. Ed. Nina Baym. Oxford: Oxford University Press, 1997.

Tacitus, Cornelius. *The Annals and History of Tacitus: A New and Literal English Version*. Oxford: D.A. Talboys, 1839.

Tennyson, Alfred Lord. *Selected Poems*. New York Penguin, 2007.

Secondary Sources

Barfield, Steven and Lisa Russ Spaar. "'Eternal London Haunts Us Still': Thirteen Contemporary Poets Reflect on London as Muse." *The Literary London Journal* Sept 2009. http://www.literarylondon.org/london-journal/september2009/russ.html.

Bettelheim, Bruno. *The Uses of Enchantment*. New York: Alfred A. Knopf, 1977.

Bibeau, Paul. *Sundays with Vlad*. New York: Three Rivers Press, 2007.

Brissey, Breia. "Cassandra Clare Talks 'Clockwork Prince' and Reveals What's Next for her Infernal Devices, Mortal Instruments Series" *EW.com's Shelf Life* 8 Dec. 2011. http://shelflife.ew.com/2011/12/08/cassandra-clare-clockwork-prince-infernal-devices.

–. "Cassandra Clare Talks 'Mortal Instruments' Movie and Teases her Other Series." *EW.com's Shelf Life* 13 Nov 2012. http://shelf-life.ew.com/2012/11/13/cassandra-clare-the-mortal-instruments-movie-city-of-bones/2.

–. "First Look: Cassandra Clare's 'Mortal Instruments' Movie." *EW.com's Shelf Life* 14 Nov 2012. http://shelf-life.ew.com/2012/11/14/mortal-instruments-movie-first-look-cassandra-clare.

Campbell, Joseph with Bill Moyers. *The Power of Myth*. Ed. Betty Sue Flowers. New York: Doubleday, 1988.

Cashdan, Sheldon. *The Witch Must Die*. New York: Basic Books, 1999.
Chevalier, Jean and Alain Gheerbrant. *A Dictionary of Symbols*. USA: Penguin Books, 1997.
Cirlot, J. E. *A Dictionary of Symbols*. New York: Dover Publications, 2002.
Clare, Cassandra, Ed. *Shadowhunters and Downworlders: A Mortal Instruments Reader*. USA: SmartPop, 2013.
Cross, Sarah. "The Art of War." Clare, *Shadowhunters and Downworlders* 20-34.
Curran, Bob. *Encyclopedia of the Undead*. New Jersey: New Page Books, 2006.
Davidson, G. *A Dictionary of Angels. Including the Fallen Angels*. USA: Free Press, 1994.
Downing, Christine, ed. *Mirrors of the Self: Archetypal Images that Shape Your Life*. New York: St. Martin's Press, 1991.
Estés, Clarissa Pinkola. *Women Who Run With the Wolves*. New York: Ballantine Books, 1992.
Fleming, Michael. "'Mortal' Getting Unique Life." *Daily Variety* 305.20 (2009): 18. *Film & Television Literature Index with Full Text*. Web.
Frankel, Valerie Estelle. *Buffy and the Heroine's Journey*. Jefferson, NC: McFarland and Co., 2012.
–. *From Girl to Goddess: The Heroine's Journey through Myth and Legend*. Jefferson, NC: McFarland and Co., 2010.
–. *The Many Faces of Katniss Everdeen: Exploring the Heroine of The Hunger Games*. USA: Winged Lion Press, 2013.
Gaster, Moses. "Two Thousand Years of a Charm against the Child-Stealing Witch." *Folk-Lore Vol 11*, London: The Folk Lore Society, 1900. 129-161.
Ginzburg, Louis. *The Legends of the Jews*. Trans. Henrietta Szold. New York: 1909. The Sacred Texts Archive. http://www.sacred-texts.com/jud/loj/index.htm.
Hanauer, J. E. *Folk-lore of the Holy Land*. Ed. Marmaduke Pickthall. London: Duckworth and Co., 1907. The Sacred Texts Archive. http://www.sacred-texts.com/asia/flhl/flh100.htm.
Hassett, Maurice. "Labarum (Chi-Rho)." *The Catholic Encyclopedia*. Vol. 8. New York: Robert Appleton Company, 1910. http://www.newadvent.org/cathen/08717c.htm.
Italie, Hillel. "Cassandra Clare Signs up for New LA Fantasy Series." Associated Press Archive 14 Mar 2012.
Jewell, Stephen. "Magical Tales Take on Life of their Own." *The New Zealand Herald*. 30 Apr 2011. http://www.nzherald.co.nz/entertainment/news.
Jung, Carl. *Collected Works*. Trans. R.F.C. Hull. Princeton: Princeton University Press, 1968.
Kent, William. "Demons." *The Catholic Encyclopedia*. Vol. 4. New York: Robert

Appleton Company, 1908. http://www.newadvent.org/cathen/04710a.htm.

Kirk, Robert. *Elves, Fauns & Fairies: A Study in Folk-Lore & Psychical Research.* London: David Nutt, 1893. The Sacred Texts Archive. http://www.sacred-texts.com/neu/celt/sce/index.htm.

Link, Kelly and Holly Black. "Immortality and its Discontents." Clare, *Shadowhunters and Downworlders* 167-184.

Lodge , Sally. "Unusual Chapter Reveal for New Cassandra Clare Novel." *Publisher's Weekly.* 7 Mar 2013. http://www.publishersweekly.com/pw/by-topic/childrens/childrens-book-news/article/56248-unusual-chapter-reveal-for-new-cassandra-clare-novel.html.

Maberry, Jonathan and Janice Gable Bashman. *Wanted Undead or Alive: Vampire Hunters and Other Kick-Ass Enemies of Evil.* USA: Citadel, 2010.

Markey, Natalie C. "The Power of Magnus Bane." *Examiner.* 16 Mar 2013. http://www.examiner.com/article/the-power-of-magnus-bane.

Minzesheimer, Bob. "Cassandra Clare Has Teen Fiction down like 'Clockwork.'" *USA Today.* 13 Mar 2013. http://www.usatoday.com/story/life/books/2013/03/13/cassandra-clare-teen-fantasy-fiction/1982437.

Molton, Mary Dian and Lucy Anne Sikes. *Four Eternal Women: Toni Wolff Revisited – A Study in Opposites.* Carmel, CA: Fisher King Press, 2011.

Nathan, Sara. "'They're Clearly in Love': Top-selling Author Cassandra Clare on Being an Unwitting Matchmaker to Lily Collins and Jamie Campbell Bower" *Daily Mail* 19 March 2013. http://www.dailymail.co.uk/tvshowbiz/article-2293560/Author-Cassandra-Clare-unwitting-matchmaker-Lily-Collins-Jamie-Campbell-Bower.html.

Patai, Raphael. *The Hebrew Goddess.* New York: KTAV Publishing House, 1978.

Pearson, Carol and Katherine Pope. *The Female Hero in American and British Literature.* New York: R.R. Bowker, 1981.

Robbins, R. H. *The Encyclopedia of Witchcraft and Demonology.* USA: Bonanza Books, 1988.

Serrano, Pepe. "Alicante, the City of Light." *Official Tourism Site of the Region of Valencia,* 10 June 2010. http://en.comunitatvalenciana.com/files/publicacion/doc/guia_alicante_en_06102010.pdf.

Squire, Charles. *Celtic Myth and Legend.* London: The Gresham Publishing Co., 1905. The Sacred Texts Archive. http://www.sacred-texts.com/neu/celt/cml/cml24.htm.

Stern, David and Mirsky, Mark Jay. *Rabbinic Fantasies: Imaginative Narratives from Classical Hebrew Literature* (Yale Judaica Series). Philadelphia, Jewish Publication Society, 1990. 183-184.

Summers, Montague. *The Vampire, His Kith and Kin.* New York, E.P. Dutton

& Co., 1929. The Sacred Texts Archive. http://www.sacred-texts.com/goth/vkk/vkk00.htm.

Stewart, J. Malcolm. "Strange Apostle: Assessing the Conflict between Today's Christianity and Modern Culture." *Teaching with Harry Potter: Essays on Classroom Wizardry from Elementary School to College.* Ed. Valerie Estelle Frankel. Jefferson, NC: McFarland, 2013. 42-55.

Trachtenberg, Joshua. *Jewish Magic and Superstition: A Study in Folk Religion.* New York: Behrman's Jewish Book House, 1939. The Sacred Texts Archive. http://www.sacred-texts.com/jud/jms/index.htm.

Tracy, Ann B. *The Gothic Novel 1970-1830: Plot Summaries and Index to Motifs.* Louisville: The University Press of Kentucky, 1981

Vilkomerson, Sara, and Stephan Lee. "Find Me a Twilight!" *Entertainment Weekly* 1156 (2011): 83-84.

Walker, Barbara G. *The Woman's Dictionary of Symbols and Sacred Objects.* San Francisco: Harper, 1988.

Walker, Mitchell. "The Double: Same-Sex Inner Helper." Downing 48-52.

Wehr, Demaris. "Animus: The Inner Man." Downing 33-47.

"What is Steampunk?" *The Ministry of Peculiar Occurrences.* Blog Post. http://www.ministryofpeculiaroccurrences.com/what-is-steampunk.

Wilkinson, Amy. "Cassandra Clare's 'Shadowhunter's Codex': Get Your EXCLUSIVE First Look At The Cover!" *Hollywood Crush* 6 Feb 2013. http://hollywoodcrush.mtv.com/2013/02/06/cassandra-clare-shadowhunters-codex/

–. "'Mortal Instruments' Author Cassandra Clare Reveals Details About New 'Dark Artifices' Series." *Hollywood Crush* 15 Mar 2012. http://hollywoodcrush.mtv.com/2012/03/15/dark-artifices-cassandra-clare-interview.

Zweig, Connie. "The Conscious Feminine: Birth of a New Archetype." Downing 183-191.

INDEX

Abbadon, 21, 70
Accords, 51, 127, 133-134
action, 12, 86-87, 94, 110, 112
Adam (Bible), 35, 48-50, 52, 61, 64, 67-68, 70
adamas, 28
adolescence, 24, 38, 40
Aeneid, 100, 124
African, 43, 82
Agramon, 34, 70
Alec Lightwood, 10, 15, 18, 22-23, 34, 58-59, 70, 78, 89, 99, 126-132, 142-145, 147, 150, 152
Alexander, Lloyd, 73, 77
Alicante, 76-78, 124
Alice in Wonderland, 5, 93, 104
allegory, 2, 4, 73
Amatis Herondale, 41, 124, 128, 134
Amazon (archetype), 14-16
Angel (TV show), 79, 84, 86
angel necklace, 39, 41, 42
Angel of Death, 60
Angelology, 49, 65, *see also* Book of the Angel Raziel, Book of Enoch, *Celestial Hierarchy, Lesser Key of Solomon, Summa Theologiae*
angels, 2-3, 8-9, 14, 16-17, 22, 25, 33, 36-37, 47-54, 60-61, 63, 65-66, 68, 71, 79-81, 86-87, 89, 98, 100-101, 113, 124, *see also* Angel of Death, Metatron, Michael, Ithuriel, Raziel
angels in pop culture 79-81

anger, 16, 28, 32, 34, 71, 79, 82, 101, 119, 132, 140, 142
anime, 88, 136
animus, 11-12, 15
Anita Blake, 74, 86
Aphrodite, 10
apples, 10
archetypes, 14, 22, *see also* Amazon, Animus, Chosen One, Dark Mother, dark side, Deceiver, Destroyer, Divine Child, Double, dreams, heroine's journey, Hetaera, Medial Woman, Predator, Shadow, unconscious
archetypes charts, 12, 15
archetypes and tarot 127-129, *see also* symbols
Artemis, 14
artist, 8, 71, 80, 109, 138, 152, 155
Ascension, 22, 45
Asian, 93, 141
Asmodeus, 70-71
athame, 25
Aunt Harriet, 38, 42, 141
authors (classic) *see* Blake, Bronte Sisters, Coleridge, Catullus, Dante, Dickens, Keats, Kipling, Milton, Rossetti, Shakespeare, Tacitus, Tennyson, Virgil
authors (popular) *see* Black, Holly; Brennan, Sarah Rees; Bull, Emma; Hamilton, Laurell K;

Johnson, Maureen; Rice, Anne; Sherman, Delia; Yarbro, Chelsea Quinn
automatons, 41, 44-45, 92-96
Ave Atque Vale, 102
Azazel, 71, 86, 103, 131
Aztec, 43, 82

Babylonia, 50-51, 68
Bane Chronicles, 148, 156
beauty, 16, 24, 53, 74, 76, 90, 101, 105, 116, 129
Being Human, 74, 84
Benedict Lightwood, 44, 96, 129, 144
Bible, 2, 25, 47-48, 50-53, 58-62, 64-66, 71, 73, 78-82, 113, 123, 125, 152, *see also* Adam, angels, apples, David and Jonathan, demons, Eden, Enoch, flood, Glorious, grail, Jacob, Jesus, Joshua, Mark of Cain. Mizpah, prayer, Ruth, serpent
Bible Books *see* Corinthians, Deuteronomy, Ephesians, Exodus, Genesis, Job, Joshua, Maccabees, Proverbs, Revelations, Ruth, Samuel, Song of Songs
binding rune, 20, 27
birds, 10, 68, 115, 118
birth, 7-8, 15, 18, 35-36, 43, 45, 68, 117, 123-124, 133, 136, 140, 142
black, 1, 16, 17, 27-28, 62, 69-70, 96, 101, 112, 118, 132, 138, 152
Black, Holly, 1, 74, 91, 92, 136, 153, 154
Blackfriars Bridge, 76, 114
Blake, 113-114
Bluebeard, 21, 29
Boadicea, 104, 119, 120
Bone Chandelier, 28
Book of Enoch, 52, 65, 71
Book of the Angel Raziel, 2, 48-50, 81
Book of the White, 133
books by Cassandra Clare
see *Bane Chronicles, City of Ashes, City of Bones, City of Fallen Angels, City of Glass, City of Heavenly Fire, City of Lost Souls, Clockwork Angel, Clockwork Prince, Clockwork Princess, Dark Artifices, Iron Trial, Shadowhunter's Codex,*
books, children's and YA
see *Alice in Wonderland, Chronicles of Narnia, Coraline, Daughter of Smoke and Bone, Divergent, Gemma Doyle Trilogy, Golden Compass, Hobbit, Hunger Games, Inkheart, Lord of the Rings, Percy Jackson, Song of the Lioness Quartet, Spiderwick Chronicles, Tithe, Twilight, Wizard of Oz, Wrinkle in Time, Young Wizards*
books, classic *see Aeneid, Alice in Wonderland, Carmilla, The Castle of Otranto, David Copperfield, Divine Comedy, Doctor Faustus,*

Myths and Motifs in *The Mortal Instruments*

Dracula, East of Eden, Frankenstein, Hidden Hand, Ivanhoe, Jane Eyre, Julius Caesar, King Arthur, Macbeth, Midsummer Night's Dream, Paradise Lost, Tale of Two Cities, Tess of the d'Urbervilles, Twelfth Night, Vampyre, Varney the Vampire, Vathek, Wuthering Heights
books, fictional *see* Book of the White, Book of the Angel Raziel, Grey Book, *Shadowhunter's Codex*
books, religious *see* Bible, Book of the Angel Raziel, Book of Enoch, *Celestial Hierarchy, Lesser Key of Solomon, Summa Theologiae*
books timeline 121
box *see* Kwan Yin box, silver box
bracelet, 42, 124
Brennan, Sarah Rees, 33, 86, 148, 156
Bridget Daly, 44
Bronte Sisters, 104, 111
Brooklyn, 5, 21, 75
Brother Enoch, 130
Brother Zachariah, 130-131, 151
Buffy the Vampire Slayer, 12, 32, 73, 84-86, 145
Bull, Emma, 73-74, 92, 153
bus tour, 156

Camille Belcourt, 23, 32, 40, 44, 78, 85, 129-133, 141
Carmilla, 73, 85, 109
Castle of Otranto, 109
Catullus, 2, 102-103
cave, 25, 36
Cecily Herondale, 45, 111, 131-133, 135, 143-144
Celestial Hierarchy, 65
Celtic, 82
Central Park, 75
Characters (*Infernal Devices*) *see* Aunt Harriet, Benedict Lightwood, Bridget Daly, Brother Enoch, Camille Belcourt, Cecily Herondale, Charlotte Branwell, Consul, Dark Sisters, De Quincey, Gabriel Lightwood, Gideon Lightwood, Henry Branwell, Jem Carstairs, Jessamine Lovelace, John Shade, Magister, Magnus Bane, Mortmain, Nathaniel Grey, Ragnor Fell, Sophie Collins, Starkweather, Tatiana Lightwood, Tessa Grey, Will Herondale, Woolsey Scott
Characters (*Mortal Instruments*) *see* Alec Lightwood, Amatis Herondale, Brother Enoch, Brother Zachariah, Camille Belcourt, Clary Fray, Consul, fairy queen, Hodge Starkweather, Inquisitor Herondale, Isabelle Lightwood, Jace Wayland, Jocelyn

Fairchild, Jordan Kyle, Luke Garroway, Madame Dorothea, Magnus Bane, Maia Roberts, Maryse Lightwood, Maureen Brown, Max Lightwood, Meliorn, Raphael Santiago, Robert Lightwood, Simon Lewis, Simon's mother, Stephen Herondale, Valentine Morgenstern
Charlotte Branwell, 39-40, 44-46, 104, 107, 110, 114, 134, 143-144, 147
Charmed, 73, 79
Chinese, 43, 72, 82
Chosen One, 4, 7-8, 18, 23, 145
Christian, 2, 47, 48, 53, 61, 65, 67, 77, 84, 141-142
Christmas, 45
Chronicles of Narnia, 2, 4, 6, 20, 30, 61
church, 53, 80, 87, 105, 136
Church the cat, 130
Cinderella, 5, 20, 22, 38, 41, 78, 105, 138-139
circle, 23, 42-43, 46, 51
Circle, 13, 18, 54, 99, 101-102
cities *see* Alicante, London, New York
City of Ashes, 9, 13, 30, 31, 34, 51, 53-54, 63, 75, 78, 92, 133, 142
City of Bones, 5-11, 16, 17, 21-22, 28, 30-31, 53-55, 70, 77-78, 89, 96, 98, 100, 121-123, 132, 135, 138, 140-141, 144-145, 149, 156

City of Fallen Angels, 11, 17, 23-27, 32, 36-37, 78, 121-122, 129-131, 135, 137, 147
City of Glass, 13, 20, 29, 31, 34, 36, 45, 51, 53-54, 56, 77-78, 99, 121, 123-124, 130, 142
City of Heavenly Fire, 45, 79, 121, 127, 133, 150, 156
City of Lost Souls, 5, 16, 23, 26-33, 35, 37, 56, 64, 71, 78, 79, 98, 103, 121-125, 130-133, 137, 146, 150, 152
Clary Fray, and the heroine's journey, 4-30; and Jace, 9-11, 26-30; and men, 11-13; name meaning, 121-122; and Tessa, 134-135; and women, 14-18
classics *see* authors, classic; books, classic
Clave, 13, 15, 21, 23, 41, 55, 64, 79, 94, 99-100, 108, 118, 126, 141, 143-144, 150
clockwork angel (pendent) *see* angel necklace
Clockwork Angel, 39, 40, 43-44, 52, 58, 78, 96, 103-104, 109-110, 113, 120, 130, 135-136, 143, 146
Clockwork Prince, 11, 26, 39-42, 47, 58, 104, 116, 118, 129-133, 139, 144, 147
Clockwork Princess, 17, 39, 41, 43-45, 56-58, 95-96, 104-106, 111, 114, 121, 130-134, 137, 140, 143-144, 147, 150, 155-156

clothes, 16, 39, 41, 75, 112, *see also* colors, disguise, gear, silvery gown, velvet coat
coffin, 24-25
Coleridge, 2, 110
colors *see* black, golden, orange, pink, red, silver, white
comics, 32, 75, 88, 136
compassion, 49
Consul, 44-45, 144
Coraline, 5
Corinthians (Bible), 53
Cortana, 64, 73, 131, 134
costume *see* disguise
Council, 13, 15, 19-23, 32, 41, 44, 63, 67, 93, 99-100, 133, 144
courage, 18, 34, 39, 57
creation, 10, 15, 25, 35, 45, 50, 54, 62, 66
creativity, 5, 11, 94
Cristina Rosales, 141, 152
cross, 82-83, 89, 93, 101
cup, 14, 17-18

dagger, 10, 25, 37, *see also* athame, Herondale knife, kindjal, seraph blade
Dante, 2, 47, 48, 99-100, 104, 137, 140
Dark Artifices, 64, 92, 121, 134-135, 137, 141, 150-151, 156
Dark Mother, 7, 22-24, 27, *see also* stepmother
dark side, 6, 14, 16, 23, 25-32, 35-36
Dark Sisters, 38, 40-45, 105, 108, 120, 133
daughter, 5, 8, 9, 20, 25, 28-29, 34, 58, 71, 77, 80, 95, 145
Daughter of Smoke and Bone, 74, 80, 149
David and Jonathan (Bible), 58, 123
David Copperfield, 137
daylighter, 31
De Quincey, 40-41, *see also* vampire ball
Deceiver (archetype), 38
deleted scenes, 29
Demeter, 4-5
demon pox, 133
demonic Shadowhunters, 18, 54, 150
demons *see* Abbadon, Agramon, Asmodeus, Azazel, Lilith, Lucifer, Marbas, Samael, Yanluo
Destroyer, 21, 26, 44
Deus Volt, 102
Deuteronomy (Bible), 61, 79
Dhampir, 87
Dickens, 105-107, 110, 114, 137
disguise, 27, 41, 95, 111, 113, 145
Divergent, 4, 138, 149
Divine Child (archetype), 14
Divine Comedy, 2, 48, 99-100, 104, 137, 140
Doctor Faustus, 103
Double (archetype), 16
Downworlders, 5, 7, 10, 13, 20, 31-33, 35, 40, 44, 51, 55, 89, 93, 100, 121, 126, 133, 134, 140-141, 145-146, *see* fairies, vampires, warlocks, werewolves
Dracula, 73-74, 83-86, 93-94, 109, 142

dreams, 9, 14, 16, 19, 26, 27, 29, 36-37, 45, 57, 68, 73, 78, 81, 104-106, 137-138
drugs, 27, 28, 29, 133
Dungeons and Dragons, 136

East of Eden, 122
easter eggs 129-136
Ecclesiastes (Bible), 48
Eden (Bible), 10, 48, 49, 63, 64, 77, 124
Egypt, 43, 70
electrum whip, 134
Emma Carstairs, 59, 131-132, 151-152
emotion, 11, 19-20, 41, 86, 109
Enoch (Bible), 50, 52, 61, 65-66, 71
Ephesians (Bible), 67, 153
Evil Jace, 26-27, 30, 37
Exodus (Bible), 61
Eye, 62-63

fairies, 2, 5, 74, 89-92, 116, 121, 140, 151, *see also* magic rings, silver bell
fairy potion, 31
fairy queen, 7, 20, 23, 27, 91-92
fairytales, 4-6, 19, 30, 39, 73, 74, 138, 140, *see also* Bluebeard, Cinderella, Frog Prince, Hansel and Gretel, Little Mermaid, Rapunzel, Six Swans, Sleeping Beauty, Snow White, stepmother
faith, 3, 13, 17-20, 36, 42, 61, 126, 137, 147, 152
fallen angels, 3, 35, 48, 52-56, 64, 65, 67, 71, 79-81, 89, 100, 119, 126
family tree, 121, 132, 134
fandom see anime, books, comics, Dungeons and Dragons, easter eggs, fantasy, Forbidden Planet, garage band, *Geektastic*, genre, *Halo*, manga, movies, rock band, television, *Very Secret Diaries*,
fantasy, 1-4, 7, 30, 40, 62, 73-80, 89, 90, 124, 136-139, 145, 153-155, see also books, movies, television
Fates, 8
fear, 12-13, 28, 31, 34, 63, 65, 70, 101, 117
Fearless, 9, 12, 70
feminine, 9-11, 14-19, 23, 24, 26-27, 38, 41, 43-45, 113, 129
feminine symbols *see* angel necklace, apples, birds, books, bracelet, circle, clothing, colors, cup, disguise, dreams, electrum whip, forest, glass, lake, mirror, ocean, Ouroboros, pentagram, ring, rose, ruby necklace, runes, Seal of Solomon, seeds, serpent, Sensor, shapeshifting, sight, thread, unconscious, voice, water, witchlight
feminism, 94, 126, 137, 143, 145, 156
fledgling, 31
flood, 52, 79
Forbidden Planet, 75, 136

forest, 74, 115
Forever Knight, 84
forgiveness, 3, 79
Frankenstein, 35, 83, 86, 109
French, 84, 88, 105, 124-125
Frog Prince, 9, 42

Gabriel Lightwood, 131-132, 147
Gaia, 43
garage band, 136
gear, 41
Geektastic, 93
Gemma Doyle, 4
Genesis (Bible), 47, 51, 59-60, 63-64, 67
genre, 1, 74, 85-86, 93, 96-97, 109, 111
Germanic, 88-89, 109
Gideon Lightwood, 45, 132, 147
girl power, 145
glamour, 7, 10, 22, 41, 90-91, 122
glass, 10, 24, 30, 62, 77-78, 124, 146
Glorious, 30, 36, 56, 64
goblin, 76
God, 14, 25, 30, 33, 38, 49-68, 71, 78-82, 88-89, 98, 101-102, 109, 113-114, 125, 127, 141
goddesses, 8, 14, 16-17, 24-25, 68, *see also* Aphrodite, Artemis, Demeter, Fates, Gaia, Isis, Ix Chel, Norns, Pandora, Persephone, Psyche, Venus
gold, 7, 9-10, 16, 18, 27, 29, 31, 37, 45, 50, 57, 77, 101, 114, 123, 127, 138
Golden Compass, 2, 4-5, 80
gothic, 77, 83, 93, 105, 109-111, 139
grail, 17-18
Greek, 43, 57, 70, 89, 101, 115, 151
greenhouse, 10, 21
Grey Book, 8, 12, 21
Grimm, 74
growth, 11, 16, 23-24, 129

hair, 9, 17, 29, 53, 81, 89, 123, 132, 138, 139
Halo, 32
Hamilton, Laurell K., 74, 86
Hansel and Gretel, 38
Harry Potter, 1-2, 4, 8, 74, 129, 136, 141, 143, 154-155
Hebrew, 50, 52, 62, 70, 82
Henry Branwell, 52, 95, 110, 131-133, 143
heroine's journey, 2, 4-30, 38-46
heroine's journey chart 21
hero's journey 30-38
Herondale knife, 27, 37
Hetaera, 14-15
Hidden Hand, 110-113
Hindu, 2, 43, 48, 89
Hispanic, 141
history, 20, 52, 63, 75-76, 87, 93, 108, 115, 127, 129, 150, 153
Hobbit, 8, 30
Hodge Starkweather, 5, 7, 15, 99, 100, 129, 140, 145
holy water, 53, 82, 87
homosexuality, 141-142, 156
honor, 47, 106, 129
Horace, 78, 103, 109

Hotel Dumort, 5, 21, 31, 84, 141
Hunger Games, 2, 4-5, 8, 14, 20, 137, 138-139, 143, 149
Hyde Park, 39, 76

Idris, 3, 10, 13, 17, 19, 21, 34-35, 41, 54, 56, 59, 64, 76, 77, 99, 100, 133-134
immoral, 26, 35, 99
immortality, 43
in hoc signo vinces, 101-102
Indian, 48, 67, 94
Infernal Devices, 1, 52, 75, 76, 80, 85, 92-93, 95-96, 108, 110, 121, 124, 129, 131, 133, 136, 151, 155
Inferno see Divine Comedy
Inkheart, 5, 8
Inquisitor, 7, 15, 34, 128, 143, 145-146
inspiration, 14, 57, 122, 128
Institute, 9, 15-16, 19, 21, 25, 27, 39, 75, 76, 87, 110, 111, 133, 134, 143-144, 146, 151
intuition, 13, 19, 57
inventions, 95
Iron Sisters, 144
Iron Trial, 153
Isabelle Lightwood, 10, 12-17, 22-23, 25, 28, 31-33, 41, 60, 92, 127-128, 132-135, 143, 150
Isis, 5, 88
Ithuriel, 45, 56-57, 131
Ivanhoe, 104
Ix Chel, 8

Jace Wayland, as Evil Jace, 26-27, 30, 37; and hero's journey, 33-38; name meaning, 122-123; and Will, 131, 134-135
Jace's childhood home, 19
Jacob (Bible), 26, 60, 138
jade pendant, 42
Jane Eyre, 104-105, 110, 139
Japanese, 48, 67, 88-89
jealousy, 12, 47, 59, 141
Jem Carstairs, 41, 42, 45, 47, 57-59, 64, 72, 76, 93, 102, 106-110, 114-117, 121, 126, 128, 131-147, 150, 152
Jessamine Lovelace, 16, 39-41, 45, 76, 107-109, 113, 117-118, 128-129, 143-144, 146
Jesus, 61, 101, 114, 123
jewelry *see* angel necklace, bracelet, jade pendant, magic rings, Morgenstern ring, ring
Jewish, 2, 48-53, 61, 67-68, 70, 84, 141-142
Job (Bible), 78
Jocelyn Fairchild, 5, 8, 9, 11, 13-24, 26, 28, 34-35, 53, 77, 78, 122, 124, 127, 129, 132, 142, 147, 150-151
John Shade, 41
Johnson, Maureen, 148, 156
Jonathan Shadowhunter, 13, 24, 58, 123-124, 129
Jordan Kyle, 48, 79, 140, 147, 150
Joshua (Bible), 52, 64, 73, 149
Julius Caesar, 98-99
Judaism *see* Jewish

Jung, 6, 11
Jungian psychology *see* Amazon, Animus, Chosen One, Dark Mother, dark side, Deceiver, Destroyer, Divine Child, Double, dreams, heroine's journey, Hetaera, Medial Woman, Predator, Shadow, unconscious, Wolff's archetypes chart

Kabbalah, 49, 62
Keats, 103, 109-110
kid power, 143
kindjal, 10, 58
King Arthur, 8, 17, 31, 63, 89, 109
Kipling, Rudyard, 57, 103, 114-115
kiss, 10, 12, 40-41, 92
knife *see* athame, dagger, Herondale knife, kindjal, seraph blade
Kwan Yin box, 134

Laban, 47
lake, 10, 13, 44, 77, 124
Latin, 65, *see also* Roman
Lesser Key of Solomon, 65-66
letters, 36, 39, 49, 50, 62, 63, 101, 104
library, 39, 129
lies, 13, 28-29, 38, 42, 56, 82, 91, 112, 147
Lilith, 7, 18, 22-27, 36, 37, 43, 61, 67-70, 80-81, 86, 103, 137
Lilith's temple, 25, 37
Little Mermaid, 4, 18, 20, 38

locations *see* places
London, 38, 44, 74-78, 80, 89, 92, 94, 95, 103, 105, 108, 113-117, 126, 130
Lord of the Rings, 8, 10, 16, 31, 73, 79, 89, 136, 148, 155
Lost Girl, 74
love triangle, 10, 42, 128, 137-140
Lovecraft, H.P., 74
Lucifer, 47, 53-55, 80-81, 89, 102, 122
Luke Garroway, 8, 10-5, 20, 23, 32-33, 36, 51, 58, 67, 75, 78, 99, 124-125, 133, 140-143, 145, 147, 150-151

Macbeth, 64
Maccabees, 125
Madame Dorothea, 7, 14, 18, 38, 70, 99, 100
madness, 13, 83, 88
Maellartach, 63-64, 133
magic rings, 27, 29
Magister, 40, 42-45, 77, 96, 106, 108, 110-114, 120, 126, 134, 137, 143, 146-147
Magnus Bane, 6, 8, 10, 12, 15-17, 21-23, 40, 71, 78, 89, 95, 100, 102, 106-107, 127, 129-133, 136, 140-142, 147-150, 156
Maia Roberts, 23, 25, 32, 70, 79, 127, 140-141, 150
Malachai Configuration, 131
manga, 136
Marbas, 131, 147
Mark of Cain, 20, 31-33, 59-60, 62, 79, 125

marriage, 11, 41, 76, 95, 144
Maryse Lightwood, 15, 33-34, 127-128, 143-44
masculine, 10-11, 14, 41, 43-44, 64, 128-129
Maureen Brown, 32-33, 78, 140
Max Lightwood, 13-14, 35, 38, 127, 136
Medial Woman, 14-15, 22, 62
Meliorn, 131
memories, 6-8, 12, 28, 40, 100
mene, mene, tekel, parsin, 51, 172
Metatron, 60, 69
Mexican, 141, 152
Michael (angel), 30, 33, 53, 55-57, 64-66, 71, 79, 81, 96, 124, 148
Midsummer Night's Dream, 91
Milton, 2, 54, 99
mirror, 38, 57, 108
misogyny, 20, *see also* feminism, prejudice
mixed-race, 93, 138, 141
mizpah, 47
Moonlight (TV show), 84
morality, 33-35, 112, 126
Morgenstern ring, 10-11, 23
Mortal Cup, 17, 21
Mortal Sword, 63-64, 133
Mortmain, 40, 42-45, 77, 96, 106, 108, 110-114, 120, 126, 134, 137, 143, 146-147
movie, 1, 86, 88, 93, 148, 149, 154, 156
movies, 3, 74, 79, 83, 93, 136, 139
Muslim, 2, 48, 77
mystic *see* Medial Woman

mystic symbols *see* athame, Ouroboros, pentagram, runes, Seal of Solomon, tarot
myth *see* goddesses, Greek, Roman

Nathaniel Grey, 40-42, 76, 104, 107, 110, 113, 118, 128, 143, 146
Native American, 43, 138
nature, 10-11, 19, 23, 30, 32, 35, 38, 42, 47, 75, 78, 81, 84, 106, 115, 126, 150
Nephilim, 2, 7, 24, 47, 51-52, 54, 57, 81, 96, 123
Nephilim (Bible), 51-52
New York, 1, 74-76, 89, 111, 130, 136
Nixies, 19, 75, 89
Norns, 8
Norse, 8, 43, 62, 88
Nosferatu, 83

obsession, 25, *see also* passion
ocean, 18-19, 50
Opening rune, 9, 19, 21
orange (color), 16
"Oranges and Lemons", 116-117
Ouroboros, 42-44, 129

painting, 28, *see also* artist
Pandemonium Club, 100, 133, 134
Pandora, 44
Parabatai, 48, 57-59, 102, 132, 134, 151-152
Paradise Lost, 2, 47-48, 53-56, 65, 77, 100
paranormal fiction, 1, 6, 74,

84, 87, 93-95, *see also* vampire fiction
parents, 4-5, 7, 26, 35, 40, 45, 58, 76, 102, 123, 142-143, 146, 152
passion, 12, 18, 57, 78, 79, 108, 110, 119, 128, 129, 132
patriarchy, 13, 15, 18-19, 21-22, 34, 41-45, 64, 110, 112
pendant *see* angel necklace, jade pendant, ruby necklace
pentagram, 66
perception, 6-11, 13, 17
Percy Jackson, 73-74
Persephone, 4
Persian, 71, 130
pink, 16, 145
places *see* Alicante, Blackfriars Bridge, the Bone Chandelier, Brooklyn, cave, Central Park, church, Forbidden Planet, forest, greenhouse, Hotel Dumort, Hyde Park, Idris, Institute, Jace's childhood home, Lilith's temple, London, New York, ocean, Pandemonium Club, river, Roosevelt Island, Sebastian's safehouse, ship, stronghold, tunnels, vampire ball, Venice, Wales, Westminster Abby, Whitechapel, Yorkshire
Portal, 133
Praetor Lupus, 132, 133
prayer, 53, 60, 67-68
Predator (archetype), 27, 30
pregnancy, 20, 24, 55
prejudice, 141-142
pride, 24, 32, 55, 89, 102
protection, 2, 6-8, 11, 39, 42, 56, 60, 62, 66, 109, 134, 143
Proverbs (Bible), 25
Psyche, 4, 38, 45

Queen of Air and Darkness, 92, 153
Queen Victoria, 94, 109

rage, 12, 19, 23, 40-41, 56, 88
Ragnor Fell, 130
Raphael Santiago, 13, 23, 31-33, 84, 125, 127
Rapunzel, 6
rat, 5, 12, 31, 132
rationality, 11, 13, 109
Raziel, 13, 17, 20, 33, 36, 48-51, 55, 60, 64, 81, 125, 141
rebirth, 6, 15, 36, 43, 108, 121
red, 10, 17, 81, 119
religion, 47-48, *see also* books, religious
rescue, 4-5, 19-20, 22, 92, 105, 110-111, 143-144
responsibility, 25, 32, 41, 102, 129-130
restraint, 12-13, 42, 137
Revelations (Bible), 53, 70
Rice, Anne, 84, 136
ring, 10-11, 29, 42, 66, 129, *see also* magic rings, Morgenstern ring
ritual, 47-48, 103
Robert Lightwood, 23

rock band, 84, 92, 136, 138, 156
Roman, 56, 77, 88, 98, 100, 102-103, 109, 115, 120, 151, *see also* Latin
romance, 2, 9, 34, 45, 74, 80, 95, 104, 110-111, 116, 139, 148, 150, *see also* love triangle, passion
Roosevelt Island, 18, 75
rose, 9, 10, 60, 118-119, 152
Rossetti, 86, 103
ruby necklace, 133, 135, 144
rune of coercion, 27
runes, 1-2, 7-9, 12, 14, 19, 20, 23, 25-27, 43, 47, 49-51, 61-62, 66, 70, 100, 121, 127, 129, 144, 147, 149-150, 153, *see also* binding rune, rune of coercion, Eye, Fearless, Opening rune, stele, tattoo
Ruth (Bible), 58, 136

saints, 56, 61, 113, 126
Samael, 70
Samuel (Bible), 58
Seal of Solomon, 66
Sebastian Verlac, 11, 13, 16, 18, 23-25, 28-30, 34-38, 54-56, 78-81, 92, 99, 103, 123-125, 127, 133-134, 141-143, 146, 150, and Clary, 26-30; and Jace, 35-38; name meaning, 123-125
Sebastian's safehouse, 133
secrets, 11, 13, 48, 50, 87, 100, 105, 108, 112, 128, 147
seeds, 10
selfishness, 23, 91

Sensor, 7, 133
seraph blade, 53, 128
serpent, 43, 53, 54, 124
Shadow (archetype), 14, 16, 23, 27-28, 32, 34-35, 37, 40
Shadowhunter's Codex, 39, 149-150, 156
Shadowhunters *see* Nephilim, *see also* Accords, Ascension, Circle, Clave, Consul, Council, Inquisitor, Iron Sisters, Parabatai, Silent Brothers
Shadowhunter tools *see* adamas, Book of the White, books, electrum whip, Grey Book, kindjal, Maellartach, Malachai Configuration, Mortal Cup, Portal, prayer, ruby necklace, runes, Sensor, seraph blade, *Shadowhunter's Codex*, stele, swords, tattoo, wards, witchlight
Shakespeare, 64, 91, 103, 123-124, *see also Julius Caesar, Macbeth, Midsummer Night's Dream, Twelfth Night*
shapeshifting, 9, 40, 42, 105
Sherman, Delia, 74
ship, 9, 19, 23, 31, 51, 78, 80, 129
sight, 5-7, 62, 69, 90, 121
Silent Brothers, 12, 44, 63, 78, 100, 126, 133, 137
silver, 16, 17, 23, 28, 37, 50, 63, 83, 85, 89, 116, 133, 134, 139

silver bell, 23
silver box, 134
silvery gown, 41
Simon Lewis, as daylighter, 31; as fledgling, 31; and hero's journey, 30-33; name meaning, 125
Simon's mother, 32
sister, 26-27, 29, 34, 35, 80, 87, 92, 124, 152
Six Swans, 4, 19
sketchbook, 7-8
slayers 85-88
sleep, 18-19, 24, 45, 114
Sleeping Beauty, 19, 24, 27, 40
Snow White, 5, 19, 24, 38, 40, 138
snuffbox, 133
son, 11, 13, 15, 34-35, 52-54, 56, 69, 71, 86, 95, 123, 145
Song of Songs, 35, 47
Song of the Lioness Quartet, 4
Sophie Collins, 45, 87, 126, 132, 143
souls, 51, 57-58, 79, 82, 101, 133, 141
Speaking Stars, 63
Spiderman, 30, 136
Spiderwick Chronicles, 8, 74, 154
spirituality, 18, 22, 128
spoils, 44
Star Wars, 4, 44
Starkweather, 44, 45, 110
steampunk, 2, 75, 92-97, definition, 94, 97; invention, 96
stele, 9, 128
Stephen Herondale, 36, 38, 172

stepmother (archetype), 4-6, 20, 24, 38, 124
stronghold, 18-19, 21, 25, 41, 44-45, 96, 111
Summa Theologiae, 65
sun, 9, 18
Supernatural, 73, 74, 81, 86
swords *see* Cortana, Glorious, Maellartach, Mortal Sword
symbols *see* angel necklace, apples, birds, books, bracelet, circle, clothing, colors, cup, dagger, disguise, electrum whip, glass, jade pendant, Kwan Yin box, lake, magic rings, mirror, Morgenstern ring, ocean, Ouroboros, pentagram, ring, rose, ruby necklace, runes, seeds, serpent, Sensor, shapeshifting, sight, silver bell, silver box, sleep, sun, sword, tarot, tattoo, thread, voice, water, witchlight

Tacitus, 151
Tale of Two Cities, 2, 104, 105-108, 126, 132-133
talisman, 8, 10, 31, 39, 69, 105
Tarot, 17-18, 127-128, 152
Tatiana Lightwood, 132
tattoo, 1, 48
television *see Angel, Being Human, Buffy the Vampire Slayer, Charmed, Forever Knight, Grimm, Lost Girl, Moonlight, Supernatural, True Blood, Twilight,*

Vampire Diaries, Xena, X-Files
temptation, 10, 28, 32, 37, 78, 85
Tennyson, 102, 103, 118, 120
Tess of the d'Urbervilles, 126
Tessa Grey, and Clary, 134-135; heroine's journey, 38-46; love triangle, 138-140; name meaning, 126
themes 136-148
thread, 10
timeline 121
Tithe, 4, 91-92, 154
tolerance, 3, 137, 156
torture, 13, 15, 25, 72, 81, 92
Trevor Project, 156
True Blood, 84, 138
truth, 25, 33-34, 44, 56, 79, 90, 100, 111, 137, 143, 147-148, 151
Tumblr, 127, 150, 152, 155
tunnels, 36
Twelfth Night, 123-124
Twilight, 1-2, 4, 26, 74, 84, 137, 149

unconscious, 9, 14, 18, 21, 26, 31, 36, 44, 66, 78, 98
underground, 19
Underworld, 86, 88
urban fantasy, 2, 75, 91-92, 153-154

Valentine Morgenstern, 5-15, 18-23, 25, 28-37, 44-45, 51, 53, 54-58, 78, 81, 86, 98-102, 122-125, 129, 134, 137, 140-143, 145, 149
Vampire Academy, 87

vampire ball, 41
Vampire Diaries, 74, 84, 138
vampire fiction see *Angel, Anita Blake, Being Human, Buffy the Vampire Slayer, Dracula, Forever Knight, Moonlight, Nosferatu, True Blood, Twilight, Underworld, Vampire Academy, Vampire Diaries, Vampyre, Van Helsing, Varney the Vampire*
vampires, 2, 5, 11-12, 31, 32-33, 40-41, 51, 59, 68, 78, 82-88, 93-95, 109, 110, 125, 131, 132, 136, 139-142
Vampyre (novel), 83
Van Helsing, 85-86
Varney the Vampire, 83, 110
Vathek, 109
velvet coat, 41
Venice, 27
Venus, 38, 53
Verne, Jules, 93, 96
Very Secret Diaries, 136, 155
violence, 12, 13, 49, 112, 141
Virgil, 100
voice, 6, 9, 13, 19, 26-28, 35-36, 39, 48, 67, 80, 113, 128, 132

Wales, 76, 77, 134
war, 9, 10, 12, 15, 21, 31, 32, 47, 48, 53, 54, 55, 64, 73, 79, 80-81, 92, 94-95, 111, 113, 115, 122, 125, 150, 152
wards, 55
warlocks, 8, 41, 42, 43, 89, 93, 103, 110, 122, 130, 151

water, 8, 18, 52, 75, 78, 90, 92-93, 124, 129, 151-152, 154
wedding, 45, 47, 58, 151
werewolves, 8, 12, 32, 51, 58, 79, 86-89, 93-95, 122, 125, 131, 141, 143
white, 17, 27, 53, 77, 119, 130, 138, 142, 145, *see also* Book of the White
Whitechapel, 76, 107, 114
Will Herondale, 2, 17, 39-45, 58, 59, 72, 76-79, 102-114, 117-118, 120-123, 126, 128-144, 147, 152
wisdom, 11-15, 20, 30, 33, 48, 62
witches, 20, 38, 60, 68, 87
witchlight, 10
Wizard of Oz, 4, 18, 22, 30
Wolff, Toni, 14-15

Wolff's archetypes chart, 15
Woolsey Scott, 133
worm, 124, 132, 144
Wrinkle in Time, 4-5, 79
Wuthering Heights, 93, 110-111, 139

Xena, 79, 145
X-Files, 73, 79

Yanluo, 72
Yarbro, Chelsea Quinn, 84
yin fen, 72
Yorkshire, 41
young adult, 1, 4, 139, *see also* books, movies, television
Young Wizards, 74, 79

Zachariah (Bible) 126-127, *see also* Brother Zachariah

Other Titles of Interest

MORE INFORMATION AT WWW.WINGEDLIONPRESS.COM

C. S. Lewis

C. S. Lewis: Views From Wake Forest - Essays on C. S. Lewis
Michael Travers, editor

Contains sixteen scholarly presentations from the international C. S. Lewis convention in Wake Forest, NC. Walter Hooper shares his important essay "Editing C. S. Lewis," a chronicle of publishing decisions after Lewis' death in 1963.

"*Scholars from a variety of disciplines address a wide range of issues. The happy result is a fresh and expansive view of an author who well deserves this kind of thoughtful attention.*"
    Diana Pavlac Glyer, author of *The Company They Keep*

The Hidden Story of Narnia:
A Book-By-Book Guide to Lewis' Spiritual Themes
Will Vaus

A book of insightful commentary equally suited for teens or adults – Will Vaus points out connections between the *Narnia* books and spiritual/biblical themes, as well as between ideas in the *Narnia* books and C. S. Lewis' other books. Learn what Lewis himself said about the overarching and unifying thematic structure of the Narnia books. That is what this book explores; what C. S. Lewis called "the hidden story" of Narnia. Each chapter includes questions for individual use or small group discussion.

Why I Believe in Narnia:
33 Reviews and Essays on the Life and Work of C. S. Lewis
James Como

Chapters range from reviews of critical books, documentaries and movies to evaluations of Lewis' books to biographical analysis.

"*A valuable, wide-ranging collection of essays by one of the best informed and most acute commentators on Lewis' work and ideas.*"
    Peter Schakel, author of *Imagination & the Arts in C. S. Lewis*

C. S. Lewis Goes to Heaven: A Reader's Guide to The Great Divorce
David G. Clark

This is the first book devoted solely to this often neglected book and the first to reveal several important secrets Lewis concealed within the story. Lewis felt his imaginary trip to Hell and Heaven was far better than his book *The Screwtape Letters*, which has become a classic. Clark is an ordained minister who has taught courses on Lewis for more than 30 years and is a New Testament and Greek scholar with a Doctor of Philosophy degree in Biblical Studies from the University of Notre Dame. Readers will discover the many literary and biblical influences Lewis utilized in writing his brilliant novel.

C. S. Lewis & Philosophy as a Way of Life
Adam Barkman

C. S. Lewis is rarely thought of as a "philosopher" per se despite having both studied and taught philosophy for several years at Oxford. Lewis's long journey to Christianity was essentially philosophical – passing through seven different stages. This 624 page book is an invaluable reference for C. S. Lewis scholars and fans alike

C. S. Lewis: His Literary Achievement
Colin Manlove

"This is a positively brilliant book, written with splendor, elegance, profundity and evidencing an enormous amount of learning. This is probably not a book to give a first-time reader of Lewis. But for those who are more broadly read in the Lewis corpus this book is an absolute gold mine of information. The author gives us a magnificent overview of Lewis' many writings, tracing for us thoughts and ideas which recur throughout, and at the same time telling us how each book differs from the others. I think it is not extravagant to call C. S. Lewis: His Literary Achievement a tour de force."
 Robert Merchant, *St. Austin Review*, Book Review Editor

Mythopoeic Narnia:
Memory, Metaphor, and Metamorphoses in The Chronicles of Narnia
Salwa Khoddam

Dr. Khoddam, the founder of the C. S. Lewis and Inklings Society (2004), has been teaching university courses using Lewis' books for over 25 years. Her book offers a fresh approach to the Narnia books based on an inquiry into Lewis' readings and use of classical and Christian symbols. She explores the literary and intellectual contexts of these stories, the traditional myths and motifs, and places them in the company of the greatest Christian mythopoeic works of Western literature. In Lewis' imagination, memory and metaphor interact to advance his purpose – a Christian metamorphosis. *Mythopoeic Narnia* helps to open the door for readers into the magical world of the Western imagination.

Speaking of Jack: A C. S. Lewis Discussion Guide
Will Vaus

C. S. Lewis societies have been forming around the world since the first one started in New York City in 1969. Will Vaus has started and led three groups himself. *Speaking of Jack* is the result of Vaus' experience in leading those Lewis societies. Included here are introductions to most of Lewis' books as well as questions designed to stimulate discussion about Lewis' life and work. These materials have been "road-tested" with real groups made up of young and old, some very familiar with Lewis and some newcomers. *Speaking of Jack* may be used in an existing book discussion group, to start a C. S. Lewis society, or to guide your own exploration of Lewis' books.

George MacDonald

Diary of an Old Soul & The White Page Poems
George MacDonald and Betty Aberlin

The first edition of George MacDonald's book of daily poems included a blank page opposite each page of poems. Readers were invited to write their own reflections on the "white page." MacDonald wrote: "Let your white page be ground, my print be seed, growing to golden ears, that faith and hope may feed." Betty Aberlin responded to MacDonald's invitation with daily poems of her own.

"*Betty Aberlin's close readings of George MacDonald's verses and her thoughtful responses to them speak clearly of her poetic gifts and spiritual intelligence.*"
　　　Luci Shaw, poet

George MacDonald: Literary Heritage and Heirs
Roderick McGillis, editor

This latest collection of 14 essays sets a new standard that will influence MacDonald studies for many more years. George MacDonald experts are increasingly evaluating his entire corpus within the nineteenth century context.

"*This comprehensive collection represents the best of contemporary scholarship on George MacDonald.*"
　　　Rolland Hein, author of *George MacDonald: Victorian Mythmaker*

In the Near Loss of Everything: George MacDonald's Son in America
Dale Wayne Slusser

In the summer of 1887, George MacDonald's son Ronald, newly engaged to artist Louise Blandy, sailed from England to America to teach school. The next summer he returned to England to marry Louise and bring her back to America. On August 27, 1890, Louise died, leaving him with an infant daughter. Ronald once described losing a beloved spouse as "the near loss of everything." Dale Wayne Slusser unfolds this poignant story with unpublished letters and photos that give readers a glimpse into the close-knit MacDonald family.

A Novel Pulpit: Sermons From George MacDonald's Fiction
David L. Neuhouser

"*In MacDonald's novels, the Christian teaching emerges out of the characters and story line, the narrator's comments, and inclusion of sermons given by the fictional preachers. The sermons in the novels are shorter than the ones in collections of MacDonald's sermons and so are perhaps more accessible for some. In any case, they are both stimulating and thought-provoking. This collection of sermons from ten novels serve to bring out the 'freshness and brilliance' of MacDonald's message.*"
　　　From the author's introduction

Behind the Back of the North Wind:
Critical Essays on George MacDonald's Classic Children's Book
John Pennington and Roderick McGillis, editors

The unique blend of fairy tale atmosphere and social realism in this novel laid the groundwork for modern fantasy literature. Sixteen essays by various authors are accompanied by an instructive introduction, extensive index, and beautiful illustrations.

Through the Year with George MacDonald: 366 Daily Readings
Rolland Hein, editor

These page-length excerpts from sermons, novels and letters are given an appropriate theme/heading and a complementary Scripture passage for daily reading. An inspiring introduction to the artistic soul and Christian vision of George MacDonald.

Christian Living

The Living Word of the Living God:
A Beginner's Guide to Reading and Understanding the Bible
Rev. Tom Furrer

This book is based on over 20 years experience of teaching the Bible to confirmation classes at Episcopal churches in Connecticut. Chapters from Genesis to Revelation.

Keys to Growth: Meditations on the Acts of the Apostles
Will Vaus

Every living things or person requires certain ingredients in order to grow, and if a thing or person is not growing, it is dying. *The Acts of the Apostles* is a book that is all about growth. Will Vaus has been meditating and preaching on *Acts* for the past 30 years. In this volume, he offers the reader forty-one keys from the entire book of Acts to unlock spiritual growth in everyday life.

Open Before Christmas: Devotional Thoughts For The Holiday Season
Will Vaus

Author Will Vaus seeks to deepen the reader's knowledge of Advent and Christmas leading up to Epiphany. Readers are provided with devotional thoughts for each day that help them to experience this part of the Church Year perhaps in a kore spiritually enriching way than ever before.

"Seasoned with inspiring, touching, and sometimes humorous illustrations .... I found his writing immediately engaging and, the more I read, the more I liked it. God has touched my heart by reading Open Before Christmas, and I believe he will touch your heart too."
    The Rev. David Beckmann, Founder of The C.S. Lewis Society of Chattanooga

Called to Serve: Life as a Firefighter-Deacon
Deacon Anthony R. Surozenski

Called to Serve is the story of one man's dream to be a firefighter. But dreams have a way of taking detours – so Tony Surozenski became a teacher and eventually a volunteer firefighter. And when God enters the picture, Tony is faced with a choice. Will he give up firefighting to follow another call? After many years, Tony's two callings are finally united – in service as a fire chaplain at Ground Zero after the 9-11 attacks and in other ways he could not have imagined. Tony is Chief Chaplain's aid for the Massachusetts Corp of Fire Chaplains and Director for the Office of the Diaconate of the Diocese of Worcester, Massachusetts.

Harry Potter

The Order of Harry Potter: The Literary Skill of the Hogwarts Epic
Colin Manlove

Colin Manlove, a popular conference speaker and author of over a dozen books, has earned an international reputation as an expert on fantasy and children's literature. His book, *From Alice to Harry Potter*, is a survey of 400 English fantasy books. In *The Order of Harry Potter*, he compares and contrasts *Harry Potter* with works by "Inklings" writers J.R.R. Tolkien, C.S. Lewis and Charles Williams; he also examines Rowling's treatment of the topic of imagination; her skill in organization and the use of language; and the book's underlying motifs and themes.

Harry Potter & Imagination: The Way Between Two Worlds
Travis Prinzi

Imaginative literature places a reader between two worlds: the story world and the world of daily life, and challenges the reader to imagine and to act for a better world. Starting with discussion of Harry Potter's more important themes, *Harry Potter & Imagination* takes readers on a journey through the transformative power of those themes for both the individual and for culture by placing Rowling's series in its literary, historical, and cultural contexts.

Repotting Harry Potter: A Professor's Guide for the Serious Re-Reader
Rowling Revisited: Return Trips to Harry, Fantastic Beasts, Quidditch, & Beedle the Bard
James W. Thomas

In *Repotting Harry Potter* and his sequel book *Rowling Revisited*, Dr. James W. Thomas points out the humor, puns, foreshadowing and literary parallels in the Potter books. In *Rowling Revisited*, readers will especially find useful three extensive appendixes – "Fantastic Beasts and the Pages Where You'll Find Them," "Quidditch Through the Pages," and "The Books in the Potter Books." Dr. Thomas makes re-reading the Potter books even more rewarding and enjoyable.

The Deathly Hallows Lectures:
The Hogwarts Professor Explains Harry's Final Adventure
John Granger

In *The Deathly Hallows Lectures*, John Granger reveals the finale's brilliant details, themes, and meanings. *Harry Potter* fans will be surprised by and delighted with Granger's explanations of the three dimensions of meaning in *Deathly Hallows*. Ms. Rowling has said that alchemy sets the "parameters of magic" in the series; after reading the chapter-length explanation of *Deathly Hallows* as the final stage of the alchemical Great Work, the serious reader will understand how important literary alchemy is in understanding Rowling's artistry and accomplishment.

Sociology and Harry Potter: 22 Enchanting Essays on the Wizarding World
Jenn Simms, editor

Modeled on an Introduction to Sociology textbook. this books is not simply about the series, but also used the series to facilitate reader's understanding of the discipline of sociology and a development of a sociological approach to viewing social reality. It is a case of high quality academic scholarship written in a form and on a topic accessible to non-academics. As such, it is written to appeal to Harry Potter fans and the general reading public. Contributors include professional sociologists from eight countries.

Harry Potter, Still Recruiting:
An Inner Look at Harry Potter Fandom
Valerie Frankel, editor

The Harry Potter phenomenon has created a new world: one of Quidditch in the park, lightning earrings, endless parodies, a new genre of music, and fan conferences of epic proportions. This book attempts to document everything - exploring costuming, crafting, gaming, and more, with essays and interviews straight from the multitude of creators. From children to adults, fans are delighting the world with an explosion of captivating activities and experiences, all based on Rowling's delightful series.

Hog's Head Conversations: Essays on Harry Potter
Travis Prinzi, editor

Ten fascinating essays on Harry Potter are divided into five sections: Conversations on 1) Literary Value, 2) Eternal Truth, 3) Imagination, 4) Literary Criticism, and 5) Characters. Contributors include the following popular Potter writers and speakers: John Granger, James W. Thomas, Colin Manlove, and Travis Prinzi.

Biography

Sheldon Vanauken: The Man Who Received "A Severe Mercy"
Will Vaus

In this biography we discover: Vanauken the struggling student, the bon-vivant lover, the sailor who witnessed the bombing of Pearl Harbor, the seeker who returned to faith through C. S. Lewis, the beloved professor of English literature and history, the feminist and anti-war activist who participated in the March on the Pentagon, the bestselling author, and Vanauken the convert to Catholicism. What emerges is the portrait of a man relentlessly in search of beauty, love, and truth, a man who believed that, in the end, he found all three.

"This is a charming biography about a doubly charming man who wrote a triply charming book. It is a great way to meet the man behind A Severe Mercy."

 Peter Kreeft, author of *Jacob's Ladder: 10 Steps to Truth*

Poets and Poetry

Remembering Roy Campbell: The Memoirs of his Daughters, Anna and Tess
Introduction by Judith Lütge Coullie, editor
Preface by Joseph Pearce

Anna and Teresa Campbell were the daughters of the handsome young South African poet and writer, Roy Campbell (1901-1957), and his beautiful English wife, Mary Garman. In their frank and moving memoirs, Anna and Tess recall the extraordinary, and often very difficult, lives they shared with their exceptional parents. The book includes over 50 photos, 344 footnotes, a timeline of Campbell's life, and a complete index.

In the Eye of the Beholder: How to See the World Like a Romantic Poet
Louis Markos

Born out of the French Revolution and its radical faith that a nation could be shaped and altered by the dreams and visions of its people, British Romantic Poetry was founded on a belief that the objects and realities of our world, whether natural or human, are not fixed in stone but can be molded and transformed by the visionary eye of the poet. Unlike many of the books written on Romanticism, which devote many pages to the poets and few pages to their poetry, the focus here is firmly on the poems themselves. The author thereby draws the reader intimately into the life of these poems. A separate bibliographical essay is provided for readers listing accessible biographies of each poet and critical studies of their work.

The Cat on the Catamaran: A Christmas Tale
John Martin

Here is a modern-day parable of a modern-day cat with modern-day attitudes. Riverboat Dan is a "cool" cat on a perpetual vacation from responsibility. He's *The Cat on the Catamaran* – sailing down the river of life. Dan keeps his guilty conscience from interfering with his fun until he runs into trouble. But will he have the courage to believe that it's never too late to change course? (For ages 10 to adult)

"*This book is a joy, and as companionable as a good-natured cat."*
    Walter Hooper, author of *C. S. Lewis: Companion and Guide*

The Half Blood Poems
Inspired by the Stories of J.K. Rowling
Christine Lowther

Like Harry Potter, Christine's poetry can soar above the tragic to discover the heroic and beautiful in such poems as "Neville, Unlikely Rebel," "For Our Wide-Armed Mothers," and "A Boy's Hands." There are 71 poems divided into seven chapters that correspond to the seven books. Fans of Harry Potter will experience once again many of the emotions they felt reading the books – emotions presented most effectively through a poet's words.

Pop Culture

To Love Another Person: A Spiritual Journey Through Les Miserables
John Morrison

The powerful story of Jean Valjean's redemption is beloved by readers and theatergoers everywhere. In this companion and guide to Victor Hugo's masterpiece, author John Morrison unfolds the spiritual depth and breadth of this classic novel and broadway musical.

Through Common Things: Philosophical Reflections on Popular Culture
Adam Barkman

"Barkman presents us with an amazingly wide-ranging collection of philosophical reflections grounded in the everyday things of popular culture – past and present, eastern and western, factual and fictional. This is an informative and entertaining book to read!"
  Doug Bloomberg, Professor of Philosophy, Institute for Christian Studies

Above All Things: Essays on Christian Ethics and Popular Culture
Adam Barkman

"Those who don't normally think of themselves as philosophically inclined will be surprised and delighted as Barkman rescues philosophy from dry classroom abstractions and reveals how it fills the glorious messiness of everyday life."
  Dr. Kevin Flatt, Assistant Professor of History, Redeemer University College

Spotlight: A Close-up Look at the Artistry and Meaning of Stephenie Meyer's Novels
John Granger

Stephenie Meyer's *Twilight* saga has taken the world by storm. But is there more to *Twilight* than a love story for teen girls crossed with a cheesy vampire-werewolf drama? *Spotlight* reveals the literary backdrop, themes, artistry, and meaning of the four Bella Swan adventures. *Spotlight* is the perfect gift for serious *Twilight* readers.

Virtuous Worlds: The Video Gamer's Guide to Spiritual Truth
John Stanifer

Shows readers specific parallels between Christian faith and the content of their favorite games. Written with wry humor, this book will appeal to gamers and non-gamers alike. Those unfamiliar with video games may be pleasantly surprised to find that many elements in those "virtual worlds" also qualify them as "virtuous worlds."

The Many Faces of Katniss Everdeen: Exploring the Heroine of The Hunger Games
Valerie Estelle Frankel

Katniss is the heroine who's changed the world. Like Harry Potter, she explodes across genres: She is a dystopian heroine, a warrior woman, a reality TV star, a rebellious adolescent. She's surrounded by the figures of Roman history, from Caesar and Cato to Cinna and Coriolanus Snow. She's also traveling the classic heroine's journey. As a child soldier, she faces trauma; as a growing teen, she battles through love triangles and the struggle to be good in a harsh world. This book explores all this and more, while taking a look at the series' symbolism, from food to storytelling, to show how Katniss becomes the greatest power of Panem, the girl on fire.

www.ingramcontent.com/pod-product-compliance
Lightning Source LLC
Chambersburg PA
CBHW020412080526
44584CB00014B/1293